Decision Making under Time Pressure

Decision Making under Time Pressure

An Experimental Study
of Stress Behavior
in Business Management

Rolf Bronner
University of Paderborn

LexingtonBooks
D.C. Heath and Company
Lexington, Massachusetts
Toronto

BF
441
.B7813
1982

Library of Congress Cataloging in Publication Data

Bronner, Rolf.
  Decision making under time pressure.

  Translation of: Entscheidung unter Zeitdruck.
  Bibliography: p.
  Includes index.
  1. Decision-making. 2. Job stress. 3. Industrial management—Psychological aspects. I. Title.
BF441.B7813   658.4'03'019   81-47626
ISBN 0-669-04696-5   AACR2

Translated from the German edition: *Entscheidung unter Zeitdruck* © Rolf Bronner, J.C.B. Mohr (Paul Siebeck), Tübingen 1973.
Translation by Leo D. Aichinger and Hermann Fink.

Index copyright © 1982 by D.C. Heath and Company

All rights reserved. No part of this publication may be reproduced or transmitted in any form or by any means, electronic or mechanical, including photocopy, recording, or any information storage or retrieval system, without permission in writing from the publisher.

Published simultaneously in Canada

Printed in the United States of America

International Standard Book Number: 0-669-04696-5

Library of Congress Catalog Card Number: 81-47626

Contents

	List of Figures and Tables	vii
	Foreword *Eberhard Witte*	xi
Chapter 1	**Decision Making under Time Pressure as a Problem of Overcoming Stress**	1
	The Mastery of Stress as a Problem of Interdisciplinary Explanation	2
	The Elements of Stress	8
Chapter 2	**The Theory of Decision Making under Time Pressure**	21
	Conditions of Time Pressure	23
	Problem Solving under Time Pressure	27
	Performance Efficiency under Time Pressure	34
Chapter 3	**Method and Concept of Investigation**	49
	The Experiment as a Method of Research	50
	Experiment Characteristics	52
	The Experimental Design	58
	Quality of the Experiment	75
Chapter 4	**Verification of the Theory**	93
	The Conditions of Time Pressure	93
	Problem Solving under Time Pressure	100
	Efficiency of Performance under Time Pressure	120
Chapter 5	**Consequences of the Theory of Decision Making under Time Pressure**	143
	The Performance Character of Decision-Making Regulation	143
	The Mastery of Problem Intensity	147
	The Effectiveness of Time Pressure	151
	Appendix	155

Bibliography 159

Index 183

About the Author 187

List of Figures and Tables

Figures

3-1	Institutions in the Experiment	63
4-1	Experimental Designs of Different Research Projects	112

Tables

3-1	Dimensions of the Neutrality of Methods	58
3-2	Formation of Groups	66
3-3	Distribution of Professional Qualifications	66
3-4	Temporal Experiment Design	75
3-5	Comparison of Time-Pressure Sensitivity of Students and Practitioners	78
3-6	Comparison of Time-Pressure Sensitivity of Students and Practitioners, Experiment Periods 1-3	79
3-7	Comparison of Time-Pressure Sensitivity of Students and Practitioners, Experiment Periods 4-7	80
3-8	Comparison of Time-Pressure Sensitivity of Students and Practitioners, Experiment Periods 8-10	81
3-9	Comparison of Time-Pressure Sensitivity in Staff and Board of Directors' Positions in Experiment Periods with Time Limitations	83
3-10	Comparison of Market-Index Values of All Experiment Sequences	84
4-1	Comparison of Time-Pressure Index Values, by Time Limitation (Staff)	94

4-2	Comparison of Time-Pressure Index Values, by Time Limitation (Board of Directors)	95
4-3	Comparison of Time-Pressure Index Values, by Problem Intensity, Periods 1-3 and 8-10	98
4-4	Comparison of Time-Pressure Index Values, by Problem Intensity	99
4-5	Decision-Making Activities	101
4-6	Decision-Making Objects	102
4-7	Comparison of Communication, by Time Limitation	103
4-8	Comparison of Decision-Making Activity, by Time Limitation	103
4-9	Activity Profile of Decision-Making Performance	105
4-10	Object Profile of Decision-Making Performance	106
4-11	Operations Profile of Decision-Making Performance	107
4-12	Degree of Performance as a Function of Time Pressure	108
4-13	Comparison of Quantity of Demand for Information, by Time Limitation	113
4-14	Comparison of Degree of Precision of Demand for Information, by Time Limitation	113
4-15	Comparison of Breadth of Demand for Information, by Time Pressure	114
4-16	Coordination of Decisions	117
4-17	Comparison of Activities in Organizing the Decision, by Time Limitation	118
4-18	Comparison of Activities for Goal Setting, by Time Limitation	119

List of Figures and Tables   ix

4-19	Comparison of Satisfaction, by Degree of Activity	123
4-20	Comparison of Satisfaction, by Quantity of Information Demand	123
4-21	Comparison of Satisfaction, by Coordination Performance (Process, Function, and Goal Regulation)	124
4-22	Comparison of Time-Pressure Absorption (in Periods 8-10), by Degree of Activity	127
4-23	Comparison of Time-Pressure Absorption (in Periods 8-10), by Demand for Information	128
4-24	Comparison of Time-Pressure Absorption (in Periods 8-10), by Coordination Performance	128
4-25	Comparison of Success (after Ten Experiment Periods), by Degree of Activity	133
4-26	Comparison of Result-Index Values, by Degree of Activity	133
4-27	Comparison of Result-Index Values, by Demand for Information	134
4-28	Comparison of Success (after Ten Experiment Periods), by Demand for Information	135
4-29	Comparison of Success (after Ten Experiment Periods), by Coordination Performance	135
4-30	Comparison of Result-Index Values, by Coordination Performance	136
5-1	Comparison of Success (after Ten Experiment Periods), by Time-Pressure Sensitivity	151

Foreword

This experimental investigation of decision making under time pressure is part of a series of projects undertaken at the Institute of Organization of the University of Munich designed to establish an empirical theory of the firm. With this work Rolf Bronner continues scientific efforts to explain problem-solving behavior in decision-making processes.

The principal tool in all our studies has been the method of field investigation. We used it to analyze a variety of basic questions concerning individual behavior in the context of information processes, learning, goal setting, external influence, and the business organization proper and to measure the efficiency of decision processes. In his study of stress behavior in decision making, Rolf Bronner uses the experimental method, an unorthodox approach, at least in the economic sciences. His methodological concept and topic are rooted in the institute's cooperative program of research whose purpose is to analyze the firm under real-world conditions, to identify patterns of problem-solving behavior and, as a consequence, to attempt an explanation of the efficiency of problem solving itself.

Bronner develops his hypotheses and transforms them into operational statements that he can test rigorously. His theoretical propositions and empirical results refer to a sequence of homogeneous, multiperson problem-solving processes, with stress as a central condition. In contrast to field investigations, stress as a situation variable can be easily controlled in an experimental setting. One can measure under which conditions time pressure arises and how it influences the problem-solving behavior of decision makers. Since stress is varied experimentally, its influence upon problem-solving efficiency can be shown. A major result is that time constraints cannot be judged merely good or bad but that their numerous effects must be carefully differentiated.

The broad scope of the results is not only of interest to behavioral research but also of great importance to the part of organization theory concerned with arranging decision processes under time pressure. Finally, it addresses decision making in actual business situations where stress is a typical concomitant variable. It is important to know which management activities are shortened under stress and which activities are intensified under time pressure.

When Rolf Bronner's work appeared in German in 1973, it was one of a few scientific contributions that analyzed stress in the context of decision making in business. Today the increasing interest and critical awareness of this problem is an important reason to publish this research in English and to make it accessible to a broader public.

I am delighted that with this translation knowledge is transferred from the German to the Anglo-American language area and not as is usually the case in the social sciences. I hope it will be the beginning of a fruitful dialogue.

Eberhard Witte

Decision Making under Time Pressure

1

Decision Making under Time Pressure as a Problem of Overcoming Stress

In all areas of human existence decisions must be made that determine individual as well as collective behavior. Man's numerous associations with his natural and social environments bring about a variety of limits to behavior that ultimately lead to a restriction of freedom of action. Any form of such behavioral restriction constitutes a reduction of personal sovereignty. As soon as people perceive these dispositional borders, the stage is set for the creation of stress.

Stress is understood here in general terms as a condition to which individuals and groups are exposed when they recognize that their freedom of action is limited. It is the expression of a situation of tension in which a person finds himself or herself under behavioral pressure. Accordingly stress can be designated as any imbalance that prevails on the biological-physical, the psychic-cognitive, or the social-interactive level of the human system.

Decisions under time pressure are characterized as those situations in which it does not suffice to find a solution to the particular problem at hand or to reach the most-effective result possible. Rather the solution to a problem must be completed within a limited frame of time. There is not only an unspecified pressure for mental achievement; a secondary condition—limited time—plays a role as well. It is therefore justified to classify decisions under time pressure in the more-comprehensive problem area of behavior under stress.

The purpose of establishing this study within a superimposed concept of behavior is to provide a more-expansive view of the problem. Of course, this in no way redirects the focus of investigation in one direction, nor is it intended solely to open up a more-expanded field of findings for analogous conclusions.[1] Rather the goal of this expansion of the problem area is to create a theoretical bridge, which allows the discovery of common points of departure for solving the problem at hand. This procedure is particularly promising if other disciplines that deal with the mastery of stress have developed and proved explanations of phenomena. The association of differentiated individual findings affords the possibility of creating fact-finding systems with a higher degree of generalization.[2] The hypotheses necessary for the specific analysis of the behavior of decision making under time pressure can then be derived from a general theory of stress mastery, and the results of closer examination—in the case of confirmation as well as falsification—contribute to understanding a nonisolated problem.

That there is no common agreement on the definition of stress in its more-expanded connotation can be explained by the fact that concrete forms of the phenomenon strongly diverge with regard to their comprehension, as well as their effects. Nevertheless, the inconsistency of terminology does not represent a weighty argument. The greater the area of validity for a theoretical statement, "the more frequently such a statement will contain concepts which are based only indirectly and remotely on empirical data."[3] This also explains why the view of the term *stress* as used in this book does not agree fully with its medical definition.

According to Selye, biological stress is the reaction of the human organism to external pressures. He defines it as "the total sum of the various procedures of homeostasis . . . which constantly occur in the human body."[4] Selye is fully aware of the problem of such a reaction-orientated definition and system of measurement, noting that the biological-physiological reactions do not actually represent stress but the overcoming of stress—that is, mechanisms of adaptation.[5] The methodic question of stress measurement will not be discussed in depth at this point. It will be given more detailed treatment in connection with the measurement of the degree of stress in decision making under time pressure.

The Mastery of Stress as a Problem of Interdisciplinary Explanation

The prerequisites under which stress is produced and the forms in which it manifests itself are the object of behavioral science in a broader sense. Medicine and psychology, sociology and economics—to mention only the main disciplines of this field of research—seek to explain the factors that influence the extent of stress as perceived and investigate the measures by which stress situations are overcome.

Biological-Physical Stress

Physical and psychic stress first became an essential part of medical research on the basis of Selye's theoretical and experimental studies.[6] He was successful in proving that different forms of stress resulted in the systematic occurrence of a syndrome. Independent from the specific qualities of the respective stressor, the reaction of the body always follows the same pattern.[7] This process of adaptation, known as the *general adaptations syndrome,* follows a three-phase course.

A Problem of Overcoming Stress

First, there is an alarm reaction, in which the biological forces of resistance are mobilized. The phase that follows is characterized by vital resistance, which is the core of adaptation. Under continuing stress the limits of the ability to adapt are reached, and the behavior enters its final phase. The adaptation acquired is lost again, and a state of exhaustion is reached. If the stress exceeds the absorption effect of the adaptation measures, collapse of the biological system inevitably follows.[8] However, Selye emphasizes explicitly that stress is in no way to be viewed only as a factor that endangers existence.[9] During the course of continuing moderate stress, the organism is capable of accommodating itself to this restriction, and it may even use stress as a vitalizing stimulus for enhanced achievement. When stress is overcome, latent energies are released, which could not have been mobilized if there had been no stress initially.

Without a doubt, the most important finding of the medical investigation of stress was that the striving for stability and balance is inherent in the system. These findings of experimental medicine are of far-reaching significance for the clinical therapeutic field of this science. The principle of homeostasis can be considered the fundamental behavioral pattern of biological systems.

While the research on somatic and psychosomatic stress is primarily concerned with the analysis of the effect of exogenous stress, occupational medicine is attempting to identify the causes of stress in addition to its consequences. Thus it pursues a fundamentally different research concept. Contrary to Selye, who sees stress as a vitalizing and thus ultimately positive element of biological processes,[10] occupational medicine views its task as being in the field of preventative and corrective structuring of working conditions in order to minimize injuries. It therefore concentrates particularly on psychic stress in the performance of industrial work, although it also has produced findings in the areas of dispositive activity and of stress occurring in mental work.[11]

Psychic-Cognitive Stress

In addition to its medical-biological approach, stress was recognized, under the strong influence of Freud,[12] as a central phenomenon of human life. New disciplines such as psychoanalysis and psychotherapy arose and led to an extension and connection of the medical and psychological areas of study.[13]

Around 1944 psychology, strengthened by the events and consequences of World War II, took up the problem of overcoming stress.[14] Thus the first studies were largely influenced by the physical and ethical stress caused by the chaotic conditions of the war.[15] Since then the field of investigation has been under constant expansion, and now an almost boundless wealth of literature exists. The field encompasses a wide spectrum of real and simulated stress situations. Natural catastrophes, impending surgery,[16] and experiencing the use of violence as well as crises in the course of civilian and military training[17] provide the basis for fieldwork and experimental research. Concepts such as fear, conflict, defense, aggression, and frustration are representative of the various aspects of the problem.[18] The strong methodic connection between this area of psychology of the individual and biological stress research is clearly discernible. Although human reactions to outside pressures are not designated as stress in themselves, they retain the character of operationalizations and evidence of stress.[19]

Festinger's *Dissonance Theory* goes beyond this theoretical and terminological framework, focusing on a condition of tension in the cognitive dimension of human behavior.[20] This condition arises when information is perceived that contradicts preexisting notions, attitudes, or actions.[21] This cognitive imbalance is described as inconsistence, or dissonance, and as understood in this book is defined as *stress*. For the mastery of this cognitive state of tension, the dissonance theory predicts a selective behavior toward information.[22] The consequent development of Festinger's approach—by way of analysis of attitudinal changes—made possible the establishment of a concept of theories of cognitive consistence.[23] Within this expanded theoretical framework, stress again became an explicitly designated central object of explanation.[24]

Cognitive stress arises when a human being's attitudes and judgments and the security connected with them are threatened by external pressure in the form of incompatible information. In such a state of tension, the entire behavior is directed at the reinstatement of internal stability. For this purpose a subtle set of regulative instruments are employed, which permit the mastery of this specific form of stress.[25] The cognitive system shields itself by rejecting inconsistent and purposive selection of consistent information and seeking information that conforms to actions and attitudes. Information contrary to the cognitive status is underrated in its relevancy, ignored, and thereby excluded from mental processing. In order to increase the cognitive value of the information the person reevaluates its source. If the existence of the stress-triggering information cannot be ignored by means of these defense mechanisms alone, a process of selective forgetting begins, which leads to the repression of inconsistent cognitive elements.

The core of the multitude of activities used for the mastery of stress consists of the stabilization of the cognitive system. As was already shown for the biological plane of human behavior, there is also in the area of cognitive orientation an obvious, natural tendency to secure balance. While physiological adaptation reactions achieve harmony in the body, the human system secures itself on its cognitive plane through measures of corresponding suitability. The human being protects his cognitive status by "self-censorship."[26]

Thus far the analysis of behavior under stress has left the manifold social ties of human beings largely unconsidered. The purpose of this attempted isolation was to present individual mastery of stress free from socially caused behavioral interferences. This fiction could not be completely maintained because in the framework of consistency theory social determinants of behavior had become apparent, but generally the individual focus remained.[27] This limitation now must be abandoned.

For the most part, human behavior is socially determined. In Festinger's formulation, this contention is valid not only for the interpersonal sphere but for the interpersonal area of cognition.[28] He designates the social comparison and the social adaptation connected with it as an elementary pattern of behavior for the achievement of personal cognitive balance. Man, in orienting the formation of his personal judgment by the utterances and expectations of his social environment, reaches a collective anchorage, which leads to internal congruency. He seeks justification for his decisions and is prepared to adapt himself to prescribed maxims.[29] By attempting to achieve social support for the reduction of cognitive stress, social obligations are assumed, which themselves can produce stress.[30]

Social-Interactive Stress

Social systems secure themselves from external interference and internal dissolution by steering the behavior of their individual members and subgroups.[31] They try to guarantee their ability to exist and the achievement of the goals of the whole group in order to maintain and, if possible, extend their autonomy.[32] To preserve their internal stability, a comprehensive repertoire of influencing techniques is available, which social psychology calls *social pressure*.[33] At the heart of this control of behavior are the group member's ties to role expectations. From the particular function and position of the individual, from his role within the social system, there result numerous imposed demands on achievement and behavior, which constitute personal stress. This stress, which grows from the requirement for role-determined conformity, is strengthened to a considerable degree by the individual's integration into a multiple network of roles.[34]

People overcome social interactive stress through "adaption and conformity" to the social environment and its behavioral norms.[35] By using "adaptive defense mechanisms," they secure their social position and at the same time achieve an internal balance.[36] The particular mechanisms that people develop for this purpose are not of primary interest in the search for a common behavior in overcoming stress, however. More important is the fundamental postulate of the sociological study of stress that "in stress conditions some mechanisms will most probably occur which can relieve these tensions."[37]

The presentation of behavior under stress thus far has proceeded from the perspective of the individual. This approach was justified because biological-physical stress and psychic-cognitive pressure affect persons as individuals exclusively. By contrast, not only does social interactive stress affect the individual person as a member of social systems, but also the system as a whole can be exposed to this form of pressure in addition to other restrictions. But since I am examining not individual behavior but problem solving by groups, an expansion of the theoretical approach is necessary. The task at hand is to test whether the behavior of groups corresponds to individual behavior.

An examination of the sociological literature on stress behavior indicates that research in individual stress mastery generally is most common.[38] Even when explicit organizational stress is discussed, the explanation focuses on the behavior of the members of the group.[39] This transfer of the problem from the microsocial to the macrosocial level is further supported by many terminological overlappings within the social sciences.[40] The resulting heterogeneous conceptual picture of stress behavior offers more confusion than insight, although at least an analogous transfer can be made of the findings from the individual analytic area into the theoretical frame of reference of collectively oriented behavioral science.

It can be tacitly assumed, therefore, that the behavior of groups is to be recognized as an additive or at least complementary function of the behavior of individuals. To the extent that this approach is not applied as an untested research finding but is used for the generation of theses still to be proved, it can be regarded as legitimate. An integration and with it a generalization of testimony can be achieved if the similarity between unipersonal and multipersonal behavior is not only imputed but also explained. The most pointed comments on this matter are provided by Hall and Mansfield.[41] They base their empirical analysis on a model of sequential relationship upon which organizational stress acts as an external factor of disturbance. This stress is first directed to the institution; by system internal transfer, however, it later becomes individual stress for its members.[42] The restriction that bears an influence from the outside is carried over to the individual. The circle of effect is closed when the stress behavior of the individual members of the system again sets off internal organizational stress.

Institutional and individual stress exist in a close, mutual correlation of effect.[43] That which represents stress to the individual, to the institution already signifies a tendential stress reduction.

The investigative interests of sociology and social psychology concern themselves primarily with the social instruments for overcoming crises. If,

A Problem of Overcoming Stress

in a search for patterns of behavior, one abstracts from the variables that are caused by the respective method and stress situation, some general measures for overcoming stress can be determined.

In this search communication and cooperation prove to be major points of departure for securing the system.[44] One of the earliest empirically marked statements concerning the general behavior of social systems is found in Pareto. He proceeds from an immanent striving for balance and formulates in reference to the condition of the system, "If we insinuate that some change is made artificially in its form [virtual movements], then if the real change is taken into account, a reaction will soon follow in the sense that the changed situation will be reverted to its original condition."[45] The same basic thought can be found in March and Simon, who developed a theory of organizational balance from the interplay of stimuli and contributions.[46] Their concept focused on the explanation of entrance, residency, and exit of the members, an essential component of institutions.

Such homeostatically based attempts at explanation are not accepted without reservation.[47] The main point of conjecture is found in the criticism of the analogous transfer of biophysical laws of the individual and particularly of the collective behavior of humans. Thus Mayntz emphasizes that "the goal-directed social system is different from the organism."[48] She goes on to say that "with organic systems one can speak of a self-preservation tendency which is also served by the homeostatic goal-orientation of the organism. This notion cannot be simply applied to a goal-directed social system."[49] Davis emphasizes his objections to an even greater degree and arrives at the conclusion that "homeostasis is not a good, universally applicable model of behavior."[50]

These reservations toward an uncritical acceptance of findings from other disciplines do not, however, result in any basic rejection of the assumption that a system tends to preserve itself. They are primarily directed against a static, automatized view. "A sociological theory which is really striving at becoming dynamic will almost always include the dimension of time in the analysis and will have to examine the differences of the rates of social change, the time sequence of decisive events, moments of inertia and delays. A mere interest in 'timeless' shifts between conditions of balance does not suffice."[51] The necessity as well as the empirically provable fact of self-preservation and the overcoming of conflict are essentially undisputed.[52] Thus it can be established that human beings, not only as individuals but also as social units of aggregation, dispose of strategies for overcoming stress. Social systems are in a position to master external pressures by adapting themselves to the changed situation, using the resources of interactive structuring. A dynamic balance and thus stability is strived for by means of reaction mechanisms, which depend on the situation and are specific to the system. The general pattern of behavior for overcoming stress can be formulated for individuals and groups in an identical manner: adaptation, stabilization, and balance form the elements of a strategy of stress behavior.

The Elements of Stress

The theoretical analysis has been aimed thus far at the determination of modes of behavior that can be isolated in different disciplines and under different forms of stress conditions. The purpose has been to uncover the common structure, that is, the strategic concept, and not the specific facts, that is, the instrumental actions. The characteristic methods of overcoming stress have been worked out in this way, in quite general terms, and it is now necessary to investigate the measurement of stress in decision making under time pressure. At the same time this second analytical step is designed to establish the managerial organizational frame of reference to the problem.

While there has been an almost boundless abundance of literature dealing with biological and socially caused stress, the frame of reference of our question of decision making under stress is being more closely defined. The thematically relevant writings allow only restricted application since the forms of stress and/or the character of problem solving are only peripherally related to our closely defined field of investigation.

Most of the underlying tasks concern simple problems whose solution requires but a few minutes and rather playful selective actions. The discrepancy between the thematic designation of the investigations and the operationalizations employed in them becomes particulary evident with Broadbent.[53] But studies of this kind do not correspond to our research approach in either content or method. They depict only insufficiently the complexity of economic selective actions and neglect the procedural characteristics of the decision.[54] References concerning the amount of stress in decisions, as they are to be investigated here, can be expected only from literature that devotes itself to complex problems of decision making. Therefore, the statements about the theory of decision making presented thus far are to be tested from this vantage.

Personal Disposition

In his psychological investigation of the individual, Thomae emphasizes that decisions of great existential significance are determined by the existence of stress.[55] He comes to the conclusion that "not a feeling of activity but rather one of passivity, namely one of existential perplexity is characteristic of the initial experience of the decision."[56] The mental involvement with the solution of the problem at hand already contains stress. "Human beings hate to make decisions. Indecision is generally more comfortable.... Decisions are painful."[57]

Witte takes up the unipersonal-oriented approach of Thomae and transforms it into multipersonal economic decisions.[58] He develops a catalog of questions that he uses to discuss the relevance of the organizational process in the view purported by Thomae. At the heart of this discussion are the consequences for decision-making behavior and the delineation of the organizational structuring of the process.[59]

Situative Complexity

In addition to these investigations of the existence and effects of restrictions on behavior, the problem of restrictions of information has become an essential question in the more-recent theory of decision making.[60] Incomplete information is regarded today as one of the central sources of pressure in performing decision-making tasks. The amount of foresight is directly related to the postulate of rationality.

Nevertheless, the classical and neoclassical models of microeconomic decision making do not offer references concerning the occurrence of decisional stress based on information. They surmise that the selective actions are performed under the availability of complete information. The data and alternatives essential for the decision are given. Furthermore, it is assumed that the rule guiding the decision is the maximization of benefit or—if oriented to a higher degree by the goal criteria of the business enterprise—the maximization of profit.[61] Both assumptions form necessary conditions for a rational decision devoid of any restriction. The criticism of this approach, which is too divorced from reality, was first directed against the theorem of certainty.[62] "Today the environment of the economic decision maker is much more complex and therefore uncertain. For this reason the assumption of perfect information, of acting under certainty—aside from extreme cases—can no longer be maintained."[63] An even more extensive view is held by Scherhorn, who considers full information not only difficult to achieve but, for considerations of theoretical probability, not necessary.[64] Both premises of the theory of decision making, the more strongly rationalistic as well as its behavioristic version deal with the question of limited foresight.[65]

The mathematically formal approach, which encompasses the so-called statistical theory or logics of decision making as well as the game theory, takes up this aspect in its calculations of uncertainty and risk. The goal of these experiments is to include the various degrees of problem complexity and intensity of negotiation. Rules of decision making are being developed on the basis of statistical probabilities, including parameters that depict the respective willingness to assume risks.[66] With rationality aids of this type intransparent problem situations are to be structured and analyzed objectively. The initially incalculable risk is delineated and brought to the fore. In this way the efficiency of problem solving—especially in spite of existing information gaps—must be intensified; the total renunciation of decision making and thus the fatalistic submission to coincidence must be prevented.

This development of the theory, characterized by more-realistic assumptions concerning the decision-making situation, leads to a fundamental change in the still-central concept of rationality. An assessment of a concept of rationality that is unilaterally oriented by a maximal goal is replaced by a relativized concept of rationality. This concept makes it possible to cope better with the cognitive pressures that develop from the actual conditions of a problem situation, that can be mastered only to a limited degree.

This framework of empirically relevant statements on decisional behavior is expanded on the basis of the works of Simon.[67] The behavioral theoretical approach proceeds from the basic tenet that people do not pursue any maximal or minimal goals at all, as is presupposed in the classical model of rational decision making. Rather, the individual overcomes problem situations by striving for satisfying solutions. Human activities in general, and particularly decision making, are oriented by the dimension of the goal one sets.[68] By setting up a basis of judgment autonomously, a person is capable of ensuring internal satisfaction and balance in spite of external performance stress. The less easily the problem situation can be mastered, the more important this mechanism of self-stabilization becomes. The concept of *bounded rationality* rests on an environment that, fundamentally, can be only partially comprehended or controlled. Defective cognitive abilities, insufficient resources for the search as well as the costs of information permit only a limited analysis of the situation. Accordingly, the striving for a satisfying solution to the problem is an embodiment of the elementary maxim of behavior.[69] It is presupposed—usually not explicitly—that a theory of collective decision making is derived directly from the decision-making behavior of the individual.[70]

The goal of the previous analysis was not to provide a representative insight into decision-making theory today.[71] Rather it was to search selectively for indications concerning the amount of stress in decisions, which will have to be observed within the framework of an investigation of decisions under time pressure.

In sum, it can be said that if one attempts to grasp and present the explicative contribution of the theory of decision making, the argument focuses on three areas. The object of the first area of comment is the person as the individual bearer of the decision. Independent of the subject matter of the decision, philosophy and psychology take up this basic question of human existence and try to reach generally valid findings. By contrast, the second area of the theory of decision making—completely neglecting personality characteristics—contains statements concerning the situation of the decision. With great emphasis placed on the respective concrete problems to be solved here, methods are developed for problem solving. The third attempt at explanation within the theory of decision making could be termed *synthetic,* insofar as it conceives of a general theory of decision-making *behavior* of individuals and groups.

While the approach that is directed at the problems of obtaining information in decision-making situations concentrates on the objective analytic mastery of uncertainty and does not explicitly treat the fact of decisional stress, the cognitive pressures assume central significance in the two other areas of the theory: in the specifically individual as well as the general decisional behavior. Decision is understood here explicitly as a dual state of tension. It always implies the existence and mastery of a problem defined by content; it also implies the existence and mastery of psychic-cognitively determined stress. The elaboration of pertinent problem solutions is understood here as a very function of overcoming stress.

Time Restrictions

The subject matter of this investigation is not the general stress involved in making decisions but the pressure produced by the time limit imposed. Thus, our interest is in a specific form of stress. Nevertheless, it was necessary to deal with the general concept of stress because our investigation also includes the relationships discussed in that connection. The reduction of the problem-solving time cannot be regarded as an isolated fact, for it leads to an intensification of pressures already present.

From the perspective of the individual decision maker who is under the influence of psychic stress, the limitation of individual reaction time means an intensification of stress. In an intransparent decision-making situation, the shortening of the time available for an analysis of the problem leads to a limitation of the information-gathering possibilities and thus to increased uncertainty.[72] Cognitive decision stress is overlapped by an additional condition of stress, so that the effects measured are always to be understood as resultants from two stress components. We call the pressure emanating from the content of the decision problem *elementary stress* and differentiate it from time pressure, which results from the limitation of the time available in making the decision. Compensatory and additive effects cannot be excluded when elementary stress itself has to be recognized as a variable.

The fact that decisions in business must frequently—if not regularly—be made under time pressure is given rather scant regard in economic literature. Although this time limitation in business firms is touched upon in studies on management, it rarely receives comprehensive treatment.[73] German as well as Anglo-American literature lack statements concerning this basic problem of decision making reality. Rubenstein and Haberstroh also recognized this problem: "One aspect of decision making that has not been sufficiently studied is the question of time constraints on decision making—the time during which the decision maker has to resolve a decision problem."[74]

The principal problem of using time resources in decision making is a new frontier in science. "Despite the extensive research on decision making, surprisingly little research has been done on the time that decision makers take to make complex decisions."[75]

With their almost-classical contribution to the theory of organizations, March and Simon probably developed the first systematic approach that included time as a determinant in the behavior of resolving problems. Time pressure constitutes one of the variables for the explanation of intraindividual conflicts. The "unacceptability, incomparability and uncertainty" that result from the available alternative solutions are the causes of cognitive stress.[76] The amount of time pressure intensifies this internal state of stress and motivates the effort to overcome the conflict. "In general, the search will be more vigorous the greater the time pressure."[77] Thus, time pressure initially is considered as unpleasantly perceived stress whose effect on attentiveness and selective perception capability must ultimately be regarded as positive.[78]

Aside from this concept of March and Simon, who are oriented toward the theory of cognitive learning and who conceive time pressure as an explicatory element of the general theory of behavior in solving problems, there are individual, strongly pragmatic representations that deal with insufficient time in decision making. Morris notes that "at present there seems to be nothing very subtle to be said about how decisions should be made under this pressure, but its existence must be clearly recognized.. . . The firm is continually under the pressure of time in many of its activities."[79] Morris identifies as the central problem the limitation of information-gathering possibilities and the consequent limitation of the development of alternatives directly connected with it. The search concentrates on finding satisfactory alternatives; and depending on the intensity of time constraint, a lowering of original goals ensues. This finding on adaptive behavior is supplemented by Morris with a structuring norm: "The obvious way of reacting to repetitive decisions made in the face of time pressure . . . is, of course, the formulation of policy which effectively predetermines the choice."[80]

The empirical data of a field investigation led Hall and Lawler to conclude that time pressure by far is the most frequently cited form of job

A Problem of Overcoming Stress

stress.[81] Nevertheless multivariate correlation analysis cannot furnish a distinct correlation of this variable with other criteria of performance. In this case time pressure assumes the position of an almost-isolated variable, which ranks high in individual consciousness but whose functional relationship cannot be proved.[82]

At first glance this appears surprising. Nevertheless, it has an explanation when we consider the following. Undoubtedly time pressure is a common restriction in problem solving, particularly within the framework of decision-making processes in business. It could also be proved that this limitation of time on decision making constitutes a pressure for the individual decision maker, as well as for decision-making groups. The ensuing state of temporal constraint as a specific form of stress causes the development of compensating mechanisms, which allow the mastery of the stress situation.

Active and passive behavior change as a result of these adaptation measures. Cangelosi and Dill speak of organizational learning, which occurs during the course of repeated confrontation with problems of the same type.[83] The positive effect of stress again becomes apparent. It manifests itself in such a way that the short-term frictions that occur with the behavior and success in problem solving are ultimately overcome and thus no longer identifiable. This consequence, which has often been proved empirically, may serve as an explanation that a functional relationship between time pressure and characteristics of achievement that have been revealed ex post cannot be verified. The negative findings of Hall and Lawler can be regarded as a virtual confirmation of the thesis of adaptation.[84]

Statements made thus far by the theory of decision making on the problem of time pressure are limited to scarcely operational assumptions. While the theoretical approach of logical decision making understands time restrictions to be a cause of incomplete information exclusively, and subsequently subordinates them, directly and in an immunizing manner, to the problem of uncertainty, time pressure, in the theoretical concept of behavior, continues to be understood as an independent variable. Although the aspect of time is shifted onto the cognitive level of problem-solving behavior, it retains its explanatory function as a stimulating element in the quest for information. Based on general consensus, behavior under time pressure is understood as a specific form of overcoming stress. This widely held view is clearly manifest in the references to basically adaptive behavior and its designation as a positive impulse for crisis mastery. From available empirical tests dealing with this question, we can derive an essential requirement for a personal methodological approach. A variable whose existence at first is perceived as strain that apparently causes processes of adaption and compensation, which ultimately lead to overcoming the restriction, can be analyzed successfully only on the basis of a long-term dynamic research approach. These findings, although sketchy at this time, are the result of a successively limiting extraction of relevant literature.

Notes

1. See analogy as a method of discovery in W. Stegmüller, *Wissenschaftliche Erklärung* (1969), p. 133; G. Klaus, *Logik* (1966), p. 415ff; R. Löther, *Vergleich* (1969), p. 103ff; and W. Segeth, *Logik* (1971), p. 272ff.

2. For the need to generalize in the form of the most-general theories possible, see particularly A. Malewski, *Reduktion* (1965), and K.-D. Opp, *Anwendung* (1967), p. 400, who emphasize the aspect of economic findings of generalization, and K.R. Popper, *Theories* (1968), p. 287, who accentuates the critical aspect of increasing falsifiability of findings. S.L. Rubinstein, *Denken* (1968), p. 28ff, and F. Richter, *Vereinfachung* (1969), discuss the procedures of abstracting.

3. Malewski, *Reduktion,* p. 374.

4. H. Selye, *Stress* (1957), p. 72.

5. See ibid.

6. See ibid.

7. The inner kidney, the thymolymphatic system, and the intestinal tract react physiologically to stress.

8. See Selye, *Stress,* p. 44ff.

9. See ibid., Foreword.

10. See ibid., p. 19ff.

11. See F. Koelsch, *Arbeitsmedizin* 1 (1963), and *Arbeitsmedizin* 2 (1966).

12. See S. Freud, *Psychopathologie* (1947), and S. Freud, *Psychoanalyse* (1953).

13. See A. Karsten, *Motivation* (1963), p. 288. These attempts at integration give the greatest emphasis to the efforts in achieving the development of general system of theories as it is represented particularly by Bertalanffy and Rapoport. See also L. v. Bertalanffy, *Theoretical Models* (1951); A. Rapoport, *Self-Organization* (1960); S.I. Cohen, A.J. Silverman, and B.M. Shmavonian, *Human Adaptation* (1959); Sir G. Vickers, *Stress* (1959); J.G. Miller, *Living Systems* (1965); H. Reinermann, *Systeme* (1970); and M.D. Mesarovic, *Systems* (1962).

14. R.S. Lazarus, *Stress* (1966), p. 9, points out that the concept of stress first appeared in 1944 in the *Index of Psychological Abstracts.*

15. B. Bettelheim, *Extreme Situations* (1958), provides an investigation on behavior under stress in concentration camps. R.R. Grinker and J.P. Spiegel, *Stress* (1945), analyze human behavior under combat conditions.

16. I.L. Janis, *Stress* (1958), devotes this study to the problems in connection with the psychic pressures of patients before, during, and after surgery.

17. D. Mechanic, *Stress* (1962), analyzes the social behavior of students directly before examinations; R. Radloff and R. Helmreich, *Stress* (1968), investigate the modes of behavior of aquanauts in an underwater research station; and Th.E. Drabek, *Laboratory Simulation* (1969), tests the behavior of policemen in a surveillance control room. An airplane catastrophe was simulated as the condition of stress.

18. See Lazarus, *Stress*, p. 1ff., and S.Z. Klausner, *Stressful Situations* (1966), p. 334ff.

19. See M.H. Appley and R. Trumbull, *Stress* (1967), p. 5, and G.E. Ruff and S.J. Korchin, *Stress Behavior* (1967), p. 297.

20. L. Festinger, *Dissonance* (1957), lays the foundation for an immense abundance of contributions to a theory of cognitive equilibrium. See also J.W. Brehm and A.R. Cohen, *Dissonance* (1962) and R.P. Abelson et al., eds., *Consistency* (1968).

21. Festinger, *Dissonance,* p. 13ff. illustrates the initially formal definition by several markedly different examples and in this way is able to sketch the span of the area of occurrence of dissonance.

22. See ibid., pp. 3, 18ff.

23. Brehm and Cohen are representatives of a general theory of consistency. See Brehm and Cohen, *Dissonance;* A.R. Cohen, *Attitude Change* (1964); and Abelson et al., eds., *Consistency.*

24. See E.L. Norris, *Stress* (1968), and P.H. Tannenbaum, *Stress* (1968).

25. See, among others, Freud, *Psychopathologie;* S. Freud, *Verdrängung* (1965); N. Miller, *Time* (1968), p. 590; E.E. Levitt, *Angst* (1971), p. 35ff.; and M. Haire, *Psychology* (1964), p. 92ff.

26. M. v. Cranach, *Selbstzensur* (1968), uses this appropriate designation to characterize the general information behavior of human beings.

27. See L. Festinger and J.M. Carlsmith, *Kognitive Folgen* (1969).

28. See L. Festinger, *Comparison Processes* (1954).

29. See F. Naschold, *Systemsteuerung* (1969), p. 66ff., and E.K. Francis, *Grundlagen* (1957), p. 62ff.

30. W.J. Goode, *Rollen-Stress* (1967), p. 269, and M. Irle, *Macht* (1971), p. 14ff.

31. See particularly K.H. Tjaden, *Sozialsysteme* (1971), for the development and span of this concept.

32. F. Naschold, *Systemsteuerung* (1969), p. 25.

33. Synonyms are such concepts as *group pressure* and *social control.* See particularly L. Festinger, *Social Communication* (1960), p. 287ff.; G.C. Homans, *Gruppe* (1968), p. 271ff.; S.E. Asch, *Social Pressure*

(1964); A.G. Athos and R.E. Coffey, *Behavior* (1968), p. 94ff.; V.H. Vroom, *Organizational Control* (1964), p. 72ff.; H.A. Simon, *Models* (1967), p. 115ff.; P.A. Hare, *Handbook* (1967), p. 24ff.; and R.M. Stogdill, *Group Ahievement* (1959), p. 213ff.

34. See W.J. Goode, *Rollen-Stress* (1967), p. 271.
35. R. Mayntz, *Soziale Organisation* (1958), p. 43.
36. F.E. Horvath, *Psychological Stress* (1959), p. 206.
37. Goode, *Rollen-Stress,* p. 272.
38. See S.Z. Klausner, *Stressful Situations* (1966), p. 334, who investigated 1,226 writings concerning behavior under stress. He determined that the majority of these publications is devoted to the behavior of the individual in military and civilian groups. Next most common are writings on purely individual behavior without social ties.
39. See R.L. Kahn, D.M. Wolfe, R.P. Quinn, J.D. Snoek, and R.A. Rosenthal, *Organizational Stress* (1964), who develop stress behavior from the concept of the social role. Also J.T. Lanzetta, *Stress* (1955), p. 29, attributes group behavior to "the behavior of individuals interacting in small groups."
40. For the dimension of content of stress research, see Ch.F. Hermann, *Crisis* (1963-1964), p. 63; Horvath, *Psychological Stress,* p. 205; and Klausner, *Stressful Situations,* p. 334ff.
41. See D.T. Hall and R. Mansfield, *External Stress* (1971), p. 533.
42. This shift of stress within the social system is also mentioned by Hermann, *Crisis,* p. 71.
43. See ibid., p. 66, and H. Oaklander and E.A. Fleishman, *Organizational Stress* (1963-1964), p. 522ff.
44. These characteristics of interaction are the focal point of the investigation by H. Guetzkow and J. Gyr, *Conflict* (1964), p. 367ff.; Hermann, *Crisis,* p. 68; and R. Dubin *Stability* (1959), p. 218ff.
45. V. Pareto, *Gesellschaft* (1971), p. 72.
46. See J.G. March and H.A. Simon, *Organizations* (1958), p. 83ff. G. Carlsson, *Funktionalismus* (1965), p. 240, also gives a similar presentation.
47. For homeostasis as a principle of the existence of organisms, see F. Alexander, *Homöostase* (1966).
48. R. Mayntz, *Soziologie* (1963), p. 43.
49. Ibid., p. 46.
50. R.C. Davis, *Homöostase* (1966), p. 486.
51. G. Carlsson, *Funktionalismus* (1965), p. 236.
52. Mayntz, *Soziologie,* p. 46ff., acknowledges self-preservation of groups as the prerequisite for existence and identifies interaction and identification as essential mechanisms of stabilization.
53. D.E. Broadbent, *Decision and Stress,* (1971), p. 4, is to be given

unlimited agreement when he states, "The most valid theory is one which works." Nevertheless, it is quite doubtful whether the simplification of situation conditions (p. 3) and reaction variables (p. 274) noted by Broadbent himself justifies the designations of "stress" and "decisions." Statements on simple motoric activities as are characteristic for psychological reaction time tests should be subject to a careful equivalence test before far-reaching generalizations are made.

E. Aronson and D. Landy, *Excess Time Effect* (1967), vary the solution time of their test items between five and fifteen minutes. W.G. Schutz, *Groups* (1955), p. 437, limits the time to sixty and thirty seconds. Even R.W. Pollay, *Decision Times* (1970), p. 459, who also objects to the transferability of results from choice-reaction-time investigations on the basis of a few seconds, employs only problems with a short solution time of eight to eleven minutes.

54. Literature on decision making in economics, however, is in full agreement on marking the character of the process as an essential characteristic. For this see H. Albach, *Entscheidungsprozess* (1961), p. 356ff.; K. Bender, *Führungsentscheidung* (1957), p. 25ff.; W.R. Dill, *Decision-Making* (1962), p. 33; G. Gäfgen, *Entscheidung* (1968), p. 100ff.; E. Kosiol, *Organisation* (1962), p. 102; E. Witte, *Entscheidung* (1964), p. 106; E. Witte, *Phasen-Theorem* (1968), p. 625ff.

55. H. Thomae, *Entscheidung* (1960), p. 88, clearly discerns decisions as "core-centered reactions" from other forms of mastering multivalent situations.

56. Ibid., p. 124.

57. H.A. Bullis, *Making Decisions* (1967), p. 127. See also O.W. Haseloff, *Risiko* (1970), p. 131, and W.J. Gore, *Decision-Making* (1964), p. 28ff.

58. See Witte, *Entscheidung*, p. 110ff; S. Biasio, *Entscheidung* (1969), pp. 9ff., 78ff. addresses decision-making behavior in connection with work psychology; however, his work is directed to the individual.

59. See Witte, *Entscheidung*, pp. 108ff., 122 ff.

60. See C.W. Churchman, *Ungewissheit* (1970); G. Gäfgen, *Entscheidung* (1968); W. Wittman, *Information* (1959); E. Witte, *Informationsverhalten* (1972), who focus on this problem in their investigations. G. Katona, *Rational Behavior* (1964), D.W. Taylor, *Decision Making* (1965), and F. Naschold, *Systemsteuerung* (1969), p. 30ff., provide an overview of the development of a widely understood theory of decision making.

61. For repeated criticism of this assumption, see Katona, *Rational Behavior,* p. 57ff., and E. Grunberg, *Wirtschaftswissenschaft* (1971), p. 75ff., who shows that a general axiom was developed from a statement originally understood to be a hypothesis. The frequently polemic attempt at justification by F. Machlup, *Marginalanalyse* (1971), proves that this dis-

cussion to justify such prerequisites is not simply the result of more-recent considerations.

62. Morgenstern was, indeed, the first to carry this assumption ad absurdum. For this see O. Morgenstern, *Wirtschaftsprognose* (1928), p. 98ff., and *Vollkommene Voraussicht* (1964), p. 257ff.

63. F. Naschold, *Systemsteuerung* (1969), p. 36.

64. See G. Scherhorn, *Information* (1964), p. 27ff.

65. W.J. Gore, *Essay on Decision-Making* (1959), p. 100, typifies both analytical directions of decision-making research.

66. F. Philipp, *Risiko* (1967), esp. p. 57ff., provides an overview on the problems and operational rules of decision making. For this also see R. Schneeweiss, *Entscheidungskriterien* (1967), p. 12, concerning the forms of uncertainty and the nature of the rules of decision making (p. 17); W. Wittman, *Information* (1959), p. 158, and D. Schneider, *Investition* (1970), pp. 63–128.

67. See H.A. Simon, *Behavior* (1957); H.A. Simon, *Rational Choice* (1964); J.G. March and H.A. Simon, *Organizations* (1958), but also Taylor, *Decision Making,* and J. Feldman and H.E. Kanter, *Decision Making* (1965).

68. See F. Hoppe, *Anspruchsniveau* (1966), p. 217ff., for the general character of this target value.

69. For the level of aspiration as a determinant of decision making, see March and Simon, *Organizations,* p. 136ff.; R.M. Cyert, H.A. Simon, and D.B. Trow, *Business Decision* (1960), p. 459; S. Siegel, *Level of Aspiration* (1964), p. 119ff., and E. Heinen, *Entscheidungen* (1971), p. 239ff.

From the same considerations, D. Braybrooke and Ch.E. Lindblom, *Strategy* (1963), p. 11ff., emphasize a pragmatic approach when generally advocating a "Strategy of Disjointed Incrementalism" (p. 81) "as a practical substitute for the calculus" (p. 225).

70. An explicit characterization of this reductionist approach is provided by W. Kirsch, *Entscheidungsprozesse*, I, II, III (1970–1971), p. 7: "However, not the organizations decide. Investigations of organizational theory therefore have to begin with the decision-making persons." He justifies such a concept under the reference to the decision premises: "Moreover, this combining function of the concept of decision premise allows the making of the theory of individual decision making the basis for the theoretical analysis of organizational systems or collective decision-making processes" (p. 94). For this see, however, J.W. McGuire, *Theories* (1964), p. 27, and J. Marschak and R. Radner, *Teams* (1972), p. 327, who emphasize the differences between individual and collective decisions. Also R. Münch, *Mentales System* (1972), p. 8ff., points out the problems of a generally reductionist approach.

71. See here Kirsch, *Entscheidungsprozesse.*

72. For this see M.F. Meltzer, *Information Center* (1967), p. 34f.

73. H. Dienstbach, *Anpassung* (1968), p. 144ff. points to the insufficient flexibility in problem solving under time pressure. See also W.T. Morris, *Management Science* (1968), p. 11; W.T. Morris, *Management Decisions* (1969), p. 33ff.; J. Bidlingmaier, *Unternehmerziele* (1964), p. 178; E. Hodnett, *Problem Solving* (1955), p. 80; and K. Bender, *Führungsentscheidung* (1957), p. 84ff.

74. A.H. Rubenstein and Ch.J. Haberstroh, *Communication* (1966), p. 375.

75. R.W. Pollay, *Decision Times* (1970), p. 459.

76. March and Simon, *Organizations,* p. 113.

77. Ibid., p. 116.

78. Ibid., p. 154.

79. Morris, *Management Decision,* p. 470.

80. Ibid., p. 473.

81. D.T. Hall and E.E. Lawler, *Job Characteristics* (1970), in a work-analytical study recorded the job characteristics of 313 executives in twenty-two research and development institutions. "Job pressures" were determined on the basis of questionnaires and interviews. Time pressure, financial responsibility and quality demands on the job formed the ranking order of the pressures mentioned.

82. For the analytic method, the statistical values, and model-like interpretation, see ibid., p. 275ff.

83. See V.E. Cangelosi and W.R. Dill, *Organizational Learning* (1965-1966, esp. pp. 175, 191ff.

84. Our methodic approach will take these circumstances into account and therefore will investigate problem mastery in its process.

2

The Theory of Decision Making under Time Pressure

The goal of this investigation is to develop a system of explanatory theories that will hold up under the test of practical application. We are thus pursuing a reality-oriented research concept whose results will be used to formulate an empirically viable theory for decision making under time pressure. For this purpose it will be necessary, as a first theoretical step, to produce the findings of the explanatory system individually and to trace their relationship to each other. Modern scientific logic does not consider the creation and construction of theories a methodological problem.[1] Correspondingly, there are no rules that demand absolute adherence. The presence of a theory is emphasized as a requirement of an observation solely under the aspect of the course of cognitive processes. "Interest precedes the observation; a question, a problem—in short, something theoretical."[2] In addition, there are no logically founded requirements for the formulation of hypotheses.[3] "Theories are seen as human inventions, constructions, which stem from human imagination. They do not bear the stamp of truth, but one may try to put them to difficult tests to ascertain if and how well they hold up."[4] Since any scientific testimony can be considered relevant only after it has been tested and verified, the methodological regulation of the creative fact-finding phase can be waived.

In order to develop our explicatory concept systematically, we will now have to examine which consequences will result in the face of this methodological vacuum. Let us first neglect the question whether accidential discoveries, in the true sense of the word *accidential,* are possible.[5] For independent of the result of such a discussion, chance, understood as the complete absence of a strategy for seeking evidence, can never be the basis of a research plan. At this point, however, we are concerned with the development of such a plan.

Only rarely do researchers find themselves in complete theoretical isolation with a specific inquiry. In most cases there are already hypotheses that are logically and factually connected with their own assertions, even if these originate from different disciplines. The extent of the transparency and agreement that exists among these contextually connected statements determines the possibility and, at the same time, the obligation of finding mutual theoretical and methodological connections. To demonstrate this point more succinctly, I will discuss two cases of high theoretical correspondence.

In total accordance with the fundamental idea of critical rationalism, a number of theories intentionally aim at refuting such hypotheses, which have already been recognized as verified and often irrevocable.[6] From the area of microeconomic theory the critical contributions by Morgenstern and Witte, among others, must be mentioned. Both men present a discussion of the theorem of certainty, although under different aspects.[7] A contradictory development of theory presupposes the existence of a fundamentally controversial parallel theory, which differs from the contradictory argumentation in as few aspects as possible.[8]

This condition, however, does not exist for the problem of decision making under time pressure. There is not a comprehensively formulated system of findings, nor do the initially fragmentary suppositions provide a uniform view of the problem. Such an approach to the development of a critical, contradictory theory can therefore not be applied to the investigation pursued here. In addition to this development of theory, which is marked by its intent to contradict, great importance is to be assigned to the deductive generation of hypotheses.[9] By deriving additional, consistent statements from a theory already in existence that carries a higher degree of generality, the scope of the previous theory will be expanded. At the same time it provides the theoretical frame of reference for the newly founded hypotheses. As does the first concept, the deductive approach necessitates the existence of a theory of reference characterized not by the same level but by a higher one. Such a possibility of derivation often exists when as yet no specific and delineated statements exist concerning an object of explanation.

The frequently expressed view that the social sciences do not have general theories at their disposal—in contrast to the natural sciences—is not justified in this generalizing formulation. As a matter of fact, verified attempts at explanation already exist in the fields of psychology and social psychology.[10] Systematic relationships between assertions are also known in economics. They are frequently formulated nonoperationally, however, and thus are not accessible to verification; and until now, they have never been subjected to empirical testing.[11] In the case of our central problem of decision making under time pressure, there is a lack not only of purely assertive testimony but also of empirically oriented findings that could be adopted without reinterpretation within the scope of an investigation of business management and organization. There are only some very general references that can be taken up as derivative approaches. But their theoretical content determines their scientific value to a lesser degree than the fact that they have been formulated in broad agreement within different areas of discipline.[12] The fundamental thesis on the mastery of stress is that modes of behavior are developed under pressure that lead to adaptation and thus ensure balance.

Because of the lack of content-equivalent testimony, it will be difficult

The Theory of Decision Making

to achieve a direct connection between our research objective and objects of other systems of explanation. It is now necessary to sketch the concept of theory development and to depict the system of hypotheses.

For the formal organization of the individual assertions, we resort to the stipulation made by scientific logic that hypotheses be structured as "if—then" sentences, so that the statement content claimed by the respective sentence will be completely clear.[13] The conditions under which an assertion is to be valid are fully contained in the "if" component of the sentence. The complete, exclusive, and explicit indication of the limits of validity of an assertion will prevent its immunization.[14] The goal of the development of theory is to formulate nomologic hypotheses of a high degree of generality and precision.[15]

The investigation of decision making under time pressure proceeds in three steps, which are represented in a closed relation of effect. In this manner we arrive at a three-stage concept of interconnected if-then relations.

Proceeding from the existence of a given exogenous time limit, it is first necessary to analyze whether and to what extent certain structural and/or objective marginal conditions influence the perception of time pressure. Suppositions must be formulated concerning the creation of time pressure. Subsequently, statements must be made about behavior in problem solving under time limitations. The third step concerns the explanation of the effects of behavior. Hypotheses will be developed that contain different efficiency presumptions for alternative decision-making behavior.

All stages of the sequential-causal system of statements are based on the same area of explanation. The explications claim validity for a problem context—and for this one only—that is marked by the following characteristics: (1) The subject matter of the theory to be developed here consists of complex decision-making problems requiring a high degree of intellectual analysis and a large amount of time and effort. (2) Within multipersonnel decision-making units, the solution of problems on the basis of the division of labor is set as the prime condition. We thus examine the overall achievement and the behavior of the unit as a whole, and not individuals' contributions to problems.[16] The framework created by these two basic conditions constitutes the invariable elements of the "if" components of each of the hypotheses. They define the structural barriers of explanation of the theoretical system by excluding all noncomplex and all individually made decisions as unexplained.

Conditions of Time Pressure

In the first chapter we observed that limited resources of time constitute one of the most serious burdens in solving decisional tasks. If and to what extent such a pressure is perceived by the bearers of the decision does not, however, depend solely on the purely time-related circumstances of the problem situation. Rather, time pressure arises only when the available time is felt to be insufficient. There are three conditions for the occurrence of time pressure.

Decision Time

A necessary condition for a point in time is a defined interval within which the decision must be made by a formal declaration of action. We call this declaration of action *resolution*.[17] The persons making the decision must be aware that this imposition of time is obligatory and that its violation will lead to a reduction in score, and in extreme cases, to the nonrecognition of the total achievement. Thus time pressure cannot arise if the participants in the decision do not learn, or learn retroactively, of the existence of time restrictions; if time pressure is considered only as part of a desirable concept of planning; or if it is declared by means of verbal instructions exclusively, without a factual time limitation.[18]

Sensitivity

It may sound almost trivial to designate a corresponding degree of sensitivity on the part of the decision makers as a supplemental condition for the rise of time pressure. The examination of intrapersonal predispositions, however, shows that this statement cannot be denied significance. Differences in the biological constitution and, particularly, different cognitive characteristics result in varying degrees of sensitivity to time pressure.[19] Research interest is directed to the collective decision-making process and not to the investigation of personality-dependent time-pressure sensitivity. Nevertheless, completely ignoring this fact would mean an unjustified simplification.

In this way a methodological reference for the later testing of the hypotheses has been formulated without consequences for the assertions ensuing from it. The danger of a systematic falsification of the measurement scores because of this variable must be eliminated. Since this factor is a variable that cannot be absolutely excluded, the only technique of controlling its influence is neutralization. This procedure is suitable since there are no indications as to how sensitivity would be measured autonomously, as to what connections exist between individual and collective sensitivity, and as to what thresholds may be exceeded or at least maximally reached.

Stress may not, on the one hand, be ignored, but on the other hand, it may not lead to a physical or psychic collapse.[20] In both cases the empirically achieved results would not be the expression of behavior under time pressure and thus would not be valid.[21]

Problem Intensity

The conditions for time pressure presented thus far—limited decision time and sensitivity to external pressures—are not sufficient for the creation of time pressure. As the third prerequisite there must be a decision situation that implies a problem for the decision-making units.

Two things become apparent at this stage. First, it can be established that time pressure is defined as a resultant of limited decision time, time pressure-sensitivity, and problem intensity of the decisional situation. Thus this is not an empirical finding but only a pure statement of fact.[22] This reference appears significant, since an experiment subsequently will be conducted to provide evidence for the initial definitional statement and thus transform it into an informative statement.

The second note deals with the relationship of effect among those elements that constitute time pressure. Preempting a neutralization of the degree of sensitivity it can be understood as a function of two independent and one dependent variables. With a given problem intensity, perceived time stress varies with the time available for decision while fixed decision time results in time pressure by a change or, better, by an increase of the problem intensity.

Although the available decision time embodies a variable requiring no further definition, it appears necessary to analyze more precisely the concept of problem intensity. In particular, it is necessary to demarcate this concept from the complexity of decisions.

Complexity was fixed as a situationally bound characteristic for the purpose of a general delineation of the area of validity of the theory sought. *Complexity* designates the objectively prevailing problem content of the decision-making situations. By contrast, the concept of problem intensity should express the evaluation of the problem from the perspective of the decision-making unit as the subjective assessment of the situation. In spite of its rather close connection, this differentiation, which might appear somewhat sophistic, is essential for the explanation of the actual problem solution achieved. Above all, the analysis of the actuating conditions of time pressure requires a separation of the two variables. In doing so, a falsely understood psychologism must be prevented and should be excluded by objectivizing the originally subjective subject matter.

The degree of difficulty of a decision is determined initially by the number of different individual decisions, that is, by the "scope of the decision". A more qualitatively oriented difficulty arises from the interdependencies between the different subdecisions. Complementing and concurring relationships between individual fields of the total decision mark the *internal weight* of a problem. The inclusion of the situational environment by which the decision is brought about and in which it must finally hold up creates a further modification of the content of the problem.

The amount of latitude by which the frame of reference in the form of information and personal alternatives of reaction can be mastered designates the *external weight* of a decision. The cognitive pressure that results when one is attempting to master a definite decisional situation is more intense if the individual initial situation imposes limits on the decision-making unit. The scarcer the economic resources, the smaller will be the firm's policymaking potential and the more difficult the elaboration of suitable alternatives. The situation is further aggravated by the fact that a firm in such a tense situation is much more dependent on the success of the intended measure, which is within fullest possible agreement with its planning. Finally, even in the case of highly complex problems, and particularly in the course of repeatedly occurring decisions, a certain routine for the mastery of decisions develops.[23] It is independent of the concrete individual case, and unspecific. The general decision routine causes relief, above all, in the organizational processing of the tasks to be resolved.

Thus problem intensity is a multilevel concept. When its content is broken down analytically into the quantitative dimension of the scope of decision making, the qualitative element of internal weight, the strategically relevant external weight, and the organizational aspect of the decision-making routine, the concept proved to be a useful empirical theoretical variable. This definition thus is simultaneously a first step toward the unequivocal operationalization that follows later.

Depending on the actual facts, several constellations may occur within this explicatory area and necessitate explanation.[24] We will therefore choose a theoretical thesis that allows a comprehensive test. In this manner the praxeological and prognostic value of the hypothesis—that is, its empirical content—can be increased.[25] Including the basic conditions of our research approach—that statements are to be made only for the complex decision-making units—the first theoretical hypothesis is thus formulated as follows:

Hypothesis 1: In complex decision-making situations, decision-making units register time pressure more intensively the higher the time-pressure sensitivity, the less the available decision-making time, and the higher the problem intensity.

The Theory of Decision Making

Problem Solving under Time Pressure

The second step of theory formation concerns problem solving under time pressure. Here we are concerned with a dual-pressure phenomenon caused by the problem intensity and the time pressure involved in making the decision. This justifies adopting a supposition of interdisciplinary fields that has already been proved valid under other forms of stress: time pressure leads to behavioral patterns of adaption.

Although this statement is much too global and is not capable of explaining anything yet, it forms the beginning of the development of hypotheses. Therefore it should be determined more profoundly what the expected adaptive behavior may be directed at so that the areas of adaptation become visible within the decision-making process. After gaining insight into this question, it must be determined how an adaptation to time pressure can be achieved.

To obtain a representative basis for observation, it is necessary to include in the analysis the total mental achievement required for the mastery of complex decision-making processes under time limitations. This in turn necessitates the creation of empirically delineable categories. For this purpose we must determine experimentally a multidimensional system of problem-solving activities that can serve as a reliable grid of hypothesis formation and testing.

Collective decision-making processes constitute the focal point of interest for management research projects. The fact that the theory for a long time has been confined exclusively and frequently to the decision of the entrepreneur as a unipersonal disposition can be based on totally different levels of argumentation. First, an isolating delineation of the effect signifies a legitimate means of scientific model forming. By renouncing considerations of the influence of the superimposition of preferences and of other decisional restrictions, an essential simplification of relationships can be achieved. "If the individual entrepreneur makes the . . . decisions, only minor difficulties occur in the analysis."[26] Access to the problem is thus simplified. In addition to this technical fact-finding argument, which implies the necessity of a theoretical extension, there is an indication of the "single-center will formation" as found in reality.[27]

But this model-like simplification contains difficulties since it provokes statements that vary with the conditions of ownership within the enterprise.[28] The assumption of entrepreneurial autonomy must be abandoned or at least modified considerably. Thus it is a mere consequence and in accordance with reality to proceed principally from collective decision finding and to explain at the same time, by renouncing organizational variables, the case of the "classical" entrepreneurial decision.[29]

From the class of decisions that form the basis of this investigation, three distinct areas of problem solving can be derived. (1) Collective and, consequently, labor-divisional task fulfillment requires the *interaction* of individuals and work teams. (2) The conditions of decision making resulting from the personal situation and position, as well as from the frame of reference of the respective environment, form the core of the solution to the problem. In order to analyze them and to conceive suitable reactions, comprehensive *information* is necessary. (3) The division of labor and the structuring of the total solution of the problem in individual steps—that is, the processual character of the decision—lead to the necessity for *coordination*. Using these points of departure for adaptive behavior in problem solving, the multilayer structure of mental achievement was successfully projected onto three different levels of explanation.[30] It is now necessary to depict the specific expectations that result from the existence of time restrictions for these different categories of mental achievement.

Interaction

The area of achievement of interaction encompasses the problem-solving activities that take place within individual decision-making units. In it the concept is used less in its sociopsychological meaning as an exchange of social activities but is used here in the literal meaning of the word "interaction." Conceptually it is very close to the term *cooperation*, which, because of its value-expressive content, is less suitable.[31] Interaction contains the active as well as the mediative element of actions as is characteristic for the division of labor in problem solving.[32]

In an achievement situation governed by time pressure, object-determined decision-making tasks and limited time resources compete with one another. A conflict results between the group-internal problem-solving activities required by necessity and their exchange and reconciliation with the work results of the other participants in the total performance. If confronted with the question as to which areas of activity can be most easily adapted to the limited time conditions, the decision makers will at first be less prepared to modify the internal mental achievement.

This will even be more difficult to manipulate since it is largely a question of problem-fixed activities. A reduction of intensity would imply the danger of achieving objectively unqualified results, which may be justified by the argument of existing time pressure, but are scarcely desirable. A further argument supports this expectation. The quantitative and qualitative limitation of mental activities presupposes a relatively small problem intensity unless it is to touch directly upon the result of the achievement. In complex decisional situations, this is the case only after a large amount of

The Theory of Decision Making

problem insight and decision-making routine has been established. Favorable conditions of this type can be expected only after repeated confrontation with identical decision-making tasks. This is the case if, after confirmation of hypothesis 1, time pressure is no longer perceived to be grave and thus the strong compulsion to reduce achievement is lacking.[33]

The more intensely mental achievement is bound to the problem context of decision-making tasks, the more intense is the search for other possibilities of relief. Thus the individual work groups within a decision unit will reduce as much as possible the required transmission of their own achievement results. Neither every individual consideration nor the multitude of arguments, but only their global results in the form of concrete recommendations for action are regarded as absolutely necessary and therefore deserve corresponding formulation and communication. The effect of adaptation consists of limiting the articulation of achievement. In this way the relief of a specific work group can be achieved without directly overburdening the partner group.

An intensification of the efforts appears fundamentally impossible, because it is a form of adaptation which is inadequate to the restrictive condition of time. More-intense activity would have to increase the pressure and thereby prevent a mastery of the time constraint. On the other hand, there are references in sociopsychological literature that an intensification of communication within a social unit becomes manifest under pressure.[34] This statement holds true for certain problem situations, but we would like to express a contradictory assumption for the field of research treated here.

The high degree of pressure for achievement that relates to the content of the problem and the motivation to master the complex decision-making tasks brings about a strongly concentrated treatment of the subject matter of the problem. Moreover, the formalization typical of collective decisions in the form of established communication structures are a considerable impediment to socially determined interactions. Both conditions—the dominance of object-related problems as opposed to the social aspects, as well as that communication which is not directly practicable—reduce the empirical weight of social actions. Therefore the interaction to be explained and empirically tested here is far less the expression of social communication than the result of cooperation determined by achievement.

After having shown activity limitation to be the only meaningful form of adaptation to existing temporal restrictions and having been able to exclude the possibility of a socially determined intensification of interaction, we are now in the position to formulate a hypothesis free from contradiction.[35]

Hypothesis 2: In complex decision-making situations, time pressure leads to the limitation of interaction within the decision-making units.

Information

While interest was directed to the problem-solving processes within the respective decision-making unit when dealing with interaction, the aspect of information leads to a perspective directed primarily to external contacts. The attempt to evaluate the complexity of the decision-making situation, of the personal position in it, the existing competitive situation and the development of alternative actions form the core of the decision-making process. The relationship between the selection procedure and its analytical foundation is reflected in the fact that "the decision-making process and the flow of information permeate each other."[36] The large number of empirically determined activities necessary to obtain information and to form alternatives in arriving at a complex decision justifies the ranking of the informational aspect as a central one.[37]

The existence of time pressure leads to a cognitive dilemma: the search for, preparation of, and concentration of information soon reach the time limits allowed and necessitate limiting the information. But this dilemma increases even more the amount of cognitive stress caused by inherent uncertainty. Time pressure and elementary stress exist in a substitutive relationship: measures taken to reduce one burden necessarily intensify the others. Which form of adaptation is selected in situations of this kind depends on whether a relief in time can be more easily achieved than a cognitive one.

Decision makers can find relief from the time pressure by shifting activities to others. But such delegation is subject to the condition that the party taking over the assignment is not exposed to time restrictions. If the party assigned part of the tasks has spare time, delegation can generally be used as an effective means of adaptation, signifying that the reduction of the burden is effected by transfer of cognitive achievement. Information thus far collected personally is now acquired from outside sources. Cognitive relief achieved by reducing elementary stress is synonymous with decreasing uncertainty. The reduction of uncertainty in turn requires procuring information previously unavailable. With the help of this information, the decision-making risk can be demarcated.[38] Thus this alternative of adaptation to existing time pressure also leads to an intensified demand for information.

Both modes of behavior for overcoming time pressure—the immediate evasion via the time dimension by means of delegation and the indirect absorption by repression onto the cognitive level of problem solving—would have to effect a corresponding and equally directed trend to intensify the demand for information. According to this concept of explanation time pressure thus leads to the fact that decision-making units, to a higher degree, attempt to obtain information from other sources. This theoretical conclusion results from the view of man as "homo informaticus."

Recent empirical research on decision making, however, has shown clearly that such a basic assumption can no longer be maintained to explain information-gathering behavior.[39] The human being is not in a position to formulate his information requirements comprehensively. Even under the most favorable information-gathering conditions, an intensification of demand can be achieved which is only temporary and narrowly restricted in content.[40] Thus it appears hardly probable that in situations characterized by time pressure the manifold cognitive and personal barriers to articulating the demand for information can be overcome. Even when it is assumed that the existence of time pressure will cause individuals to reduce their psychic reservation in posing questions, there remains the argument of limited abilities to analyze the problem, as well as the need for information.[41] This argument gains relevance in this type of restricted decision-making situation in which the analytic care, by necessity, will be impaired.

In view of these difficulties, it appears to be more appropriate to expect a continued demand for information. Moreover, taking into consideration that the formulation of the information requirement itself takes time and thus aggravates the pressure, even an absolute limitation of the articulation of demand must be reckoned with.[42] Finally, even if inquiries are promptly processed by the respective addressees, waiting times will be inevitable. Such delays could be prevented only by careful time planning by the decision-making units. Only when the information requirement can be systematically structured by objects of information and their respective time of need within the decision-making process can problems of this type be avoided. Nevertheless, because decision makers in complex decisions under time pressure lack the necessary objective perspective and the mental detachment, the occurrence of waiting time when gathering information cannot be avoided. Even if waiting times are necessitated by the subject matter and even if information could not be made available faster the fact that waiting is required aggravates stress. Even under the primacy of time such an escalation of stress is not acceptable if qualified information can be obtained from outside.

After it was established that restrictive behavior in information gathering under time pressure does not undergo change and that the time needed for the articulation of the requirement for information causes an additional obstacle to the demand and because the unavoidable waiting times during the procurement of information would increase the existing pressure even further, the following hypothesis is formulated.

Hypothesis 3: In complex decision-making situations, time pressure leads to the limitation of the demand for information on the part of the decision-making units.

Coordination

Two levels of consideration have been identified by this analysis of the many levels of problem-solving activities within a complex decision. The activity areas of interaction and information encompass the total problem-directed achievement of the decision-making units. In contrast, achievement-directed control is measured under the aspect of coordination. From the processual nature of decision making ensues the organizational need to coordinate achievement, a genre of activities superimposed on the implemental actions. The variety of activities, the participation of several persons, as well as their timely and capacity-dependent use, require systematizing their individual activities. "In this context coordination means the direction of activities toward a definite goal."[43] The general goal is, of course, the successful completion of the decision-making process.[44]

Coordination implies a dual regulation of activities. It affects the control of the problem-solving process in that it creates the formal framework of the course of the decision making by setting organizational markers.[45] A coordination of those participating in the decision and their contribution can be achieved by prescribing certain norms of behavior.[46] In doing this, a predisposition of the problem-solving content is striven for, which exceeds the control of the process. A strategy is formulated and fixed.[47] In the area of business-management decision making, it is the task of the company policy to develop decision-making programs that serve as goals for action and as maxims of behavior.[48] Both measures—the organization directed to the course of decision making and the strategy conceived for determining the decision content—cause a coordination of the collective mastery of the problem. A coordination in this sense may standardize the activities to be performed by the decision-making unit and thus reduce the problem intensity of complex decisions.

In a decisional situation affected by time pressure, problem solving must be achieved without delay and in an appropriate manner. Under these conditions, organizational regulation of the course of decision making and company policy guidelines are not only meaningful but necessary.

From the standpoint of rational behavior, coordination is necessary in overcoming time pressure.[49] As far as this statement postulates the presence of a regulatory system, it may be left undisputed. We cannot, however, support the expectation that coordinative activities are taken up spontaneously as a direct consequence and for the mastery of acute time pressure.

When there is time pressure, activities that initially are necessary to solve the problem must be restricted. It is thus apparent that time pressure leads to an adaptive behavior in the form of a simple reduction of achievement. If this form of reaction is already characteristic of these areas of activity that are as necessary for the decision as are those of interaction and information, it does not appear plausible to expect an intensification of the coordinative activities. This is, by no means, to make a statement concerning the effectiveness of coordinative measures but only to sketch a partial prognosis about the problem-solving procedure under time pressure.

Time pressure causes a concentration of absolutely necessary tasks, such as the evaluation of decision-making materials and the securing of calculable alternatives. Based on the time allotted for decision making, this concentration is put to use for informative and interactive performances in an undefinable ratio. Acute time pressure necessitates a short-term work orientation. There is no room for fundamental considerations of a prestructuring of the mental performance. Even if there is an awareness of the necessity of coordination, the urgency of problem-related decision-making tasks does not allow any consideration of or even directed measures for a long-term conceptual framework.

This investigation is thus based on the view that supposes an adaptation to existing time pressure generally in the form of a restriction of activity. It contradicts the opinion that stress leads to an excessively compensatory performance by increased activity, as Hare and Miller contend.[50] Both authors arrive at their conclusion by reinvoking the organic defense reactions explained by biological stress research. They do, however, reinterpret the process classified as resistance into a theory on the course of activity. In this way more than an analogous transformation of information takes place; a massive change of the original testimony ensues. Selye, a mentor of biological stress research, explicitly emphasizes the bivectorial character of stress mastery as containing both an aggressive and a defensive element: "We see therefore that these two antagonistic mechanisms do give us three possible reactions: retreat, advance and stabilization, each of which can be useful."[51] This emphasis on situative dependency of the measures for stress mastery also forms the basis of this explicative approach. As in the case of the activity areas of interaction and information, the considerations of coordination were also developed from the situational conditions of a decision under time pressure. As the result we formulate another hypothesis.

Hypothesis 4: In complex decision-making situations, time pressure leads to the limitation of coordinative activity within the decision-making units.

Thus three hypotheses are produced that explain problem-solving behavior in decision making under time pressure. A congruent concept of activity concentration results from the specific kind of stress for the performance areas of interaction, information, and coordination.

Performance Efficiency under Time Pressure

The hypotheses developed thus far are the result of a two-phase approach. First, we explained how time pressure results from the specific conditions of the decision-making situation that functioned as elements of the if component. Thus, time pressure alone represents the then component of the condition in hypothesis 1. Second, the variable of time pressure, together with the general conditions of decision complexity and multipersonal performance, assumed the function of the if component in three further hypotheses. The problem-solving activities depicted in the then components of hypotheses 2 to 4 were differentiated accordingly by their interactive, informative, and coordinative contributions to the decision.

In accordance with the methodic concept of reaching a closed system of interconnected if-then sentences, a third step now develops assertions about the efficiency of problem solving. In this step, the assertions concerning activity that were previously set up as then components now move into the if component, serving as an explanation of the efficiency of decision making under time pressure.

Efficiency is generally understood as the degree of goal attainment achieved by material or mental performance. Accordingly, the analysis of efficiency signifies a comparison of performance and goal as measured. For the area of empirical analysis, however, the existence of explicitly and clearly defined goals cannot always be presupposed. Hamel was able to determine in a field investigation that in complex decisional processes, the goal formation regularly takes place as a partial process parallel to the actual problem solving process. Goal formation thus can be construed as an ingredient of a comprehensive problem solution but not as its requisite. In this sense goals are not set a priori; they are worked out, formulated, and revised in the course of the decision-making process.[52]

Proceeding from these empirical conditions, Gzuk develops a fundamental concept of efficiency measurement in his investigation of the field of managerial decision-making efficiency, which thus far has received only scant attention.[53] Gzuk illustrates the theoretical and pragmatic possibilities of quantitatively delineating and operationalizing efficiency variables even for the case of insufficient goal articulation. Of interest is the derivation of internal standards out of the problem context of the individual decision. However, if valid reference factors cannot be determined empirically, there still remain two methods of efficiency analysis. First, testing can begin with the generally recognized objective external standards, which are independent from the singular empirical case. Or second, the satisfaction achieved during the course of the mental process and, particularly, after the conclusion of the decision can be used as a direct measurement of efficiency.

Both auxiliary techniques—orientation on general values that are inde-

The Theory of Decision Making

pendent of the process and the use of subjective expressions of satisfaction—represent the use of goal surrogates. Statements on efficiency are formulated only with the help of goal surrogates when there are no explicit goals in the sense of internal standards. These theoretical considerations of efficiency form the basis of the subsequently developed conception of efficiency analysis of decision making under time pressure. From the character of the investigated decisions and the specific conditions under which problem solving takes place, there result three different areas of efficiency:

1. Because the decisions are managerial in nature, economic goals are in the foreground of scientific interest. Thus the solution to the problem can be evaluated as successful if a high degree of economic efficiency of the decision can be achieved.
2. A second approach to determining efficiency results from the time restrictions. One of the main goals in a situation under time pressure is to reduce or even overcome the pressure. Besides applying economic parameters, the efficiency of problem solving can be assessed by measuring the degree of stress mastery. The more intense the time-pressure absorption achieved, the higher the degree of temporal efficiency of the decision.
3. A third plane of efficiency analysis focuses on the person making the decision. But ultimately no complete transparency of the problem can be achieved in complex decision-making processes. The decision maker therefore cannot form an absolute judgment of performance. Therefore he evaluates the performance, which we classify as *personal* efficiency, by means of his satisfaction.

Decision making under time pressure is thus subjected to an efficiency analysis of management organization which encompasses the personal, temporal, and economic aspects of problem solving, a multiple approach that avoids a unilateral assessment of the effects of time pressure.[54] These factors represent the levels of a three-dimensional aggregate variable, which allows the characterization of differently structured efficiency profiles. Depending on the problem-solving activity of the individual decision-making units, different efficiency profiles are to be expected.

In order to develop efficiency hypotheses, the differentiation of the decision-making activities by interaction, information, and cooperation will not be applied for the time being. In the following we shall only speak of activity. This coordination of different contributions to decision making into an aggregate variable of performance appears justified because the same efficiency effect is predicted for all three performance contributors. In operationalizing and testing, it will be necessary to ensure that this expectation will be a controlled and not an uncorroborated one.

Personal Efficiency

For those who may doubt the relevancy of this person-oriented sub-question to business management, we would emphasize explicitly that personal satisfaction of decision-making persons with the result of their performance is in no way regarded as the primary goal of problem-solving processes. Also, this investigative approach does not attempt to make measurements for the purpose of developing levels of aspiration.[55] It is rather the task of this partial analysis to gain knowledge about the extent of stress mastery.

It has been already shown that cognitively determined elementary stress is always linked to complex decisions. It is the result of the rather limited insight into the problem which results from the strong interdependence of the action parameters and the marked interference of the effects of the action. In particular, this largely uncontrollable influence of external decisions, as is characteristic of "strategic games,"[56] causes a high degree of cognitive decisional pressure. An additional aggravating factor is that the success of the decision does not become apparent immediately, although the decision maker will always attempt to make an immediate judgment so that he will not be exposed to permanent cognitive stress. This person must at least conclude the decisional situation temporarily in order to acquire the mental freedom for new solutions to problems. Accordingly, the expression of satisfaction can be seen from a dual perspective: it is the expression of a judgment on the outcome of the problem, and it reflects the willingness to perform subsequent activities. In this sense the determination of personal efficiency yields important information about processes within the decision-making unit that are hardly, if at all, accessible to external analysis. Personal efficiency therefore is valuable in indicating the internal, organizationally relevant course of performance.

Since an objective judgment based on facts is impossible, performance variables independent of the realization of success of the decisions are useful. Such variables are the personal contribution to the activity of the decision-making unit and its recognition among the other members as well as the assessment of the performance of the decision-making unit as a whole.

In the absence of other parameters of success, interactive, informative, and coordinative activity forms the main point of reference of the personal judgments of performance. Any reduction of these activities is interpreted as a reduction of decisional performance. Therefore, because performance is limited by time pressure, less-positive performance assessments will have to be expected. The problem-solving behavior is not at fault; it has been affected by external circumstances. Because the other members of the decision-making unit do not expect a high performance, there is no need to justify behavior. Thus, the individual decision maker finds it acceptable to admit to having made a negative satisfaction judgment. Since the risk

The Theory of Decision Making

of failure becomes particularly evident in decision making under time pressure, a positive performance judgment could easily be construed as a faulty evaluation. For this reason it is also obvious that a minimization of satisfaction articulation must be reckoned with. Our hypothesis therefore is:

Hypothesis 5: In complex decisional situations under time pressure, lower personal efficiency is achieved with decreased performance than with higher performance.

Time Efficiency

One of the results of empirical efficiency research has established that definitions of effectiveness vary with the performance conditions of the respective problem solutions under investigation. A working definition can be formulated, but only in a very general diction and must be concretisized again for the individual case.[57]

There is agreement, however, that aside from the complexity of the problem to be mastered, the greatest importance is attached to the temporal performance characteristics in the evaluation of efficiency.[58] The time required for performance thus can assume different analytic functions within an investigation of efficiency. The concept of temporal efficiency presented here requires clarification.

First, time may serve as an internal variable of the dynamic analysis of the course of problem solving. Time here assumes a completely passive function as a purely attributive unit; it provides the grid that orders the organizational course of the problem solving. The various activities, partial results, and resources of performance form a process that occurs within a temporal structure. The result is a sequence. Wossidlo was able to make statements about efficiency by analyzing the sequence of activities in decision-making processes.[59]

Another concept uses performance time explicitly as a factor of input and as an economic object of consumption. Time is partially viewed as an independent goal, expressed as the effort to minimize processing times.[60] Often time also serves as a substitute measurement for the unquantifiable use of personnel and material, particularly in complex decisions.[61] In this way the duration of problem solving becomes an essential characteristic of the results of performance.

The aspect of time becomes a focus particularly in investigations of the speed of problem solving. The analysis of decision making under time pressure follows this basic approach by fixing the timely conclusion of decision making as a strict secondary condition of performance. Thus, the speed of performance is central. Accordingly, the time needed in making decisions could be considered as the measurement of temporal efficiency.[62] Our study, however, is not concerned with this aspect of the use of time; rather it investigates problem mastery under the condition of present decision time. As such, decision-making time is to be understood as a causative variable, as an element of the if component of statements concerning decision-making behavior. Thus perceived time pressure forms the basis for measuring temporal efficiency. In a situation of limited decision time, temporal efficiency is all the greater the less that time pressure is registered. This means that under objectively the same time conditions a stronger absorption of time pressure is possible.

The hypothesis has already been developed that time pressure limits the total problem-solving activity. Evidence for this form of adaptive behavior was based on the expectation of the decision maker to be able to reduce time pressure. This purely behavior-related statement does not include a statement on efficiency, however; it is based only on an expectation of efficiency. The praxeologic value of a theory increases, however, if in addition to descriptions and predictions of action, the effects of activities are proved.[63] Because the arguments on the causal substantiation of temporal efficiency are identical with the expectations that were used to explain problem-solving behavior, they will not be discussed again. Instead they will be adopted from the derivations used for the behavioral hypotheses.[64] They constitute an additional hypothesis:

Hypothesis 6: In complex decision-making situations under time pressure, a greater temporal efficiency is achieved with little performance than with high performance.

Economic Efficiency

Our concept thus far has led to an organizational approach, a direct result of the processual aspect of decision making, which requires a strongly process-oriented and thus dynamic analysis. Moreover, it rests on the general assumption that organizational evidence is not neutral in purpose but is efficiency effective.[65] Business-management problems have thus been discussed with an emphasis on organization. Consequently, personal efficiency is an early indicator of successful problem solving from the perspective of those participating in the decision. In addition, the measurement of temporal efficiency includes the partial aspect of solving performance tasks independently from the content of the problem. A third step in efficiency analysis is to explain how decisional behavior will hold up under purely economic criteria of evaluation.

Determinants of economic efficiency will be parameters of the financial, profitable, and distributional effectiveness of the decision made. These are the most-important components of company performance within a free-market economy.[66] Here efficiency is evaluated exclusively on the basis of values *realized,* thus ensuring a high degree of accord with testing conditions of the company's operations. Therefore, the market constellation with its fluctuating effects of demand and competition is incorporated in the analysis in an adjusted state.[67]

Any problem-solving activity contributes to the determination of a decision. The interactive and informative performances are directly aimed at a comprehensive cognitive exploration of complex relationships. Performance is controlled by efforts to ensure a complete, objectively balanced, and timely development of all phases of the solution. A limitation of this decision activity means the renunciation of contributions of performance necessary to solve the problem and results in the expectation of a reduction of the economic efficiency. This argument implies two basic prerequisites of completely different character. The first axiom postulates a direct and positive relation between the mental performance effort and its result. Without this condition and for the time being only, coincidence could be a causative element. Explanations in the actual sense and praxeologic conclusions would then be impossible.[68] In its effect, the second prerequisite is similar to the first assumption. In its character, however, it is an empirical, measurement-related condition: In analyzing several observation units, differences of activity must be determined among them.[69]

The analysis of personal and temporal efficiency could be made independently for the individual decision units with the effects achieved explained exclusively by the individual behavior of the respective unit. An isolated analysis of this kind is, however, unsuitable to the determination of economic effects. The fact must be taken into consideration that the success achieved results not only from individual performance under the aspects of company policy but—depending on the degree of competition—to a considerable extent is also influenced by the activity or inactivity of the competitor in the market.

Completely homogeneous decisional behavior does not permit explanatory statements of efficiency. If no divergences of behavior and no differences in efficiency occur among the decision units, the statement of efficiency in such a constellation cannot be tested. This in no way falsifies the statement; it simply remains untested. If, however, there are heterogeneous efficiency data with coinciding modes of behavior, or the same effects of performance in spite of different levels of activity, the validity of the performance axiom and also the explanation of efficiency is disproved. On the basis of this theoretical discussion of efficiency the following hypothesis on economic efficiency is formulated:

Hypothesis 7: In complex decisional situations under time pressure, a lower economic efficiency is achieved with little performance than with high performance.

This provides a theory of decision making under time pressure that fulfills the following requirements of a reality-oriented scientific system of explanation.[70]

> The statements are made in the form of empirically testable hypotheses to ensure that the analysis will be based on neither pleonastic nor tautological sentences.
>
> The individual statements of theory are in an explicatory relationship that follows a stepwise mode of explanation. First, an assertion is developed for the causative conditions. There follows a derivation of adaptive problem-solving activities for overcoming decision-making situations under time pressure. Finally the effectiveness of the decision is investigated.
>
> The system of statements claims an explicatory value for complex decision-making processes under time pressure that are carried out in a system of division of labor. These borders of validity are formulated explicitly and thus exclude an immunization of the theory.

In attempting to illuminate a problem of undisputed relevance to the reality of decision making in business enterprises, we tried to make the assumptions available to empirical testing. Findings from investigations treating similar subjects of inquiry were examined as to the relevancy of their method and content to the approach presented here so as not to neglect any theoretical connections. In doing so, we were unable to detect any close connection with the problem of mastering complex decision making under time pressure in economic situations of action.

Notes

1. K.R. Popper, *Logik* (1969), p. 7, and H. Albert, *Wissenschaftslehre* (1967), p. 45, refuse to accept the development of hypotheses as an explanatory task of the logics of findings. R.S. Rudner, *Philosophy* (1966), p. 4ff., also clearly differentiates between the scientific method of proving from the findings of hypotheses, which he describes as a scientific technique. See also K. Holzkamp, *Voraussetzungen* (1970), p. 111ff., and V. Kraft, *Erkenntnislehre* (1960), p. 241ff.

2. K.R. Popper, *Naturgesetze* (1964), p. 88; P.M. Blau and W.R.

Scott, *Organizations* (1963), p. 8ff.; G. Ekman and I. Lundberg, *Theorie und Messung* (1969), p. 163; R. Pagés, *Experiment* (1967), p. 446; K. Holzkamp, *Theorie und Experiment* (1964), pp. 10, 27; H. Parthey and W. Wächter, *Theorie* (1965), p. 36; H. Vogel, *Experiment und Theorie* (1965), p. 49; C. Selltiz, M. Jahoda, M. Deutsch, and S.W. Cook, *Untersuchungsmethoden* (1972), p. 46. F.A. Hayek, *Primat* (1970), p. 304, characterizes this prerequisite as an "abstraction."

3. The postulate of logical consistency is directed to systems of theory and is understood as a methodological criterion of testing but not as a criterion of the rise of theories. For this see Popper, *Logik,* p. 7.

4. H. Albert, *Theoriebildung* (1964), p. 17. See also H. Albert, *Traktat* (1969), p. 26.

5. Popper, *Naturgesetze,* p. 87ff., emphasizes that an observation without even a rudimentary form of theory—in terms of hopes, prejudices, expectations—is unthinkable. The individual horizon of expectation prejudges the observation. Observation thus is always selective. According to this view, there is no accidental discovery "free from theory."

6. H. Albert, *Theorie* (1970), p. 4ff., in this way characterizes the concept of science as developed and presented by Karl Popper and himself.

7. See O. Morgenstern, *Vollkommene Voraussicht* (1964), who describes the logical problem of the assumption of perfect information, and E. Witte, *Informationsverhalten* (1972), in whose writing the implicit concept of an imperfect information supply is contrasted with the explicit theory of an imperfect information demand.

8. The term *parallel theory* is to be understood in terms of an alternative of explanation that is to be substituted by the countertheory. Only one of the two explanations can be valid. By contrast, physics, in its treatment of the dual character of light (as wave and material), concerns itself with a problem that can be explained in another sense as alternative or parallel. Wave theory and corpuscular theory contradict each other, although each approach is a closed theory. For this see A. Einstein and L. Infeld, *Physik* (1956), p. 78, and W. Heisenberg, *Der Teil* (1969), p. 113, who classifies this partial contradiction (drawing on Niels Bohr) as "complementarity" of theories.

9. The deductive method is employed here as a systematic approach to the obtaining of a theory and not as a procedure to test hypotheses. For the deductive examination of a theory, see Popper, *Logik,* p. 7ff., 31ff.; K.R. Popper, *Historizismus* (1969), p. 94ff.; as well as Albert, *Theoriebildung,* p. 51ff.

10. In this context Albert, *Theoriebildung,* p. 52, and Albert, *Theorie,* p. 12, also refer to the theory of elementary social behavior, the theories of level of aspiration, and the dissonance theory.

11. For this see P.R. Wossidlo, *Reservierung* (1970), p. 29, who pre-

sents the insufficient empirical foundation of management theories as well as the resulting consequences for the state of findings of the field.

12. Here a paradox of scientific logics becomes manifest. If one follows the theoretical maxims implied in the findings for the formulation of scientific statements, the theories that result are highly general and marked by a high degree of falsification; therefore they contain a large amount of empirically explicative content and claim almost unlimited validity. Statements of such a comprehensive nature are called *laws*. Under the aspect of falsifiability they are diametrically opposed to tautologies, which are completely unfalsifiable. The borders of triviality in statement making are finally reached by an advancing generalization of laws. Extremely general theories lack substance, much as tautologies do. For this see Popper, *Historizismus*, p. 97ff., and Popper, *Logik*, pp. 77-81, 98-103.

13. See Albert, *Theoriebildung*, p. 22ff., and W. Leinfellner, *Wissenschaftstheorie*, p. 96ff.

14. For the problems of immunization, see the criticism by Albert, *Theoriebildung*, p. 30ff., and J.M. Buchanan, *Ceteris paribus* (1971). Holzkamp tries to weaken this criticism. He emphasizes the "degree of burden" of empirical data and testimony contained in the "principle of exhaustion" to justify the nonrejection of falsified hypotheses. See K. Holzkamp, *Theorie und Experiment* (1964), p. 20ff,; K. Holzkamp, *Voraussetzungen* (1970); and R. Münch and M. Schmid, *Konventionalismus* (1970).

15. Popper, *Logik*, p. 77ff., illustrates the direct connection between information content or empirical content and degree of provability. From this he concludes the demand for the establishment of easily falsifiable theories. For this see also Albert, *Theoriebildung*, p. 24ff., and Holzkamp, *Theorie und Experiment* (1964) p. 23, who understands the scientific value of a statement to be the product resulting from "integration value" and "empirical value." H. Parthey and W. Wächter, *Theorie* (1965), p. 37ff., in the same context speak of the "acceptance value of hypotheses," which is constituted by the explicative value, the degree of provability, and the degree of verification of hypotheses.

16. Thus, the methodic concept is consciously based on a nonreductionist research approach. It corresponds to a higher degree to the management organizational issue and causes fewer difficulties in generalization to be expected than does a reductionist conception.

17. See E. Witte, *Entscheidung* (1964), p. 120ff., and *Entscheidungsprozesse* (1969), col. 498. For a clearer contrast of partial and predecisions, E. Witte, *Phasen-Theorem* (1968), p. 634ff., designates this process-concluding act as "final decision."

18. Th. Bartmann, *Zeitdruck* (1963), p. 10, bases his experimental investigations on a concept directed to the declaration of time pressure. Such an induction is fundamentally different from our experiment design.

In addition to actual time limitation, Bartmann is able to intensify stress and, in the case of objectively sufficient time allotments, a verbal influence of a stress character. Time pressure is understood (untested) as an independent variable. In contrast, our experiments are based on factual time allotments, without additional references to restriction; time pressure here is also understood, tested, and explained as an independent variable.

19. M. Rokeach, *Mind* (1960), explains cognitive behavior with the aid of an ideal typical polarization as "open mind" and "closed mind." In a similar manner P.S. Holzman and R.W. Gardner, *Ausgleichen* (1966), p. 331, differentiate between the behavioral types of "compensator" and "aggravator." (The original terminology of "leveler" and "sharpener" to me appear less prone to misunderstanding.) See also the experimental investigations by J.E. Sieber and J.T. Lanzetta, *Individual Differences* (1966), and M. Karlins and H. Lamm, *Information Search* (1967).

20. The problem of the pressure-triggering threshold of sensitivity is touched upon in J.T. Lanzetta, *Stress* (1955), p. 35ff., and W.C. Schutz, *Groups* (1955), p. 442, as well as by M.H. Appley and R. Trumbull, *Stress* (1967), p. 10. P.A. Hare, *Handbook* (1967), p. 265, speaks of "catastrophic collapse." Appley and Trumbull, *Stress,* p. 3, expect "a stage of exhaustion" as a result of over burdening.

21. The methodological requirements connected with the testing of hypotheses are treated in detail in chapter 3.

22. For the theoretical scientific problems of definitions and hypotheses, see Popper, *Logik,* p. 42ff., and Albert, *Theoriebildung,* p. 19ff.

23. This expectation is directed principally to all decisions irrespective of their aiming at different or congruent objects. However, the routine effect will be all the larger the more the repeat decisions resemble each other. See V.E. Cangelosi and W.R. Dill, Organizational Learning (1965–1966); O. Grün, *Lernverhalten* (1973), p. 103; and B. Liebermann, *Experimental Studies* (1962), p. 206.

24. If the variable of sensitivity, l, reflects an alternative markedness, the variable of decision time, m, may acquire various conditions, and if n different degrees of problem intensity exist, there will be $l \times m \times n$ explicative variants of time pressure.

25. See Popper, *Logik,* p. 83ff.

26. H. Albach, *Wirtschaftlichkeitsrechnung* (1959), p. 134. In a similar manner, H. Hax, *Koordination* (1965), p. 21, also abstracts from the existence of several decision bearers.

27. Albach, *Wirtschaftlichkeitsrechnung,* p. 134.

28. Ibid., p. 141, concedes "The differences between the preference function of the individual entrepreneur and of the business manager [are] . . . easy to recognize. More than the individual entrepreneur, the business manager will emphasize the safety component of the uncertainty preference

function and less the profit component." Albach therefore expands his approach to the investment decision by the "multi-centered formation of will."

29. W. Kirsch, *Entscheidungsprozesse* 3 (1970-1971), 53ff., points to the semantic content of the term *collective decision* by defining it more comprehensively as "group decision." A group decision is characterized by the direct personal interaction of individual members of a group. This requisite is absent in collective decisions.

30. For an empirical delineation and operationalization of the three genres of performance, see pp. 100ff., 109f., and 115ff.

31. The term *cooperation* carries a strong value judgment. Cooperation suggests a positive connotation; lacking cooperation imposes negative judgments. This value judgment becomes most apparent in formulations such as "lack of cooperation," which characterize the insufficiently positive aspect.

32. The close connection between the work-performing and communicative character of actions within a group is emphasized particularly by G.C. Homans, *Gruppe* (1972), p. 59ff.

33. From the perspective of the external observer, J.T. Lanzetta, *Stress* (1955), p. 42, also arrives at the empirical result of a stress-independent activity.

34. See J.T. Lanzetta, *Stress* (1955), p. 42; P.M. Blau and W.R. Scott, *Organizations* (1963), p. 135; and D. Mechanic, *Stress* (1962), pp. 109ff., 140. In contrast, I. Sarnoff and Ph.G. Zimbardo, *Angst* (1969), p. 147, find that fear does lead to an intensified tendency of affiliation, but that anxiety leads to a more-isolated social behavior.

35. F. Naschold, *Organisation* (1969), p. 76ff., also expects a "member participation kept consciously low" and thus a reduction of social interaction for political crisis decisions, which he characterizes as having little available time.

36. H. Albach, *Entscheidungsprozess* (1961), p. 357, and J.M. Pfiffner and F.P. Sherwood, *Organization* (1960), p. 305ff. O.W. Haseloff, *Risiko* (1970), p. 139, points to the mutual bond of decision and information while emphasizing the aspect of time.

37. E. Witte, *Phasen-Theorem* (1968), p. 632.

38. See J.G. March and H.A. Simon, *Organizations* (1958), p. 154, who characterize time pressure as a stimulus of selective perception and the enhancement of attentiveness.

39. E.Witte, *Informationsverhalten* (1972), proceeds from the fact that people basically articulate less demand for information than the problem requires. This general thesis can be proved on the empirical basis of field investigations and experiments.

40. R. Bronner, E. Witte, and P.R. Wossidlo, *Experimente* (1972),

The Theory of Decision Making 45

p. 195, can prove that the vitalization of the demand for information does not transcend the immediate context of supply. Witte, *Informationsverhalten,* p. 82, proves that "no lasting increase in the level of the quantity of demand can be achieved by an intervention in supply."

41. See Witte, *Informationsverhalten,* p. 62ff.

42. H. Dienstbach, *Anpassung* (1968), p. 144ff., found the same assumption on role behavior that prevents attempts at problem solving by reverting to prepared solutions. See Naschold, *Organisation,* p. 77, who transfers the same thought to political crisis decisions, and J.G. Miller, *Living Systems* (1965), p. 395.

43. H. Hax, *Koordination* (1965), p. 9, and A. Meier, *Koordination* (1969), col. 893.

44. When a decision-making process is regarded as concluded is not yet considered. It should, however, be pointed out that the formal result in the form of a decision as well as the "result of realization"—understood as the result of action on the basis of the decision—can be selected as the basis for the assessment of efficiency. For this see particularly R. Gzuk, *Effizienz* (1975), which considers this question in detail.

45. See E. Witte, *Ablauforganisation* (1969), and E. Witte, *Entscheidungen* (1969).

46. Hax, *Koordination* (1965), p. 73ff., demands these for the procurement of information, for communication, and for the selection of alternatives.

47. The original military-science concept of strategy includes determining in advance the goal toward which action is to be directed. While C. v. Clausewitz, *Vom Kriege* (1960), p. 32, emphasizes the military reference exclusively, H. v. Moltke, *Militärische Werke* (1960), p. 205, indicates a general understanding of the concept. He outlines the aspect of alternatives and freedom of action: "Strategy is a system of improvised assistance, . . . the art of acting under the pressure of the most difficult conditions." The increasing complication of strategic considerations due to the inclusion of economic and technical arguments is shown particularly by O. Morgenstern, *Strategie* (1962), p. 19.

48. See J. Bidlingmaier, *Unternehmerziele* (1964), p. 17ff.; E. Heinen, *Zielsystem* (1966), p. 17ff.; H.A. Simon, *Management Decisions* (1969), p. 5ff.; C. Sandig, *Betriebswirtschaftspolitik* (1966), p. 20; H. Ulrich, *Die Unternehmung* (1968), p. 187ff.; and E. Witte and J. Hauschildt, *Interessenkonflikt* (1966), p. 81ff.

49. W.T. Morris, *Management Decisions* (1964), p. 473, classifies "the formulation of policy which effectively predetermines the choice" as a natural way of reacting in repetitive decisions under time pressure.

50. See P.A. Hare, *Handbook* (1962), p. 265, and J.G. Miller, *Living Systems* (1965), p. 390.

51. H. Selye, *Stress* (1957), p. 111.
52. See W. Hamel, *Zieländerungen* (1974).
53. See R. Gzuk, *Effizienz* (1975).
54. R.M. Stogdill, *Group Achievement* (1959), p. 225, chooses a similar methodological approach to efficiency analysis by demanding that "productivity," "morale," and "integration" be treated as elements of group performance that are independent of each other. See also P.E. Mott, *Effective Organizations* (1972), p. 17ff.
55. For this see H.A. Simon, *Models* (1957), p. 266ff., and H.A. Simon, *Rational Choice* (1964).
56. For this see O. Morgenstern, *Strategie* (1962), p. 218ff., who presents the problem of limited transparency under a military-political accent but leaves sufficient room for interpretation of management-policy considerations, particularly in the area of market behavior.
57. H.B. Pepinsky and P.N. Pepinsky, *Productivity* (1961), p. 217, define "productivity as a measured amount of successful task accomplishment by an actor or a team of actors." Productivity thus represents the most-comprehensive concept of performance effectivity.
58. For this see Th. Bartmann, *Zeitdruck* (1963), p. 3ff., 48; Pepinsky and Pepinsky, *Productivity,* p. 225; C. Hendrick and J. Mills, *Decision Time* (1968), p. 313ff.; R. Carzo, Jr., and J.N. Yanouzas, *Effects* (1969), p. 183; R. Carzo, Jr., *Effectiveness* (1962), p. 399; D.W. Taylor and W.L. Faust, *Efficiency* (1962), p. 209; D.G. Trull *Decision Success* (1966), p. B-272; and R. Pollay, *Decision Times* (1970), p. 462ff.
59. See P.R. Wossidlo, *Reihenfolgen*, (1976).
60. See P. Stahlknecht et al., *Operations Research* (1970), p. 121ff.
61. E. Witte, *Innovationsentscheidungen* (1972), p. 82ff., chooses the duration of decision-making processes as an independent efficiency criterion of problem solving.
62. Decision-making time as a dependent variable occupies the central position in the works of Bartmann, *Zeitdruck;* Carzo and Yanouzas, *Effects;* Hendrick and Mills, *Decision Time;* and Pollay, *Decision Times.* These investigations are based, however, on experimental designs, which comprise only relatively simple problems with solution times between eight and twenty minutes.
63. See T. Kotarbinski, *Praxiology* (1965), p. 22ff.
64. See the derivations on interactive, informative, and coordinative behavior under time pressure, pp. 29ff.
65. This efficiency theorem of organization is found explicitly in F. Eulenburg, *Organization* (1962), p. 12; T. Kotarbinski, *Praxiology* (1965), p. 1ff.; E. Witte, *Ablauforganisation* (1969), col. 20; and J. Zieleniewski, *Organisation* (1966), p. 47.
66. See E. Heinen, *Zielsystem* (1966), p. 59ff.

67. Pepinsky and Pepinsky, *Productivity,* p. 219, clearly emphasize, "Effect is the modification of productivity resulting from another actor's strategies."

68. Part of the essence of the explanation is the reduction of consequences to causal, not accidental, factors of effect. For this see H. Albert, *Theoriebildung* (1964), p. 47; Popper, *Erfahrungswissenschaft,* p. 73ff.; Popper, *Logik,* p. 31ff.; and W. Stegmüller, *Wissenschaftliche Erklärung* (1969), p. 82ff.

69. The variation of values within an observation unit (during the course of time) goes without saying and finds its expression in the conditional structure of each hypothesis formulation.

70. See H. Albert, *Theorie und Prognose* (1971), p. 126ff.; Popper, *Logik,* p. 31ff.; W.J. Goode and P.K. Hatt, *Methode* (1966), p. 71ff.; and W. Leinfellner, *Wissenschaftstheorie* (1967), p. 103ff.

3 Method and Concept of Investigation

Empirical scientific testimony written as empirical statements "must, in addition to the requirement of incontestability meet another condition: They must be falsifiable."[1] Statements that do not meet these requirements must be considered as nonscientific, metaphysical comments.

Not all statements within the class of real-theory statements have the same explicatory quality. When selecting theories that are to serve as the basis of explanation and prognosis, applicability or empirical strength decides on the ultimate value as a theory.[2] The empirical strength of a statement is determined by two qualities, which are not completely independent from each other: the degree of testability[3] and of varifiability. The criterion of testability expresses the possibilities of falsification; the rate of verification represents a result of falsification.[4] The higher the degree of testability and the better the rate of verification of the sentence or theory, the stronger the statement. Since simple, general statements are characterized by a higher degree of potential for falsification, the following relationship can be established: "The verification rate of a theory of great *generality* can thus become better than that of a less general (and less falsifiable) theory. Similarly, theories of greater *definiteness* verify themselves better than less definite theories."[5]

The degree of generality of the present investigation is determined by its area of validity. This area includes statements explaining the behavior of majorities of people, in the labor-divisional mastery of problems, within the framework of business-management decisions, and under time pressure.

The degree of definiteness of this research attempt has not yet been developed in detail since it is essentially influenced by the specific marginal conditions of the respective testing area. The then elements already sketched of the rise of time pressure, activity under time pressure, differentiated according to interactive, informative, and coordinative performance, as well as personal, temporal, and economic efficiency achieved under these conditions, can be operationalized only after the presentation of the method of investigation.

The question of which contribution a single investigation can make to the verification rate of a given theory has remained largely unanswered thus far. If Popper's view is followed, even the theory of probability does not give an answer.[6] Mathematical procedures are not alternatives to a suitable methodological conception.[7] There is a lack of clear and valid, scientifically logical norms that allow the definition of the "degree of severity of tests"[8] or of a binding set of technical research instruments.[9] A first, although still vague, reference can be found in Popper:

> The verification rate will increase with the number of verifying cases. In this we usually assign much greater significance to the first cases which show verification than do later ones: If the theory has proven itself well, the later cases increase its verification rate only little. This remark is, however, not true if the "later" cases are much different from the "earlier" ones, i.e., if the theories verify themselves in another area of application; in this case they can greatly enhance the verification rate.[10]

Albert supplements this by saying, "For the verification of a theory a change of the area of application, a variation of the test environment, is more important than the continuous repetition of observations under the same circumstances since the latter does not contain any new risks for the theory concerned."[11]

These considerations lead to the following conditions necessary for our approach:

1. The development of a theory does not also require its test. A test—and particularly the first test—is, however, of fundamental importance for the empirical relevance of the statements; it provides an important indication of the verification rate of the theory. A theory that does not fail in the course of its first verification test has proved its very justification of existence. Such a theory is recognized as verified until it is later defeated.
2. An initial verification in no way proves an absolute validity. Rather, a theory must constantly be open to critical testing by repetitions or simple postexecution.[12] It is therefore necessary to note in detail the method used so that others will be able to reproduce the test.
3. So that the empirical framework will be clearly understood, the method chosen must permit the planned design and control of the test situation.
4. The number of cases under verification constitutes an essential indicator of the degree of verification of a theory. Thus, testing should not be done exclusively by means of a singular empirical unit of investigation. Therefore, a verification concept must be selected that subjects several nonidentical test groups to the test.

These are the fundamental conditions on which we are basing the methodology of investigation.

The Experiment as a Method of Research

There are several research procedures available for the empirical investigation of a specific problem. "Wherever experimentation is possible, the

Method and Concept of Investigation

experimental method is the most fruitful empirical method because it achieves the closest and the most stringently verifiable contact between theory and reality."[13] Spinner, however, points to methodological, natural, and practical limits of experimentation.[14] Thus the experimental method is not necessarily always the preferred one. The method of research should not be chosen until the specific problem and the empirical conditions have been considered.

Criteria for Selection of a Method

Decision making under time pressure doubtlessly is so widespread that the field-study method could be considered.[15] Under the aspect of access to the practical problem situations, field investigation, however, might prove to be useful. There still are certain reservations on the part of practical economics to being unreservedly open to field research and this skepsis does not appear to be entirely inappropriate.

On the one hand, science often views declaration of consent to participate in a field study as being more than a declaration of toleration. It interprets assent not only as a permission but also as a willingness to assume frequently comprehensive, unfamiliar, and often burdensome work. This form of cooperation cannot be expected and frequently is the primary reason for low quotas of assent and return of questionnaires and similar material.

Better conditions for cooperation can be created by a clear presentation of the relevance of the research project to the persons and institutions concerned. Science and practice do not always agree in their view of the problem. Therefore, it should not be surprising if excessively "theoretical" questions do not gain support. Research questions whose practical relevance cannot be proved successfully or that cannot be specified, or for various reasons, should not be revealed, will scarcely stimulate interest.

Those who support actively or even tolerate passively research efforts expect to be informed of the results. The circulation of interim reports, working papers, and other publications on the problem are necessary for eliciting continued cooperative research. Violations of these customs generally impair any field research.

This relation between the actual problem areas and their scientific opening, however, appears to be a surmountable obstacle to research. By comparison, two other arguments, which directly result from the nature of field investigation, prove to be much-more-massive barriers.

The investigation of processes such as decision making under time pressure can proceed in two fundamentally different ways, designated *acute analysis* and *historical analysis*. Acute analysis observes a process while it is occurring. Thus the process to be investigated and its scientific recording take place simultaneously. However, such a research process is quite susceptible to disturbance.[16] Particularly because of the almost unavoidable influence of the observer on the process and also because of the influence of the actual happening upon the observer, an acute analysis often cannot be carried out in a sufficiently controlled manner.[17] For our problem, the obstructions of such a research concept become particularly apparent because the risks of a real decision under time pressure cannot be estimated at this time; no one can be asked to assume responsibility for the social and economic consequences of a stress-burdened decisional situation; and the acute analysis—because of a parallel-occurring observation—has a largely uncontrollable influence on the amount of stress of the decision and thus the decisional behavior as well.[18]

Although these disadvantages are not present in a historical analysis, there are other important reservations, which should not be overlooked. The use of questionnaires or interviews is unsuitable for the recording of processual and other strongly time-dependent characteristics of problem mastery.[19] The technique of document analysis, which is more closely related to the object under study, by contrast, represents a more-reliable research procedure.[20] Its methodic value is the greater the more completely and reliably the event is documented as it occurs.

We therefore arrived at these conclusions concerning our experiment:

1. Since a highly time-related problem is the focus of our investigation, only an acute method of research can be considered. Historical analyses will fail because of lack of reliability.
2. The risks involved with the specific decisional situation and the resulting responsibility forbid a reality-based investigation.
3. The interfering influence of the testing conditions, which is closely connected with acute research procedures, requires that the manner of observation be carried out carefully so as not to influence the process.

After examining the general scientific-methodic requirements and the technical characteristics of social-scientific research approaches, the experiment was determined to be the most suitable method of research for our investigation.

Experiment Characteristics

In the natural sciences, the experimental method traditionally occupies a position of highest rank. From the beginnings of an exact science, this classical research tool has been increasingly refined and made useful to numerous areas of application in scientific analysis.

Theoretical and other developments have led to a continually progressive use of experimental techniques.[21] In contrast, the experiment was first used in the social sciences approximately fifty years ago.[22] The experiment was adopted only hesitatingly into economic research, and even today it is not a common method for national economics or for management investigations.[23] Therefore in order to explain the test concept used here, it is necessary to fall back on general characteristics of the experiment. (Of course, it cannot be the task of this writing to give a comprehensive characterization of the experimental method in its manifold forms and areas of managerial application.)[24] Nevertheless, we deem it necessary to explain the methodological approach used here.

To provide a more detailed classification of forms of scientific experiments, the laboratory experiment is contrasted with the field experiment. This classification first expresses the site of the experiment. Another important aspect concerns how much control of the influencing factors is possible or even desirable, which also reflects on the fidelity to reality present in the experiment.[25] Classifications such as exploratory experiment, experiment of application, and decision experiment are more strongly oriented to the direct research purpose.[26] *Decision experiment* and *critical experiment,* used synonymously, refer to experiments designed to provide information on the verification of a hypothesis that has already been developed.[27] Lienert adds the *interference experiment* as an interesting version whose most-striking characteristic is the directed creation of pressures.[28] In consideration of this terminological framework, our methodic approach can be classified as a laboratory experiment, which at times is also an interference experiment and is always a decision experiment.

More important than the rough categorizing of different types of experiment is the preparation of generally valid characteristics of our research procedure. In doing so, we will attempt to probe the essence—that is, the specific character of the experiment. As a result of technical experimental and philosophical considerations, several criteria have been extensively accepted.[29]

The free and exclusively purpose-oriented design of the testing conditions is peculiar to experiments. "Experimenting is acting planfully governed by theory."[30] The researcher plans and constructs the conditions under which the hypotheses to be tested are exposed to the experimental test of verification. He is in the position to intervene purposefully and effectively in the events that he has set into motion. He can control the conditions of the experiment sequentially.[31]

The possibility of isolating variation is closely connected with this "principle of arbitrariness." The experimenter gains control over the situation by structuring the influence on the existence and effect of the influencing factors.[32] For this purpose he uses various techniques, which he applies according to the type of factors concerned. All influencing factors not belonging to the explanation represent interference variables and must be completely eliminated, parallelized or randomized within comparison tests.[33] Absolute control of the situation is an ideal; it is not a typical characteristic of the experimental method. Control is rarely total. In addition to the characteristic of situation design—a term used synonymously for the valueladen concepts of arbitrariness and manipulation—the repeatability of the test is the third characteristic of the experimental method. Methodological discussion about this aspect has shown that here the question can not be that of an absolutely analogous repetition. The methodic characteristic thus expressed corresponds to Popper's basic postulate of the scientific theory of permanent testability. Also in the theory of methods it is not understood as being a quasi-identical repetition.[34]

The characteristics presented thus far are components of the classical characterization of the traditional scientific view that is oriented by the unifactorial causal experiment. With a stronger reality-oriented reference of scientific statements, this isolative form of explication turns into multifactorial attempts at explanation. The expectation that one—and only one—triggering condition will lead to a certain effect is relinquished.[35] A real scientific theory does not exclude this extreme case; it generally bases its assumptions on a (multivariable) explicative context. This theoretical demand for a complete and explicit designation of the if component thus is not only a necessary condition of repeatability in the sense of an intersubjective reproducibility; it is also the technical experimental prerequisite of situation design and of situation control. Moreover, this rule of transparency marks the basic view of modern real-theoretical understanding of scientific theory. The classical statement of causality of necessity contains the explicative ingredients of cause and effect, without which the statement would be syntactically incomplete and incomprehensible. The demand to reveal the if component is, however, not an elementary syntactical rule. It gains its significance from the supposed existence of several "causes" of one "effect".[36]

The expectation of several triggering factors within the marginal conditions of an explanation and the praxeological difficulties in transferring experimental results to true situations have led to the development of an additional methodic characteristic of the experiment. *Representativeness* is a criterion requisite to an empirically viable testing arrangement.

The degree of conformity to reality that an experiment is capable of achieving is an unsolved problem of the experimental method.[37] A meaningfully understood representativeness will thus have to be looked for within the limits of a depiction of actual situational conditions that is still technically and experimentally possible and is necessary for the prevention of misinterpretations and insufficient generalizability. It thus becomes appar-

Method and Concept of Investigation

ent that the relationship of the criterion of experimental control with representativeness is a limited one. Representativeness can be achieved only as much as the controllability of the influences allows.[38]

Problems of the Experiment

One of the primary requirements of scientific analyses is the neutrality of the research method applied in relation to the results of the investigation. This norm stipulates that the results obtained should reflect the actual relationships and should contain no interfering influences brought about by the method used.

This requirement doubtlessly touches a methodic problem that is particularly evident today in the social sciences.[39] Consequently, it is often assumed that it is a characteristic inherent to social-scientific and, especially, experimental methods which allows them to satisfy the claim of neutrality either not at all or insufficiently. The reason is that the subjects are aware of the observation. Thus the process of behavioral analysis is part of the social situation.[40] The person who is the object of the investigation sees himself as exposed to both a problem situation and an observation situation. The problem-solving behavior is overshadowed by an observation behavior and thus becomes distorted. These problems, however, are by no means unique to the social sciences. They affect the exact sciences too, and become more significant the more analysis detaches itself from the macroview and explores the microarea of the respective disciplines.[41]

> The performance of a measurement in a physical process always constitutes an intervention in the happening. In classical physics, i.e. in the area of macro-bodies, the disturbance caused by the measurement can either be completely eliminated by the appropriately selected fine instruments of measurement or can be taken into account afterwards by corrective calculation. . . . When taking measurements in atomic occurrences, i.e. in the realm of the microworld, conditions are entirely different. A deep, incisive change due to the measuring process is unavoidable.[42]

The development of nuclear physics shows that the sentence "observation disturbs the phenomenon" has yielded to the opinion "that the word 'phenomenon' cannot be used at all without stating precisely at the same time which experiment arrangement or which means of observation is to be anticipated in it."[43]

The influence of the measurement process on the results of the measurement cannot be accepted principally as an objection to the method of the experiment.[44] Of course, a great deal of methodic strictness must be demanded because the strength of conclusions drawn from findings obtained experimentally is—aside from the definiteness of the basic premise or hypothesis—determined by the experimental model (research design) and the measuring technique used.[45] Despite the difficulties of a terminological and practical investigative delineation,[46] the "basic methodological qualities"[47] that are to be guaranteed within our concept of the investigation will be presented briefly in an attempt to derive them from the postulate of neutrality of method and to concretize them with reference to the variables of the investigation, the investigative process, and the people involved in the investigation.

Validity: Neutrality of the method of research within experimental investigations means that the experiment must be capable of rendering a true explication of the behavior under investigation. This primarily refers to the conditions that are real behavioral influences. The more one succeeds in answering the principal question of the problem by means of the best representation possible of the conditions of behavior, the more valid is the testing concept. The validity of a test is determined by the degree of accuracy by which it "actually measures that mode of behavior which it is supposed or claims to be measuring."[48] This rather general definition of validity has led (partially for reasons of external control) to an analytical splitting of the content of meaning of this methodic norm.[49] In it predictive validity has proved to be particularly relevant. It characterizes the prognostic value of the data obtained and is thus a measurement for the praxeologic content of the findings.

The objective of our investigation is to analyze, by experiment, an actual problem and to obtain research results that can be used. Thus we will have to create experimental conditions of problem content, personnel and time that are characteristic of behavior in actual decision-making situations under time pressure. It is impossible to replicate such components completely, but we will try to do so to the highest degree possible.

Reliability: While "validity" contains a methodic demand for agreement of object of explanation and object of measurement, reliability refers to the accuracy of the measurement taken. It thus designates the reliability of the measurement procedure in relation to the object of measurement. Whether the right choice was made—that is, whether the object of measurement is suitable to deliver the explanation sought—remains unconsidered. Scheuch delineates the two norms by defining validity as "material accuracy" and reliability as "formal accuracy."[50]

Reliability signifies measurement accuracy in general and stability of measurement in particular.[51] Although this differentiation has been discussed intensively, especially in the literature on psychological testing, thus far only differentiations of this aspect and evidence of reliability could be

Method and Concept of Investigation

gained. As the most important facet for our concept of measurement, we adopt from it the closest possible temporal connection between the experiencing and the evaluating of a situation.[52] Particular attention will have to be given to obtaining the most direct measurement possible. If this cannot be achieved, an evaluative statement will be considered as such and cannot be interpreted as a direct measurement.

Immunity: The selection of the variables investigated in the experiment—those purposely varied as well as the controlled ones and the factors of influence considered to be "dependent" or "causative" variables—is depicted as a problem of the validity of method. Reliability was discussed as a methodic demand on the measuring instruments. Now the position of the experimenter is the third aspect of the neutrality of methods. The experiment has already been characterized as a method that allows a high degree of process regulation and situation control. The central position of the experimenter in the experiment comes directly from this characterization. Based on the transfer of behavioral scientific findings onto behavioral scientific methods, the expectations, information, and social relationships, particularly with reference to the experimenter, are causes of method-determined interferences.[53] If only the personnel-determined measurement errors are to be considered, the problems of uncertainty connected with the experimenter are justly rated second to reliability. However, as soon as it must be assumed that modes of behavior ensue from the position of the experimenter which are not to be expected without his existence, it becomes necessary to discuss the aspect of personnel neutrality as an independent methodic quality in addition to those of validity and reliability.

The fewer interferences that result from the person and function of the experimenter's influence on the situation, the higher will be the personal neutrality designated here as immunity. Immunity thus has two meanings. Except for the measures named in the experiment design, no behavioral interventions by the experimenter take place, and the capability of the experimenter to judge will not be affected by the situation at hand.[54] It becomes evident that insufficient immunity of the experimenter can produce problems with both validity and reliability. For the sake of validity and reliability it is therefore essential that the experimenter maintain a low profile.

The basic qualities demanded in this context are summarized as dimensions of the neutrality of methods in table 3-1. The demonstration of these methodic demands is done here for two reasons:

1. Validity, reliability, and immunity, which is conceived here as an independent norm, are principally the methodic problems of empirical research. Therefore, they constitute necessary ingredients of a characterization of the experiment as a method of research.

**Table 3-1
Dimensions of the Neutrality of Methods**

Area of Reference	Neutrality of Method
Variable	Validity
Measurement procedure	Reliability
Experimenter	Immunity

2. In addition to this purely formal argument there is the methodological one of "critical transparence." The clearer the methodic claim is formulated, the more effective the development and presentation of the methodic procedure will be. It is therefore consistent to articulate this methodic claim prior to formulating the arrangement of the experiment.

The Experimental Design

The presentation of the arrangement of the experiment describes the conditions under which the hypotheses which have already been developed will be tested experimentally. The task of this section is to present in detail the basis for the situative framework, the structure of personnel, and the regulation of the course of the experiment.[55]

Simulation Model

The goal of this investigation is the elaboration of practically relevant data concerning decisional behavior under time pressure. Therefore it is necessary to design the decisional situations in the experiment in such a way as to assure a qualified problem-solving activity by the decision-making persons. Numerous objections to the practicality of the experiment as a method of research can be removed if one succeeds in detaching oneself from the frequently and virtually "banal situations" and to work on the basis of less-simplified experiment conditions.[56]

The significance of the decisional situations represents a first determinant that is essential for the praxeological value of experimentally obtained findings.[57] Feger expects it to be all the greater, the more the result of the decision develops from the activities of the decision-making persons and the more the consequences can be anticipated. Moreover, the significance is higher if the decision makers are affected by the problem situation, if the decisions have a far-reaching effect, and if information on the type and extent of the consequences is available.[58]

Method and Concept of Investigation 59

Because of the management context, a second condition of the experimental decisional situation is a focus on economic decision-making problems. To provide the most representative possible design of the content and conditions of the problem, the problem context must be realistic. Therefore the model seeks goals corresponding to the demands placed on executives in actual management situations. Accordingly the simulation model must combine sufficient problem complexity with limited transparency. A further requirement is that the reactions of the models themselves be objective and always take place free from arbitrariness so that the validity and the reliability of the simulation will be guaranteed.

Decision-Making Model: Some currently available business games combine the demand for significance of the decisional situation as well as the correspondence of the problem content with actual decision-making conditions. These games are used primarily for training, but their suitability as a research instrument is being discussed increasingly.[59] Because detailed descriptions of the model are already available, the business game Topic 1, which we selected as the decisional framework, will be described only briefly.[60] We limit ourselves to those structural characteristics of the system of action that are important for the testing of hypotheses and forgo a characterization of the parametrical relationships within the mathematic system of reaction. The limitation is legitimate since the type of the internal function remains without influence on the decisional behavior if the complexity of the decision-making conditions is secured. The model is thus neutral in its effect.[61]

The market structure provides for four enterprises that have been operating for a long time and compete in five markets under oligopolistic conditions. Four fully identical markets are arranged as relatively sparsely populated regions around a more densely populated, city-type market. Each business is exposed to the same local market conditions. Each enjoys advantages of low transportation costs, market share, and reputation in the market of its location. At the beginning of the experiments, all of the businesses reflect the same level of achievement; thus the economic preconditions are equal. Changes in the market situation result from three different types of economic activity. First, the market outlets respond to the individual activity of the operating enterprises by reacting to the respective measures of the company policy. Because of the competitive relations among the individual microeconomic units, changes in the market situation also ensue from the competitors' activities. Due to this influence, the consequences of the activities are no longer exclusively the result of internal decisions but are determined, additionally, by the effects of external decisions. In this way there is a guarantee that each business reaches only a limited measure of transparency of the situation and the desired complexity of the decision-making conditions can be secured. A third source of market structuring is the exogenous regulation of the economic data by means of experiment direction. This regulation of the framework is necessary for several reasons, which will be discussed in detail later. Suffice it to say here that all of the related interventions were made according to a standardized self-contained concept and always for the market system as a whole.

The firms produce products that are identical to those which all the competitors offer. Gradual improvements in quality are possible as the result of investments made in product research. Thus, a differentiation in quality among the individual suppliers may ensue in the course of the decision sequences. A total change of the assortment of products by the addition of or exchange with other products is not possible. The product can be characterized as a common household appliance with a market value of approximately $150. Its production takes place in a factory at the firm headquarters; changes in company location or establishment of new plants are excluded. The mode of production is the same in all of the firms. Nevertheless, changes in procedure are possible by means of investments in procedural research in the form of rationalization. Thus, the firms are in a position to reduce manufacturing costs and in this way gain a competitive edge. The centralized production necessitates the transportation of the products to the market outlets. The model does not include transportation times. Transportation costs, however, arise in different proportions according to the geographic location of the markets to be supplied.

The economic transactions are determined by a system of decisions based on company policy. These decisions form the activities of the functionally structured areas of company operations of plant (procurement and production), marketing (acquisition and sales), and finance (disposition of capital and securities).

The business enterprises may make decisions in the area of procurement and production directed toward amount of raw material, personnel levels, capacity of plant facilities, volume of production, procedural research, product research, and miscellaneous expenditures.

In addition to the general market expectations, such as demand and the buyers' ideas of price and quality, the raw material prices, wages, transportation, and storage costs function as particular parameters of the expectations of these dispositions.

Within the marketing area, the firm drafts its sales policy for the individual markets. Conditions of competition—in the form of the behavior of the competitors in the market and its own market position—and the market resistance resulting from the degree of market saturation, the buyers' price and quality expectations, and the transportation costs form the particular context of the expective parameters. Each firm determines its individual marketing policy by the definition of advertising expenditures, distribution

Method and Concept of Investigation

expenditures, and sales prices differentiated according to the five markets. To this is added the quality of the product as an acquisitory instrument of company policy.

The basis for the decisions in the area of finance are the financial equivalents of the individual economic activities as well as the expectation parameters of market development. Credit conditions—interest and amortization payments, criteria of solvency of the capital investors, modes of payment in procurement and distribution, and interest and exchange value of securities—are particularly important here. Often decisions made in this area affect decisions made in the other areas. Decisions resulting from this context are acceptance and amortization of medium- and long-term credits and buying and selling of stocks and bonds (with no participation in competing firms).

A decision concerning appropriations is made quarterly. This measure determines the distribution of profits to the shareholders, as well as tax liability.

Clearly a great variety of decisions must be made regularly by each of the firms acting as a decision-making unit. The breadth of the decisional spectrum shows also the overlapping effects that result from the competitive nature of the conditions of action.

The decisional model is highly complex because of the numerous parameters and manifold, mostly multivariable, nonlinear connections. The internal validity of the model is assured by a defined mathematical system of function whose reactions to the decisions made can be calculated reliably with the help of a computer. This guarantees that the consequences of the solution to the problem are to be attributed exclusively, objectively, and free from error to the model chosen as the basis.

Information Model: The description of the decision model has not yet fully depicted the framework for the testing of hypotheses created by simulation. The aspect of decision support by information has been intentionally neglected thus far. The business game provides principally for the decision makers to be informed, but the research goal as pursued here required considerable modifications of the information conditions that were primarily conceived for training purposes. Therefore the treatment of the newly designed information model is clearly separated from that of the unmodified decision model adopted.[62]

In order to reconstruct the most-realistic conditions possible for decision making within the experiment, the decision-making units were split into two individual work groups in accordance with the staff-line concept. There was less emphasis placed on exactly duplicating the frequently criticized, formal circumstances of hierarchy and competency.[63] Rather, the aspects of indirect communication and hampered accessibility to information were the foremost considerations of design. Realistic working conditions, which result from the dimensional and organizational conditions of the division of labor, had to be created. The work groups that were to cooperate—designated as staff or board of directors—were separated spatially and could communicate with one another only by standardized forms.[64] This yielded object-related, empirical documentation material that allows a high degree of objective content analysis.[65] Communication among the competing business enterprises was excluded. The staff was given the following tasks: critical analysis of the actual economic situation, procuring information on future economic development, and providing the directors with information and advice. The board of directors of each company was entrusted with the exclusive authority for the formulation of goals and the making of resolutions. The board was not bound to the recommendations of the staff; however, it could not base its decisions on any other forms of decision-making aid.

The decisions that were formulated by the four boards of directors were fed to the computer for simultaneous evaluation. As the result of model reactions, there were several reports of findings that were partially given to the businesses as feedback information and that were partially reserved to the game directors as regulating material.

The regularly distributed routine reports were made available exclusively to the staff groups. They contained necessary decision-making data about the plant and financial areas in a form that corresponds to that of a typical financial statement. The report includes: statement of raw materials on hand, statement of finished products on hand, storage expenses for raw materials, storage expenses for finished products, raw material prices and storage costs, postcalculation of manufacturing costs, standard full-cost calculation, standard marginal-cost calculation, overview of present and predictable plant capacity by machine-operating hours and units, units manufactured and plant investments, expenses arising from procedural research, and expenditures for personnel.

In the area of finance, data were made available on: profit and loss statement, periodic balance sheet, development of the means of payment, credit limitations and interest liabilities, rate of exchange and interest rates of securities, and modes of payment for raw material and finished products.

In addition to these routine reports on the plant situation and the market conditions (bearing in mind again that these went only to the staff of each firm), there was open access to a central information source. This information center could provide within a short time, upon request, and against payment of the cost incurred, data that exceeded the realm of the individual firm. Requests for information from the staff had to be made in writing. It was always ascertained that the answer corresponded to the substance of the question. The information bank contained data that were rele-

Method and Concept of Investigation 63

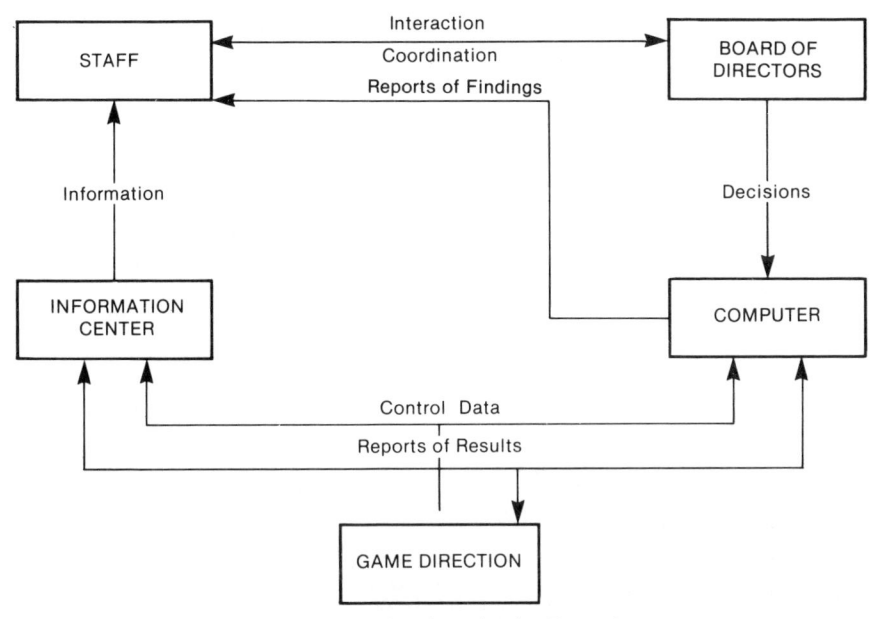

Figure 3-1. Institutions in the Experiment

vant to the decision, objectively correct, and therefore adequate to the problem at hand.[66]

The information model is outlined in figure 3-1, which clearly shows the efforts to keep the game direction aloof from direct interaction with the institutions contained in the simulation model.

Personnel

The description of the personnel requirements in the experiment presumes two methodological problems: the postulate of representation reflects a personnel component, and the demand for immunity embodies a condition that is directed to the researcher. The experiment concept meets these two demands in the following ways.

Experiment Directors: Quite often the theoretical tasks as well as those of experiment design and experiment execution are in the hands of a single scientist. Particularly for reasons of research economy, this is a common procedure; however, it often encounters criticism, particularly by pointing out the monopoly that the experimenter may practice.[67] The danger of surrendering the experiment director's immunity is certainly stronger in such a situation than it is when there is a personnel separation of the experiment directors. For this reason the procedure of strict distancing was used in the experiment.

The character of the business game as a training instrument was intentionally retained throughout the duration of the experiment so that the participants believed that they were involved in a university seminar regulated in the usual manner by a seminar directorate. The questionnaires, necessary for securing empirical data on the experiment, were generally explained as a device to help develop efficient training procedures. Students usually distributed the questionnaires. The seminar directors faced the participants only as game advisers and always as a group. I was the only one who was both a member of the game directorate and informed of the hypotheses and variable of interest. In this way, any influence on the situation of the experiment or the subjects was excluded.

Similarly the written communication within the firm's subgroups, as well as between staff and information center, was taken care of by students who were unaware of the theoretical expectations and relation of details. The information center was made known and was visible to the test persons. It was operated by a student who was trained expressly for this job and who was continuously briefed.

Experiment Groups

An additional source of insufficient representativeness is in the selection of the subjects in the experiment. For economic and technical considerations, the experimental social sciences frequently use students as subjects, an approach that has been sharply criticized, especially in psychological research, because it cannot always be determined how much the subjects took on behavior-controlling influences during the course of their training in methodic questions.

Another problem concerns the comparability of actual entrepreneurial behavior and decisional behavior as practiced by students. Sauermann and Selten are willing to recognize that there is insufficient behavioral concordance between students in experimental situations and entrepreneurs as an argument against a direct generalization of experimentally obtained data. They emphasize, however, that "there are no indications yet that participants in business games, who in reality hold an executive position in business, behave fundamentally different from, for example, students."[68] This expectation was confirmed in recent experiments on information behavior by means of complex business games.[69] From these results, therefore, neither a principle objection against the experimental method as a whole appears to be derivable nor do they seem to justify a massive argument against the use of business students in economic decision experiments. Nevertheless, actual business executives are included in our investigation.

Two methodic goals are to be reached with this arrangement of the subjects. The first is to depict actual decision-making conditions. The second is to arrive at more-precise data concerning behavioral divergencies between different genres of test persons than has been available thus far.

Altogether 112 subjects in three testing sequences were exposed to the experiments on decision making under time pressure. Of these, 72 executives were recruited from the business world and 40 students from the field of economics. In order to achieve the most-homogeneous personnel conditions possible within one testing sequence, the students were put together in a single sequence. The second testing sequence had 32 executives of the same level from eight business enterprises from different branches. Forty economists from the middle management of a large business concern formed the third testing sequence. This resulted in an almost identical group size in the twelve decision and observation units simulated.[70] (See table 3-2.)

The professional qualifications of those participating in the experiment—particularly among the business executives—were not uniform. There were considerable differences in their professional training and occupations. This fact should, however, in no way be construed as a methodic obstacle. Rather, it offered the opportunity to depict actual conditions of job placement in the experiment. The students disposed a largely homogeneous educational background and training so that problems of grouping as a result of different qualifications could be neglected. In the two testing sequences with business executives, the formation of groups was arranged so as to achieve the most heterogeneous group of subjects concerning backgrounds. In this way it was possible to give each of the business enterprises in the experiment almost the same structure of qualifications. The professional education of the participants was selected as the ordering criterion, with categories being formed in accordance with the professional emphasis and the level of training.[71] The portion of academically trained persons in testing sequence 2 was 44 percent. In sequence 3, 68 percent were university graduates. (See table 3-3.)

The age structure showed an understandably large discrepancy between the testing sequence composed of students and the other two consisting of practicing business executives. The students (in their fifth or sixth semester of study) showed an average age of twenty-five years (with a scattering of two years over and under this figure), while testing sequences 2 and 3 reflected an average age of thirty-six years (with age maximums of thirty-one and thirty-nine years, respectively). Sequences 2 and 3 were completely identical concerning age.

The placement of students and practicing business persons in separate testing sequences was necessary for methodological considerations. Differ-

**Table 3-2
Formation of Groups**

	Testing Sequence			
Experimental Design	1	2	3	Total
Enterprise	4	4	4	12
Test persons				
Number	40	32	40	112
Type	Business students	Business practitioners	Business practitioners	
Group size				
Enterprise	10	8	10	8-10
Staff/board of directors	5	4	5	4-5

**Table 3-3
Distribution of Professional Qualifications**

	Testing Sequence 2 Enterprise				Testing Sequence 3 Enterprise				
Training or Qualification	5	6	7	8	9	10	11	12	Total
Merchant	2		1	4					7
Graduate in business administration		2	5[a]		2	2	1	2	14
Engineer	4	3	1	3	3	3	4	3	24
Graduate engineer	2	3	1	1	5	5	5	5	27
Total	8	8	8	8	10	10	10	10	72

Translator's note: Merchant = vocationally (not academically) trained; engineer = usually engineer holding a three-year academic degree.

[a]Because of the communicatively closed group, the risk of the dominance of professional economic training had to be assumed.

ences in age, professional experience, modes of behavior based on position, and the amount of professional knowledge needed to be taken into consideration as principal characteristics of differentiation. To what extent significantly different forms of problem mastery actually result from these different prerequisites remains to be investigated. Measures for the design of the personnel framework other than those discussed were not taken.

It is of particular importance to note that the selection of the participants was not made by the directors of the experiment.

Method and Concept of Investigation

Regulation of the Course of the Experiment

In addition to the characterization of the experiment conditions according to problem content and personnel factors, a third step is to present the processual aspect of the experimental design. In doing so, the dynamic and economic character of the simulated decision sequences must be described.

Total Duration and Periodization: The problem context of the experimental tasks is a system of decisions based on company policy. The relationships existing in this system are of an objective as well as of a temporal nature. While the objective interdependence formed the foreground in the depiction of the simulation model, we are here interested in the dynamic relations of the individual decision sequences. In principle, also a narrow sector of time—in the extreme case even a single sequence (consisting of one definite initial situation, a number of decisions to be made only once, and their results)—could be imagined as an experiment condition. Numerous experiments are based on such single-phase situations. For three reasons our investigation selected a multiphase concept.

1. The majority of decisions made in actual business enterprises do not occur as singular problem situations. Despite a changing constellation of conditions, they are repeatedly encountered as being of the same type. The decisions that have already been developed within the framework of the simulation model are typical tasks of this genre.
2. It is to be expected that the mastery of decisions under time pressure will cause modes and changes of behavior that become pronounced only after repeated dealings with the same problem situation. A successive change of transparence and changing forms of the problem solution resulting from it can be anticipated. An initial or one-time confrontation with restrictive decisional conditions will not trigger immediate and directly effective measures for the mastery of the situations.
3. In the case of a statistically oriented methodic approach, the empirical analysis of problem-solving processes may result in findings on fact and dimension but not on the type of problem mastery. A purely comparative assessment of the initial and final situations prevents insight into the course of the happening.[72] Particularly, organizational activities directed toward the regulation of the process of achievement remain unassessed.

The representation of actual decisional conditions, the dynamics of behavior in complex situations, and the assessibility of the process of problem solving require a course of experimentation that includes several sequences of decision making. For that reason, ten decision-making sequences were subjected to uniform investigative experimentation in all of the experiment sequences. In the interest of homogeneous conditions, an absolutely identical design of the temporal succession in all of the experiment sequences would be desirable, but the other responsibilities of the test subjects concerning school and work set certain limits on this ideal. The subjects' workload at school and on their jobs limited a completely free time design—that is, oriented purely by experimental requirements. Since long-term participation by the same test subjects was necessary, the different occupational realities of students and executives had to be taken into consideration, and a totally identical design of the temporal experiment conditions had to be waived.

As a result of this requirement, the decision-making meetings of the student testing sequences, permanently taking place on the same half-day, were scheduled over a ten-week sequence during the course of the semester. And in an attempt to avoid as much organizational burden as possible, the decisions in the testing sequences of business executives were made on ten successive half-days. All groups, however, had the same amount of time for problem solving.

Design of the Economic Framework: An essential ingredient of a business game is the necessity to make decisions under changing economic constellations. Variations of internal and market-related conditions result from the economic activity inherent in a firm, from the competitors' activity, from the overall economic data of the politicoeconomic framework, as well as from the expectations and modes of behavior of potential buyers. In the simulation model, the last two parameter classes were part of the regulatory tools of the game directors. Since they are an essential part of the behavior conditions, it is of basic methodological significance to depict the type and extent of the economic influence of the game directors.

A total renunciation of intervention in the economic environmental conditions of the enterprise was rejected, for several reasons. First, the fact that the experiment was a long-term one forced us to maintain the complexity of the decisions to be made. By dealing repeatedly with problems of the same genre, increasing transparency was achieved in full accord with actual working conditions. This allowed us to arrive at more qualified solutions. This effect of experience was in no way undesired in the experiment; on the contrary, it was explicitly sought and measured. However, the decision-making routine thus acquired is not to lead to a decrease in intellectual effort, to a reduction of activity to habitual behavior within the framework of the issue investigated here. To ensure validity of the findings obtained, it is necessary to stabilize the mental engagement, the personal ego involvement, on the highest level possible. The variation of the concrete economic situational characteristics in the form of market terms appeared to be a suitable way to achieve this.

The quality of this type of simulation of the conditions of management decisions is all the better the more it reflects actual problem situations as an objectively consistent system of conditions. In the economic regulation, particular care was taken that the parameters defined as an entity were free from instrumental contradiction. That means that the simulated economic situation was always plausibly conceived as the expression of the reaction of the state and the consumers to the actual market situation and the market behavior of the firms. Taken in this sense, the decision-making situations that were created by the intervention on the part of the experiment direction were not contrarily opposed to the expectations and experience of the decision-making subjects. The frame of constellation of each case reflected a consequent and continual relationship with the management policy activities within a testing sequence. Moreover, the decision makers possessed information which was to be regarded as evidence of the existing or impending economic situation. Data on raw-material prices, interest on liabilities, securities exchange rates, and conditions of payment proved to be reliable and were valuable planning aids if properly observed and interpreted.

The variation of the specific market parameters of demand was done in terms of growing expectations concerning quality at declining price conceptions with the buyers who, on their part, gained increasing market transparency in the course of the decision sequences. This simulation of general consumer behavior also took account of those advertising activities of the enterprises, which resulted in an increase in aspirations as well as in a stronger ability of discrimination with respect to the quality and prices of the products offered by the competing firms. One unambiguous function of the sales realized in the individual markets was a permanently increasing market saturation. On the whole the firms saw themselves successively confronted with less-accessible markets, which placed increasing demands on the quality of market-policy decisions.

Since each testing sequence represented a field of competition of four companies and since each of the firms pursued independent strategies within this framework, the overall course of the economic situation of a testing sequence did not develop according to any determinable concept. The extensive freedom of the decision-making units, together with the interferences of action and effect that are characteristic of competitive situations, led to a constellation of individually dynamic conditions that was typical for each of the testing sequences. For this reason a standardization of the exogenous decision conditions had to be waived in the interest of a regulatory framework that corresponded to the situation. The regulation of the situation by the experiment direction thus was subjugated to the actual conditions of a testing sequence to a certain degree.

In spite of and particularly because of these incompletely standardized interventions in the economic context of the course of the experiment, it had to be made certain that the structuring measures were always taken as a whole for a particular testing sequence. Measures tending to prefer or disadvantage certain firms economically were excluded. The model guaranteed this neutrality of effect for the aggregate economic-trend parameters of purchasing power, payment conditions, and capital market variables (interest rates and securities exchange rates). The possibility of a regulation aimed at specific individual markets as contained in the model was waived. Market parameters were varied equally only for all the markets so that no discrimination toward other competitors resulted from the simulation-determined position of a firm. In this way the necessary neutrality of the experimental regulatory frame and, at the same time, the assurance of an adequate situational representation of economic decision-making conditions were achieved.

Induction of Time Pressure

The experimental design characterized thus far provided the general working conditions of the decision-making situations created by the simulation. But since the specific question of this investigation is directed at time pressure, this central variable of time pressure has to be discussed in detail as the last component of the experimental design. This discussion is, however, not yet to describe the concrete measurement, but only the experimental induction for the creation of time pressure.

The analysis of behavior under time pressure presupposes the existence of time pressure. This basic requisite, which appears trivial, means that it must be possible to create conditions that cause time pressure. Since time pressure is to be understood as a perception of the individuals who register stress within the conditions of achievement, time pressure in no way can be identified with definite, predetermined time allowances. It is, rather, so that these—together with other influences of achievement—have to be understood as triggering conditions for the occurrence of time pressure. This connection, which has already been theoretically founded, clearly shows that the design of the temporal decision-making conditions does not necessarily trigger time pressure.

The explicative value of statements concerning behavior under time pressure increases if the results obtained are not exclusively derived from situations burdened by time but can be based on the comparison between performance conditions that carry a high degree of time burden and those that carry a lesser temporal burden or none at all. Because both constellations are to be created within the framework of this investigation, the second basic requisite in addition to the time restriction is that of its systematically directed variation.

Method and Concept of Investigation

Forms of Time Pressure: Each of the decision-making units which functions as a business enterprise was given a predesigned, organizationally institutional structure. The form of labor division that resulted between the groups designated as staff and board of directors furnishes the experimental structural approaches for the induction of time pressure.

The activities of each of the business enterprises took place in a three-fold manner. First, mental problem-solving activities that are not directly discernible by means of the research tools chosen took place within the two subgroups of a decision-making unit. On this basis both working groups (staff and board of directors) cooperated with each other in the form of written communications. In addition to this internal communication, there were consultative outside relations between the staff and the information center of the same process type. Each of the three classes of decision-making activities can be temporally restrained as a definitely delineable type of performance and as such can be potentially subjected to time pressure. Since, however, no limitations should be imposed on the informational support rendered by the information center,[73] there remain only two restrictive approaches: group internal performance and group connecting communication. From this result the following definitions of the experimental induction variables are given.

1. Performance time pressure exists when the time available for the processing of the internal tasks of a work group is recognized by the group members as insufficient.
2. Communication time pressure prevails when the time available for the exchange of performance contributions with the respective partner group is estimated by the respective group members as insufficient.

Although the two variables can be defined in an analytically independent manner and can be subjected to empirically separate measurement, they have a basic connection, which must be observed in the design of the experimental conditions. Part of the activities performed in internal group work in principle also need to be coped with by communication. This relation becomes even more distinct in the concept of limited communication time and unlimited internal working time. Group internal performance and communication are to be understood accordingly as at least partially substitutive forms of work. In which way this substitutability actually exists depends on the concrete tasks as part of a specific problem. The general assumption of a mutual exchangeability of performance time and communication time—that is, of a compensatory effect between performance time pressure and communication time pressure—therefore must be examined in the respective area of application.

This relationship is of fundamental importance for the question of time pressure. A careful preliminary investigation of alternative time conditions is particularly imperative for the experimental measures designed to create time pressure. If such a measurement is not made, a serious impairment of validity might exist if in spite of definite time limitations, time pressure does not arise in the course described although its existence is taken for granted and the researcher believes he or she is measuring its behavioral effects. Another argument in favor of preliminary testing is the necessity of references concerning the degree of effect. If, for general reasons of method, effectiveness is to be examined, a pretest on the extent of the experimental interventions can be conducted to provide a preliminary estimate of the research success to be expected.[74] This research success will be small if the experimental design provides for interventions that are too strong or too weak. An intervention is to be viewed as too strong when it prevents behavior adequate to the problem by the experiment subjects. This would be the case if the participants in the experiment were exposed to time restrictions that made every effort at problem solving appear to be illusory from the outset. Frustration, resignation, and mental distancing would have to be expected as the most minimal consequences. In another way there is a threat of failure of an experiment if the inductions are allocated too indistinctly. Such a faulty design does not cause any quantitatively determinable differences with respect to the focal variables. The results do not reach the necessary discrimination thresholds of significance, which are required for a separation of effect and coincidence.

Time-Pressure Variation: Selection, placing, and dosage of interventions are part of the technical research tools of the experimental method. They add the dynamic element of the experimental process to the institutional, apparative, personnel, and temporal framework of the experiment arrangement. The interventions must be performed in a predetermined arrangement and must allow the unlimited testing of the hypotheses.

The limitation of time in which to arrive at decisions, which is necessary for the induction of time pressure, must be fixed with respect to the type of restriction, as well as its variation. This context raises numerous questions of technical design. The course of the experiment can be determined only after these questions have been answered.

After it has been decided to establish observation intervals with and without time pressure within the whole sequence of the experiment, the researchers must determine how the variation of the time allowances is to be accomplished. Basically, varying the interventions by the testing sequence, by business enterprises, and by decision sequences will be suitable. Because of the difficulties in comparing the efficiency of the observation units, the first two alternatives are not to be recommended. Imposing different spans of time on specific testing sequences and thus on selected business enter-

Method and Concept of Investigation

prises or even imposing different time spans on individual enterprises within each testing sequence would result in an unequal determination of competitive opportunities. It is doubtful that a purely economic elimination of this disturbing influence is possible. Besides the theoretical and mathematical difficulties of correlating decision time available equivalent with the imaginary value of competitiveness, completely uncontrollable consequences from the social sphere of the field of investigation must be anticipated. Therefore the variation of interventions is made by testing periods.

The next technical detail of the experiment concerns the points in time of the experimental interventions. Our goal is to restrict decision sequences in such a way that the dynamically explainable adaptation and absorption effects of time pressure can be proved. Moreover, the participants in the experiment must not be overburdened by continuous, narrowly limited time allowances. These considerations result in a design that provides for time limitations in the first and last three decision sequences, while the four intervening periods are kept free from such time restrictions. This arrangement satisfies the methodic requirement and uniformly provides the basis for all testing sequences.

The final element of the design intervention is fixed by the allocation of the time allowances for the individual periods of experiment. The experience of many years of application of business games has shown that three hours are sufficient for the mastering of given problems without time pressure. In order to ensure that time pressure will not occur in the experiment unintentionally, three and a half hours of working time was set as the norm for the pressure-free periods. Exceeding these time allocations was generally permissible and possible. To measure a restrictive structuring of time, the critical time was tested in the preexperiments in order to determine a reliable time allocation norm for the induction of time pressure.[75] The result showed that a time allowance of about two hours was only scarcely enough to make the obligatory decisions completely and with sufficient preparation. Therefore, in the decision sequences for which the experimental design provided for time pressure, a working time of 120 minutes was set for all staff and board of directors groups.[76] At the beginning of the respective testing period the groups were told there was a time limit, made necessary by the technical requirements of access to a computer. Time extensions were declared to be inadmissible and were not granted.

In order to check the substitutive connection between performance time and communication time, it is necessary to establish and fix an unambiguous relation between the two variables of time in the experiment. In the interest of a valid experiment arrangement, it must be guaranteed that the induction of time pressure aimed at is ensured and not interfered with by uncontrolled compensating effects. Therefore it is also necessary to allocate the communication time available for cooperation within a decision unit in the same way as this has already been done with regard to performance time. Experience in business games has shown—and the preexperiments confirmed this—that two and a half hours is sufficient and that one hour is hardly sufficient to master the communication activities that occur in the framework of the task-divisional decision. Thus the time available for communication was set at sixty minutes in addition to the time limitations for group-related internal performance. This additional restriction causes the time-pressure situation to become particularly distinct, and it thereby stabilized the arrangement of the experiment. Table 3-4 shows the course of the experiment regarding the induction of time pressure. Because all sessions began in the same way, no information on the experimental manipulation of the decision-making conditions was apparent prior to the respective experimental period. In addition, the fact of overlapping working time for both subgroups of an enterprise corresponds to the processual conditions of labor division in task completion. It appears to be meaningful to begin sessions with the situation analysis without simultaneously and immediately transforming the individual results into strategies of entrepreneurial policy.[77] Experiment regulation therefore provided for each of the staff groups to begin their sixty minutes earlier than the board of directors groups. The temporal experiment regulation thus does not contradict common views and consequently can be regarded as methodically neutral.

Measurement of Time Pressure: Within the framework of the present investigation, time pressure acquires central importance. The theoretical explanation first examines the causes for the occurrence of time pressure. This approach consequently views time pressure as a variable. In more-extensive explanatory steps it is understood as an independent—or as a causative—variable.[78] Seen from the experimental-technical viewpoint, time pressure is to be conceived of as a variable of induction and as such as a design problem.

Since it cannot be taken for granted that time pressure can be produced by measures as already presented for the regulation of time in the experiment, an adequate validity test is indispensible. In this way the effectiveness of experimental induction is tested. The theoretical concept that contains the variable of time pressure as an element of the then component and also as an element of the if component requires a direct measuring procedure. Particularly because time pressure is assigned an explanatory function, its measurement must take place independently. That means that the existence of time pressure may neither be concluded from specific antecedent conditions, nor may it be operationalized by the prevailing of specific modes of behavior. Such an approach would lead to a purely logical transformation of empirically meaningless sentences and result into a tautology instead of a scientific explanation.

Method and Concept of Investigation

Table 3-4
Temporal Experiment Design

Testing Period	1 2 3	4 5 6 7	8 9 10
Intention of test	Time pressure	No time pressure	Time pressure
Length of test	120 minutes	210 minutes	120 minutes

For the most objective measurement possible, a physical equivalent would be desirable for the time stress perceived.[79] In the absence of another suitable, methodically secure measuring technique, the participants in the experiment were asked, by means of a questionnaire, for their estimate of the temporal working conditions. The questioning took place immediately after each experiment period. Data of each person were recorded for their estimate of both the time available for performance and for communication:

What is your opinion of the time allotment?
a. for working on your assignment?

```
    fully                                completely
|-------+-------+-------+-------+-------|
  sufficient                           insufficient
```

b. For communication with your staff of board of directors?

```
    fully                                completely
|-------+-------+-------+-------+-------|
  sufficient                           insufficient
```

Rating on both parts of the question was done by a continuous six-point scale of polar anchoring.[80] In order to achieve the highest possible precision in the measurement, the graphic markings were converted, for numerical evaluation, into a two-digit decimal value, varying from 10 to 60.

The separate estimates were condensed to an arithmetic mean and in this form represent the measurement of the individually registered time pressure. Then the individual time-pressure values obtained in this way were reduced—again by determining an arithmetic mean—to a time-pressure index for each work group. Thus, for each period and each of the twenty-four work groups, a value of a total of 240 indices was obtained for further analysis.

Quality of the Experiment

At this point we do not want to make the inappropriate attempt to judge the methodic conception as a whole and ultimately. Neither the state of the previous discussion nor the scarcely avoidable bias of the author appeared to allow such an undertaking. Rather, this section has the task of examining two essential elements of design of the experiment in their effect on time pressure: Participation of different subjects and the position-determined disparity of the tasks in both subgroups of each decision-making unit. An effect on the relationships to be explained cannot be excluded a priori and thus must be tested to determine to what extent the team personnel and the specific form of the division of work reflect differences in the occurrence of time pressure. This question is not directed to explaining influences which result from experimental marginal conditions; it is directed to their control. Only after it has been proved that neither the personal nor the positional aspect affects the explanation of time pressure can the neutrality of the group formation be confirmed. But if significant and structure-determined differences in influence become apparent in the test, then the latter will require a differentiation of the results. In that case the generalizability of the findings concerning decision making under time pressure is limited.

Personal Validity

In the hypotheses, individual sensitivity to stress was developed as one of the triggering conditions. The attempt at an ex-post control of the methodic quality of the experiment now reverts to this approach. In doing so, the concept of sensitivity is not being redefined; rather it provides an additional stimulus. The theoretical value of these personality variables remains completely unaffected by the discussions below.

Time-pressure sensitivity is a complex variable that is difficult to define. As an individual characteristic of personality, it falls into the area of explanation of psychomedical stress research and would have to receive at least measurement-technical support from that area. In addition to the organizational research difficulties of such an interdisciplinary consultation, it must be emphasized that this investigation is directed not toward individual persons but toward work groups. Since the individual groups were so composed as to achieve a uniform distribution of professional qualification and the latter does not reflect any relationship to sensitivity, it can be justly assumed that these variables in the experiment are parallel. Therefore an examination of sensitivity to stress in the original sense is not to be and cannot be undertaken.

The use of different types of test subjects—students of economics and practicing economists—poses the question of the uniformity of entry requirements in the experiment. The assumption appears to be close at hand that in both classes of persons different constitutions prevail which, however, are equal in type. Consequently, different reaction to the experimental

Method and Concept of Investigation

conditions could be founded on such natural disparities, which are extremely difficult to identify in detail.[81] Direct measurements of such characteristics face the same difficulties as the recording of individual degrees of sensitivity. Therefore, a more-modest testing concept must be pursued. A measurement is needed which allows the identification of structural differences between alternative types of persons.

Measurement: The determination of a suitable indicator is based on the following considerations. Time pressure is triggered by the three complementary variables of decision time, problem intensity, and sensitivity. The first two variables are controllable; the third variable can neither be influenced systematically nor be measured directly. It therefore represents an unknown in the common-language and mathematical sense of the word. If the effect of the three influencing factors can be measured and the causative share of the two controllable variables can be duly considered, then the functional relationship may be dissolved; the unknown can be defined.

Determining the sensitivity degrees is bound to the present experimental framework. Sensitivity can be determined only as an aggregate value for definite testing groups. The experimental design determines the content of the findings on sensitivity. The findings made possible by the procedure described are therefore designated as structural sensitivity. It does not intend to and cannot claim to be surrogate for unrecordable individual sensitivity. Since a direct measurement of structural sensitivity is not possible, perceived time pressure will be used to help determine this variable. Dissimilarly high time-pressure index values are a reliable indicator of structural sensitivity if conditions otherwise are identical.[82] Since all testing sequences were exposed to exactly the same time-pressure conditions and also since the conditions of the economic framework may be considered homogeneous because of their very minor differences, the reliability of the measurement is assured.

Testing Design: The time-pressure index values of the experiment periods serve as test data with and without time limits. The measuring values are differentiated according to the genres of person as students and practitioners. The determination of differences between these classes is based on a comparison of mean values by means of the student t test. A margin of error of 5 percent is fixed as the value of confidence of the statistical significance test. Findings that reflect higher error coefficients are rated accordingly as not significant. The examination is limited to the staff groups.

Finding: Table 3-5 compares the time-pressure index of the students for all ten experiment periods with the corresponding indexes of the practitioners. The empirical findings show that the practitioners' perception of time pres-

Table 3-5
Comparison of Time-Pressure Sensitivity of Students and Practitioners

Test Values, Periods 1-10	Students: Test Sequence 1	Practitioners: Test Sequences 2-3
Mean value	31.30	27.79
Standard deviation	12.44	9.56
Number (n)	40	80
Significance	$p = 0.090$	

sure in principle does not differ from that of the students. The difference of the mean values does not satisfy the demands of the test and therefore must be classified as not significant. This is the result of the analysis of the question of whether the students and practitioners in the experiment differ from each other in their time pressure sensitivity. A test question of this kind is called "undirected" since it aims solely at the fact and not at the kind of difference of values. A difference is established independent of whether the deviation is positive or negative. In the terminology of testing statistics, the test is thus a bilateral one. [83]

If the theoretically confirmable assumption had been present that practitioners perceive time pressure to a lesser degree, a directed hypothesis would have had to be submitted to a unilateral test. The statistical examination of this question would have yielded a significant confirmation. In this context, this is in no way an arbitrary interpretation of results. Rather it shows the purely instrumental function of the statistical test of providing qualitatively different results according to the precision of the question. A directed test question is unequivocal and as such statistically easier to answer. Undirected assumptions, on the other hand, encompass more uncertainty, which is consequently reflected by the statistical test in the form of a higher probability of error. The nature of the data does not yet permit a definitive judgment with regard to the hypothesis purported.

Situations of this kind, which are quite common in empirical investigations, require a more-extensive evaluation. Insofar as the data allow a differentiation, the opportunity for a more-profound analysis should be taken. A retroactive finding-regulated reformulation of the initial question must, however, be rejected as a violation of scientific conventions of method. Renouncing a critically continued investigation above all harbors the danger of a false conclusion.

In a further step of the sensitivity analysis the attempt is made to probe more intensely into the data from the experiment. The testing sequences,

Table 3-6
Comparision of Time-Pressure Sensitivity of Students and Practitioners (Experiment Periods 1-3)

Test Values	Students: Test Sequence 1	Practitioners: Test Sequence 2	Practitioners: Test Sequence 3
Mean value	44.42	40.75	30.83
Standard deviation	4.21	8.44	7.60
Number (n)	12	12	12
Significance		$p\ 1/2 = 0.181$ $p\ 2/3 = 0.005$ $p\ 1/3 < 0.001$	

divided into groups with students and groups with practitioners, and the experiment periods, structured heterogeneously in time, are characteristics of stratification. This division of the empirical material leads to a stronger differentiation of the category of practitioners, and leads to a systematic order of the testing periods in accordance with their respective time pressure. (See table 3-6.)

The findings supplement the results achieved under undifferentiated observation in the following way:

1. It can be proved that the sensitivity of students' time pressure does not differ from the corresponding measurement values of the practitioners in testing sequence 2. The coefficient of error, $p = 0.181$, is far above the preestablished confidence level so that the minor discrepancy between the two values cannot be regarded as significant.
2. The comparison within the two testing sequences with practitioners leads to a serious modification of the initial results. The category of practitioners proves to be nonhomogeneous concerning time pressure sensitivity, which is distinctly and differently marked in *testing* sequences 2 and 3. The statistical test confirms the finding of essential differences on a high significance level, $p = 0.005$.
3. This result simultaneously explains the third result which seemingly contradicts the finding shown in table 3-5. Students reflect a highly and significantly stronger sensitivity to time pressure than do the practitioners in testing sequence 3.

As a first conclusion from these data, it can be said that the testing of sensitivity of different types of test subjects constitutes a justified and necessary step of structural analysis. Therefore, in order to gain the most-

Table 3-7
Comparison of Time-Pressure Sensitivity of Students and Practitioners (Experiment Periods 4-7)

Test Values	Students: Test Sequence 1	Practitioners: Test Sequence 2	Practitioners: Test Sequence 3
Mean value	18.75	20.13	23.63
Standard deviation	2.66	3.50	4.75
Number (n)	16	16	16
Significance	$p\ 1/2 = 0.221$	$p\ 2/3 = 0.024$	
		$p\ 1/3 = 0.0012$	

comprehensive picture possible of the connections, the sensitivity analysis (which is stratified according to periods and testing sequences) is to be enlarged in a second step.

Table 3-7 gives unlimited support to the findings as result from table 3-6. The testing values of testing sequence 3 as opposed to those of the other two testing sequences are clearly and markedly different. The high degree of correspondence of the sensitivity values of the students and practitioners in the second testing sequence also corroborate the validity of the previous results.

The final step in sensitivity testing is based on the last three periods of the course of the experiment. In accordance with the experimental design, the allotted decision time was limited during this testing interval.

As table 3-8 shows, there are no differences in sensitivity between students and practitioners in the last experiment periods of testing sequence 2, nor can any essential disparity of values be determined within groups of practitioners. Both results are above the admissible level of probability of error so that no significant differences can be established for the respective matching groups compared. The high deviation between the sensitivity of the students and that of the practitioners in testing sequence 3, however, remains unchanged in the final periods. The convergence of the sensitivity values occurring toward the end of the course of the experiment does, thus, not hold true for the two polar testing sequences 1 and 3.

The results clearly show that the question of different degrees of time-pressure sensitivity cannot be explained by the characteristics of the two classes of test subjects. This finding has two consequences for the investigation. First, it is no longer necessary to differentiate between students and practitioners. Thus a higher degree of generalization is permitted. Second, the research task of explaining the different time-pressure values that occurred despite the homogeneous framework of conditions must be directed

Table 3–8
Comparison of Time-Pressure Sensitivity of Students and Practitioners (Experiment Periods 8–10)

Test Values	Students: Test Sequence 1	Practitioners: Test Sequence 2	Practitioners: Test Sequence 3
Mean value	34.91	29.67	24.00
Standard deviation	9.51	10.38	5.48
Number (n)	12	12	12
Significance	$p\ 1/2 = 0.207$	$p\ 2/3 = 0.109$	
	$p\ 1/3 = 0.002$		

toward the processual aspect of problem mastery. That means an opening up of a work-divisional decision-making process as it takes place within the simulated enterprises. Although the findings in table 3–5 have not refuted the obvious assumption that students and practitioners reflect differently pre-marked degrees of sensitivity, the additional findings furnish the proof that this assumption is only seemingly justified.[84] It is true that sensitivity to time pressure is not a specific genre characteristic of students or practitioners.

Functional Validity

The result of the preceding validity test enhances the justification of a process-oriented approach. The course of problem solving within the framework of decisions under time pressure thus becomes the focal point of further efforts. By comparison, the aspect of the decision-making person clearly loses much of its explanatory value in this experiment. For this reason, it is necessary to examine the time-pressure effect of those structural factors of the experimental design that might influence the work method. The division of each enterprise into two subgroups is one such exogenous experiment condition. The position-dependent tasks necessarily cause disparity in the character of the performance. It must be expected that the specific functions within the staff groups will lead to an increased sensitivity to time pressures. In that case, the predetermined structure of the task distribution in the experiment would not be without effect on the respective measurement values. Since, however, not the performance effects of the specific order of experiment are to be analyzed but the decision under time pressure is to be investigated as much as possible without distortion, the influence of the division of functions must be analyzed. This analysis is designated the test of functional validity.

Measurement: Functional validity is all the higher the less the experimental working conditions characterize behavior under time pressure. Accordingly, a rigorous validity test would have to investigate alternative testing arrangements for their time-pressure effect. But since the entire experiment, including the preexperiments, proceeded under constantly maintained structural conditions, this method of control is not possible. Instead, testing by differences between the time-pressure values realized in the staff groups and/or the board of directors' groups lends itself. The more the respective comparative values deviate from each other, the more intense is the influence of the specific separation of functions by preparing and fixing decisional subtasks. In this case a discriminate evaluation and depiction would be indispensable.[85] Sensitivity as developed in the preceding validity test again serves as the measure for the evaluation of functional validity. Since the temporal as well as the economic secondary conditions are always applicable to both subgroups of a decision-making unit in the same way, the time-pressure index value is a reliable measure for time-pressure sensitivity now dependent on position.

Testing Design: The time-pressure index values from the staff and board of directors' groups are compared with each other as testing classes. By means of the student t test, the mean values are compared for the determination of differences. The statistical significance test is based on an admissible probability of error of 5 percent. The test includes the values obtained from all testing sequences; it is conducted for all experiment periods in which time is restricted.

Findings: Table 3-9 shows that the function groups of staff and board of directors reflect significant differences in sensitivity. Thus, the form of division of work indicates an influence on the perception of time pressure.

Since the investigation of structural sensitivity was done without any directed initial expectations and therefore theoretical explanations of the results are absent, retroactive explanatory approaches can be developed only in the form of new hypothetical considerations. With reference to table 3-9, it is to be assumed that the information-intensive performance profile of the decision-preparing activity that results from the selected design will require a greater amount of time input than does the critically utilizing performance in the decision-making panels, which is based on it. The necessity of common decision making as stipulated by the simulation model compels mutual consultation, which implies the same communicative pressures for both groups.

Table 3-9
Comparison of Time-Pressure Sensitivity in Staff and Board of Directors' Positions in Experiment Periods with Time Limitations

Test Values: Periods 1-3, 8-10	Staff	Board of Directors
Mean value	34.38	29.79
Standard deviation	10.26	9.09
Number (n)	72	72
Significance	$p = 0.003$	

These results do not require a revision of time pressure operationalization. Time pressure continues to be understood as the multiple measure of pressure produced by limited decision-making time available. The more profound investigation had the sole purpose of revealing essential work-technical components of time pressure and thus, at the same time, different levels of sensitivity. The methodic justification for a separate rewording of the two time-pressure components is a secondary result.

Situative Validity

The need to vary the conditions of the economic framework results from the character of the simulation model. Moreover, changes of the overall economic parameters are connected with the demand for a representative depiction of managerial decision-making situations. External regulation should, however, be done in such a way as not to distort the experimental interventions. A methodic neutrality so understood can exist only when it can be successfully proved that the indispensable regulation of the overall economic situation does not influence the rise of time pressure in the experiment. The statement is to be understood solely as a methodic comment; it does not dispute the theoretical relevance of problem intensity as a determinant of time pressure. If, however, a parallelization of the situational data can be proved—which for reasons of experimental control is desirable—this variable loses its explanatory value for the results of the experiment reported later.

The course of the experiment is subject to two simultaneously effective forms of intervention: indispensable regulation of the economic framework and variation of time allotments. In order to determine to what degree the two measures can be considered as independent from each other, it is necessary to compare both interventions.

Measurement: For the purposes of characterizing the economic constellation, an index value is selected that is composed of two parameters contained in the simulation model. One regulation variable determines the total nonspecific market and product demand, that is, the aggregate economic situation. The second regulative parameter represents the conditions of payment in the procurement and sales areas of the enterprises. Since both parameters are closely related and were always established together in the experiment, their combination in one aggregate expression can be justified. Multiplicative combination yields a valid measure for the aggregate economic situation. The market index thus determined comprises a variation range of twenty-three to seventy-seven value points. The decision-making conditions are valid for the four enterprises of each experiment sequence. High index values correspond to favorable framework constellations; a low market index signifies a tense economic situation. The situative validity is considered assured if the test values of the market index in the experimental testing intervals do not differ appreciably. In this case, alternative time-pressure values cannot be explained from the situational factors of the aggregate market.

Testing Design: In order to test the situative validity, the test values of the market index obtained in experiment periods with strict time limitations are compared with the corresponding data obtained in periods without limitation of decision-making time. The statistical test is directed to a comparison of the respective class mean values by means of the t test. The threshold value of significance is set at an admissible 5 percent probability of error.

Findings: The test equivalents for situative validity are shown in table 3-10. The apparent finding is corroborated by the result of the statistical test. Aggregate economic regulation of the experiment course reveals differences only to such a degree that does not satisfy the claim for confidence and therefore must be regarded as insignificant. Accordingly, conditions of

Table 3-10
Comparison of Market-Index Values of All Experiment Sequences

Test Values	Periods without Time Limitation	Periods with Time Limitation
Mean value	58.25	64.55
Standard deviation	10.47	18.41
Number (n)	12	18
Significance	$p = 0.250$	

economic framework in periods with strict time limitation were basically the same as in periods without such time limitation. This eliminates the aggregate market situation from the set of influencing factors explaining time pressure.

Notes

1. K.R. Popper, *Logik* (1969), p. 59.
2. For the formal equivalence of explanation and prognosis, see H. Albert, *Theoriebildung* (1964); H. Albert, *Theorie und Prognose* (1965), p. 126ff.; W. Leinfellner, *Wissenschaftstheorie* (1967), p. 168ff.; K.-D. Opp, *Methodologie* (1970), p. 67ff.; as well as W. Stegmüller, *Erklärung und Begründung* (1969), pp. 155, 198.
3. Popper, *Logik,* pp. 76ff., 100ff., calls the "degree of verifiability" the "degree of falsifiability" and the "empirical content" and identifies the latter with the "simplicity" of a theory.
4. For the "rate of confirmation" as a criterion of completed testing, see ibid., p. 214ff., and H. Albert, *Wissenschaftslehre* (1967), p. 53ff.
5. Popper, *Logik,* p. 215. For the relationship of "generality," "definiteness," and "precision," see Albert, *Theoriebildung,* p. 25, and Popper, *Logik,* p. 85ff.
6. See Popper, *Logik,* pp. 216ff., 259, 339ff.
7. In this context Albert, *Theoriebildung,* p. 36ff., criticizes the erroneous belief in the efficiency of mathematics.
8. Popper, *Logik,* p. 339.
9. P.F. Lazarsfeld, *Wissenschaftslogik* (1971), regrets the isolation of theoretical scientific research from actual scientific research practice.
10. Popper, *Logik,* p. 214ff.
11. Albert, *Theoriebildung,* p. 59.
12. See Popper, *Logik,* p. 198, and R. Meili, *Experiment* (1963), p. 17.
13. H.F. Spinner, *Modelle und Experimente* (1969), col. 1007.
14. See ibid.
15. For the method of field investigation, see K. Katz, *Field Studies* (1953).
16. For observation as a research method, see especially R. König, *Beobachtung und Experiment* (1967), and *Beobachtung* (1967), who advocates a broad view on the concept of observation. See also P. Atteslander, *Methoden* (1969), p. 123ff.
17. The methodological problem of the relation of observer and object of observation is discussed particularly in R. König, *Beobachtung* (1967), p. 124ff.; H. Hartmann, *Sozialforschung* (1970), p. 120ff.; W.R. Scott, *Field*

Methods (1965), pp. 266, 273ff.; A Schwartzbaum and L. Gruenfeld, *Subject-Observer—Interaction* (1969); H. Kreutz, *Sozialforschung* (1972), p. 92ff.; R.W. Heyns and A.F. Zander, *Observation* (1953), p. 413ff.

18. In principle this critical argument is also valid for experimental investigations. Within the frame of our methodic approach it will be given careful attention.

19. For questioning as a research technique widely used in the social sciences, see E.K. Scheuch, *Interview* (1967); P. Atteslander, *Methoden* (1969), p. 70ff.; R. König, *Interview* (1957).

20. For the same reasons E. Witte, *Komplexe Entscheidungsverläufe* (1968), p. 590ff., chooses this technique of data collection for the analysis of decision-making processes. See also A. Silbermann, *Inhaltsanalyse* (1967); Atteslander, *Methoden,* p. 46ff, and J. Szczepanski, *Biographische Methode* (1967).

21. Only in recent times has there been success in testing the hypothesis directed to the space-time relationship in Einstein's Theory of Relativity. The apparative prerequisites to measure very fast and long-range movements by aircraft had to be supplemented by highly sensitive measurement devices (chronometers powered by atomic energy).

22. See K. Eyferth, *Gruppenstrukturen* (1963), p. 388ff. For the development of the experimental method see R. Pagés, *Experiment* (1967).

23. H. Sauerman and R. Selten, *Experimentelle Wirtschaftsforschung* (1967), p. 1ff., designate the historical developmental conditions of the economic sciences as barriers of method and sketch possibilities for mastering them. For the present standing of microeconomic experimental research, see H. Sauerman (publisher), *Wirtschaftsforschung,* vols. 1 and 2 (1967, 1970); J. Hesselbach, *Verhaltensforschung* (1970), and R. Bronner, E. Witte, and P.R. Wossidlo, *Experimente* (1972), p. 165ff.

24. For this see B. Runzheimer, *Experiment* (1966), and A. Picot, *Organisationsforschung* (1972).

25. See P.M. Blau and W.R. Scott, *Organizations* (1963), p. 19ff.; G. Eberlein, *Experiment* (1964), p. 119; W. Siebel, *Logik des Experiments* (1965), p. 20ff.; J.R. French, *Experiments* (1953), p. 98ff.; J. Hesselbach, *Verhaltensforschung* (1970), p. 656; W. Janke, *Experiment* (1969), p. 97ff.; J.E. McGrath, *Theory of Method* (1964), p. 540; Pagés, *Experiment,* p. 439; A. Picot, *Organisationsforschung* (1972), p. 59ff.; Bronner, Witte, and Wossidlo, *Experimente,* p. 166ff.

26. R. Meili, *Experiment* (1963), p. 4ff., uses the designations "testing," "methods," "application," and "critical experiment" from A.L. Edwards. See also G.A. Lienert, *Belastung* (1964), p. 13, and W. Janke, *Experiment* (1969), p. 105.

27. See Popper, *Logik* (1969), p. 185, and Spinner, *Modelle und Experimente,* col. 1007.

29. For this see Janke, *Experiment,* p. 96ff., as well as the literature indicated there.

30. Popper, *Logik,* p. 224, and analogously Spinner, *Modelle und Experimente,* col. 1006. R.B. Cattell, *Experimental Design* (1966), p. 20, advocates a more-extensive view; to him the criterion of experiment structure does not represent a necessary characteristic of definition. K. Holzkamp, *Theorie und Experiment* (1964), p. 24ff., calls the experiment "creating realization" and speaks of the "moment of creating" gradually differing structuring interventions.

31. For the problem of the temporal sequence of occurrences as evidence of causal relationship, see Janke, *Experiment,* pp. 98, 100, as well as the general discussion on causality in Popper, *Logik,* p. 31ff.; E. Durkheim, *Regeln* (1965); W. Stegmüller, *Kausalität* (1960); W. Stegmüller, *Wissenschaftliche Erklärung* (1965), p. 92ff; W. Heuer, *Kausalität* (1935); Cattell, *Experimental Design,* p. 22ff.; Runzheimer, *Experiment,* p. 30ff.; and C. Selltiz, M. Jahoda, M. Deutsch, and S.W. Cook, *Untersuchungsmethoden* (1972), p. 97ff.

32. Control as a constitutive characteristic of the experiment is emphasized particularly by L. Festinger, *Laboratory Experiments* (1953), p. 137; K.E. Weick, *Laboratory Experimentation* (1965), p. 198ff.; E. Aronson and J.M. Carlsmith, *Experimentation* (1968), p. 10ff.; W. Siebel, *Logik des Experiments* (1965), pp. 22ff., 66ff.; D. Wahl, *Anwendung* (1965), p. 106ff., and E. Greenwood, *Experiment* (1967), p. 191ff.

33. Janke, *Experiment,* p. 100ff., points to the close methodic agreement between the technique of parallelizing, balancing, and randomizing. The last control procedure differs from the other two techniques only in that the experiment director does not produce the neutralization by means of a direct intervention with the structure; instead a consciously accidental order of the test groups brings about self-balance. See also Runzheimer, *Experiment,* p. 44ff.; B. Runzheimer, *Situationskontrolle* (1968); Pagés, *Experiment,* p. 432; J.A. Wiggins, *Laboratory Methods* (1968), p. 392ff.; W. Siebel, *Logik des Experiments* (1965), p. 66ff.; and Selltiz, Jahoda, Deutsch and Cook, *Untersuchungsmethoden,* p. 117ff.

34. See Janke, *Experiment,* p. 97; Popper, *Logik,* pp. 21, 214ff.; as well as Albert, *Theoriebildung,* p. 58ff.

35. Siebel, *Logik des Experiments,* p. 92ff., and Wiggins, *Laboratory Methods,* p. 390, contradict the validity of the causal law. Pagés, *Experiment,* p. 436ff., and H.M. Blalock, *Theory Building* (1968), p. 155, in the same context criticize the excessive empirically irrelevant simplification present in monofactorial experiments.

36. Modern scientific theory clearly distances itself from a "cause-effect-assumption" in terms of the classical theory of findings. For this see Popper, *Logik,* p. 31ff.

37. See Festinger, *Laboratory Experiments,* p. 152ff.; Weick, *Laboratory Experimentation,* p. 199ff.; Holzkamp, *Theorie und Experiment,* pp. 30ff., 89ff.; Aronson and J.M. Carlsmith, *Experimentation* (1968), p. 22ff.; and Janke, *Experiment,* p. 103ff.

38. See Bronner, Witte, and Wossidlo, *Experimente,* p. 177ff. Instead of control of "internal validity," Wiggins, *Laboratory Methods,* p. 391, speaks of and uses the designation "external validity" or "concept validity" synonymously for "representativeness." He emphasizes, "Sometimes internal and external validity conflict." Wiggins designates "internal validity" as the methodic strength of the laboratory experiment and "external validity" as its weakness (p. 393).

39. For the objectivity of social-science research, see R. Meimberg, *Willkür* (1964), and G. Myrdal, *Objectivity* (1971), whose criticism aims at the procedure as well as the problem of valuing.

40. See Heyns and Zander, *Observation,* p. 413ff.; Riecken, *Experimente,* p. 26ff.; Janke, *Experiment,* p. 105ff.; Holzkamp, *Theorie und Experiment* (1964), p. 81ff.

41. Stegmüller, *Wissenschaftliche Erklärung,* p. 456, emphasizes that "the border between macro- and micro-occurrences . . . is closely related to the difference between that which is directly measureable and that which is not directly measureable."

42. J. Kolb, *Erfahrung im Experiment* (1963), p. 16; analogously also Selltiz, Jahoda, Deutsch, and Cook, *Untersuchungsmethoden* (1972), p. 117.

43. W. Heisenberg, *Der Teil* (1969), p. 146, and analogously J. Kolb, *Erfahrung im Experiment* (1963), p. 17, as well as J. Müller, *Isolation* (1965), p. 171ff., and A. Picot, *Organisationsforschung* (1972), p. 195ff.

44. For skepsis toward the experiment, see Bronner, Witte, and Wossidlo, *Experimente,* p. 165ff.

45. Ibid., p. 177.

46. See E.K. Scheuch, *Interview* (1967), pp. 173-180.

47. F. Buggle, *Diagnostik* (1969), p. 72.

48. G.A. Lienert, *Testaufbau* (1969), p. 16; see also Scheuch, *Interview,* pp. 173, 188ff; Buggle, *Diagnostik,* p. 80; H. Peak, *Objective Observation* (1953), p. 283ff.

49. See particularly Scheuch, *Interview,* p. 174.

50. Ibid., p. 173.

51. See Peak, *Objective Observation,* p. 292ff.

52. See Scheuch, *Interview,* p. 175ff.

53. H.W. Riecken, *Experiments* (1962), p. 28, characterizes "the experiment as a social situation" and emphasizes above all the regularly existing role ties to the professional, disciplinary, and social authority of the experimenter. Wiggins, *Laboratory Methods,* pp. 396-403 discusses this

circle of problems under the topic of validity (but he also summarizes aspects of reliability under it). He views the behavior of the experimenter as a variable to be controlled. See also J. H. Davis, *Experimenter Presence* (1968).

54. Besides identifying the objectivity of the evaluator, Buggle, *Diagnostik,* p. 73ff, points to the reliability of the testing procedure. Thus he differentiates implicitly between a personal and an instrumental reliability. J. Kolb, *Erfahrung im Experiment* (1963), p. 12ff. emphasizes impartiality as an expression of mental freedom and supplements this personal prerequisite with professional knowledge and care of the experimenter. See particularly R. Rosenthal, *Experimenter's Hypothesis* (1971), and Aronson and Carlsmith, *Experimentation,* p. 66ff.

55. The present investigation is based on the same simulation model as contained in the works of Witte, *Informationsverhalten,* and Bronner, Witte, and Wossidlo, *Experimente.* It declares a high degree of structural agreement with the research design. Deviations result from the different problems under investigation and from the selection of other variables.

56. H. Feger, *Bedeutsamkeit* (1968), p. 69.

57. Ibid., p. 16ff., emphasizes the basic influence on behavior by the experimental conditions. He places "significance" at the focal point of his investigation as one of the most essential situational variables.

58. Ibid., p. 36ff.

59. See K.J. Cohen and E. Rhenman, *Management Games* (1961); K. Bleicher, *Simulationsmodelle* (1962); E.H. Sieber, *Planspiel* (1963); M. Shubik, *Experimental Gaming* (1964); B.M. Bass, *Experimental Techniques* (1964); B.M. Bass, *Business Gaming* (1964); K.J. Cohen and R.M. Cyert, *Simulation* (1965); K. Bleicher, *Unternehmungsspiele* (1966); A.Y. Lewin and W.L. Weber, *Management Game* (1969); and M. Shubik, *Gaming* (1972). For the general aspect of simulation, see particularly R.C. Meier, W.T. Newell, and H.L. Pazer, *Simulation* (1969), p. 179ff.; M. Shubik, *Decision-Making* (1964), p. 47ff.; Ch.F. Bonini, *Simulation* (1963); Ch.F. Bonini, *Simulating* (1964).

60. See P. Lindeman and H. Koller, *Unternehmungsspiel* (1969); P. Miottke, *Marktmodell* (1967); and Bronner, Witte, and Wossidlo, *Experimente,* p. 167ff.

61. See also Bronner, Witte, and Wossidlo, *Experimente,* p. 179ff.

62. The designation "information model" corresponds to that part of the simulation frame designated as "modified model" elsewhere. For this see ibid., p. 170.

63. See particularly M. Irle, *Macht* (1971), p. 31ff.

64. Due to this determination of the communication conditions, the analysis of alternative forms of communication is no longer applicable. However, see H. Guetzkow and H.A. Simon, *Communication Nets* (1960).

65. By making copies, the experiment conductor guarantees an uninterrupted, chronologically ordered, and unambiguously coordinated written composition. In this way, the reliability of the data recording will be more secure than by observation of the communication. For this see Festinger, *Laboratory Experiments,* p. 164ff.

66. The mode of operation of the information center, the scope of the information potential, and the method of measuring quantity, precision, and breadth of content of the information are comprehensively treated in Bronner, Witte, and Wossidlo, *Experimente* (1972), p. 170ff.

67. For this see particularly Rosenthal, *Experimenter's Hypothesis;* Carlsmith, *Experimentation,* p. 66ff.; Holzkamp, *Theorie und Experiment,* p. 81ff.; and Picot, *Organisationsforschung,* pp. 137ff., 195ff.

68. Sauermann and Selten, *Experimentelle Wirtschaftsforschung,* p. 7. See also Picot, *Organisationsforschung,* p. 159ff.

69. See Bronner, Witte, and Wossidlo, *Experimente,* p. 184ff. Irle, *Macht,* p. 205, arrives at similar results concerning conformity of behavior.

70. With the foregoing study, the size of the group represents a structuring element of the experimental design and not a variable to be investigated. In contrast to this, see R.F. Bales and E.F. Borgatta, *Size of Group* (1962), who place this aspect at the center of their analysis.

71. With reference to a meaningful group formation, the management participants were requested to give their personal data on a questionnaire. The information on position "title" and "occupation and rank" was arranged in four categories of qualification characteristics. Doctoral degrees were recorded under the respective professional university degrees.

72. See D.T. Hall and E.E. Lawler, *Job Characteristics* (1970), p. 275ff, who, in an ex-post analysis (for reasons of method) are unable to determine a functional relationship between stress caused by time and criteria of performance.

73. Limiting the time for the external procurement of information would act as an uncontrollable aggravation of the time allotted for internal group performance. Moreover, there could be a lasting loss of confidence in capabilities and willingness to perform on the part of the information center, which is also an uncontrollable factor of interference.

74. The pretest is recognized as a legitimate instrument designed to uncover sources of error in the technical procedure. Nevertheless, there are frequent objections to the pretest, which are aimed particularly at experimental research. The core of this criticism is the danger—occasionally formulated even as a reproach—that it is not aimed at improving the experimental control in an unbiased way but at achieving a tailoring of the theoretical question or the experimental design independent of the findings. See particularly D. Mechanic, *Methodology* (1962), p. 173ff.

Within the frame of the present investigation, the pretests were conducted according to a predetermined and constant theoretical conception. They were directed exclusively to the attainment of a reliable program. For the consequences of the pretests on the allocation of decision-making time, see p. 72ff.

75. A concept of four categories of time pressure had been initially tested within the frame of the preexperimental investigators. Allocated time periods were 3½, 3, 2½, and 2 hours. It could be determined that the middle categories did not lead to a reliable discrimination of the pressure values but that strong, minor, or even no pressures at all were perceived. The attempt at a continual regulation was given up in favor of a dichotomous structuring of the conditions regarding time.

76. This uniform measure of the time allotments for both subgroups of a decision-making unit guaranteed that staff and board of directors are exposed to the same temporal conditions.

77. To avoid misunderstandings, these assertions are no statement regarding the actual and/or efficient course of decision-making processes. They are only to give an idea of the course of problem solving as it has been anchored in the minds of numerous decision-making persons. For the discussion of an immanent course of decision making, see E. Witte, *Phasentheorem* (1968).

78. It becomes apparent in this connection that the explicative character of a variable does not exist a priori but results from the respective intent to explain. Accordingly, a definite variable is not independent or dependent, effecting or effected; in specific questions it may function in various logical capacities as explicator or as explicatee.

79. Humanistic research has developed numerous, exact measurement values for the recording of stress or for the quantification of behavior under stress. See H. Selye, *Stress* (1957), p. 66ff.; F.E. Horvath, *Stress* (1959), p. 213ff.; S.I. Cohen, A.J. Silverman, and B.M. Shmavonian, *Human Adaptation* (1959); E.W. Bovard, *Stress* (1959); and E.E. Levitt, *Angst* (1971), p. 53ff. A transfer of these highly sensitive procedures to our experimental conditions encounters considerable difficulties, with regard to the apparative prerequisites. Above all, basic methodic considerations preempt their application within the frame of this investigation.

80. For the content and structure of the questionnaire see the Appendix.

81. In addition to age, personal status, interest in self-protection, motivation to perform and compete as result from the social context are important.

82. At this point it seems appropriate to note that the operationalization chosen does not constitute a circular explanation. Individual sensitivity remains—although untested—as an ingredient of the theoretical explanation of the occurrence of time pressure. It is not identical with the structural sensitivity investigated here and operationalized by time pressure perception.

83. For the distinction between directed and undirected or unilateral and bilateral examination of a question, see J.B. Winer, *Statistical Principles* (1970), p. 20ff., and E. Mittenecker, *Planung und Auswertung* (1970), p. 58.

84. Even the possible antithesis that practitioners respond less sensitively to time pressures than do students would be a false conclusion. The concrete example illustrates the risk of error of an ex-post explanation that is dependent on results.

85. In order to ensure this possibility, the recording and evaluation of data were done separately for the staff and board of directors.

4 Verification of the Theory

Since the formulation of the theory of decision making under time pressure was done independently from a specific testing constellation, the individual hypotheses are not directly related to the experimental facts. Such a narrow tailoring of the hypotheses would oppose the attempt at a general theoretical explanation of decision making under time pressure. However, the scientific test of this theory requires the alignment of the if component and of the then component with the specific conditions of the experiment. In order to accomplish this, the general demand for explanation will be retained and the testability of the hypotheses will be established by an intensifying derivation of concrete experiment-related testing theorems.

The Conditions of Time Pressure

Within the framework of the theory formation, the limitation of decision time, the problem intensity of the decisional situation, and a nondeterminable sensitivity to time pressures were developed as the triggering conditions for time pressure. At this point we will return to the first hypothesis.

Hypothesis 1: In complex decision-making situations, decision-making units register time pressure more intensely the higher the time-pressure sensitivity, the less the available decision-making time, and the higher the problem intensity.

Individual sensitivity provided a conclusive impulse concerning experimental methods although testing its explicative value proved to be impracticable.[1] Further considerations must therefore be waived. By comparison, decision-making time and problem intensity are vital parts of the conditional hypothesis and justify the formulation of specific testing theorems.

Decision-Making Time

An isolated statement on the effect of decision-making time can be derived from hypothesis 1 and the peripheral experimental conditions of the experiment design chosen.

Theorem 1.1: In experiment periods with strict limitation of decision-making time, the decision-making units register a higher degree of time pressure than in periods that are free from such restrictions.

Measurement: The measurement value for the quantification of time pressure has already been established so no independent measuring problem arises. The time-pressure index represents the amount of time pressure recorded in a decision-making unit.

Testing Design: Corresponding to the experimental design, which limits the available decision-making time in the first and last three experiment periods, two comparative classes are formed. The first class comprises the time-pressure values of periods 1–3 and 8–10. They are compared with the values obtained in periods 4–7 with no pressure. The values from the staff and the board of directors' groups of all testing sequences are entered separately. The determination of time-pressure differences is done by comparison of the mean values. The significance test is based on the student t test and fixes the admissible probability of error at a maximum value of 5 percent.

Findings: The time-pressure values obtained in the restricted testing periods are compared with the corresponding values in the periods without limitation in tables 4–1 and 4–2. The comparison made initially on the basis of the measurement values from the staff groups is directly supplemented by the testing of the time-pressure values recorded in the board of directors' groups.

Table 4–1
Comparison of Time-Pressure Index Values, by Time Limitation (Staff)

Test Values	Periods without Time Limitation	Periods with Time Limitation
Mean value	20.83	34.38
Standard deviation	4.19	10.26
Number (n)	48	72
Significance	$p < 0.001$	

Table 4-2
Comparison of Time-Pressure Index Values, by Time Limitation (Board of Directors)

Test Values	Periods without Time Limitation	Periods with Time Limitation
Mean value	22.44	29.79
Standard deviation	5.55	9.09
Number (n)	48	72
Significance	$p < 0.001$	

The test data of the staff groups, as well as those of the board of directors' groups reveal obvious time-pressure differences according to the differing time allotments. The statistical test verifies these findings and a high level of significance. Thus it can be proved that a higher degree of time pressure arises in decision-making periods with strict time limitation than in periods without such restriction. Theorem 1.1 is thus verified. In this way, the statement made in hypothesis 1 that the decision-making time available is a condition in determining time pressure is supported.

Because this result so clearly corresponds to a plausible expectation, it must be asked what significance can be attributed to the result, which appears almost trivial. First, it would be wrong to interpret it only as a confirmation of definitory stipulations. The formulation of hypothesis 1 and that of theorem 1.1 were not explicitly intended to be definitions but explanations of time pressure. The result, therefore, is an empirically informative tenet, even if of a modest value. Additionally it corroborates the subsequent steps of the investigation in a methodically significant point. The planned variation of available decision-making time is the most important regulative measure in the experiment. Problem solutions both under time pressure and under no time pressure are to be induced. Only if this experimental manipulation is successful and depending on its extent can the arrangement of the experiment satisfy the claim for validity. Since it is obvious that the structuring of time determines time pressure, the success of the experimental induction is confirmed. The verification of theorem 1.1 is thus successful in explaining the rise of time pressure and in proving the existence of time pressure in the experiment.

Problem Intensity

By isolating an additional determinant from the context of hypothesis 1 and by simultaneously embedding it into the peripheral conditions of the experiment, a testable assertion concerning the influence of the situation-determined problem intensity on time pressure can be derived:

Theorem 1.2: In decision-making situations of high problem intensity, the decision-making units register a higher degree of time pressure than under less problem-intense conditions.

Measurement: The problem intensity of the decision-making situation represents a measure for qualitative pressure in coping with various sub-aspects of the decisions demanded. Because of the variety and complexity of the problem relationships, it will be difficult to reduce it to one single measure. A segmentation of the problem into its factors is advisable. In doing so, varying aspects should be considered, if possible. Since the number of the decisions to be made, as well as their mutual dependence, is analogous and constant in all cases under investigation, these two characteristics escape the determination of problem intensity. The aggregate economic situation indisputably is one of the basic components of management decision making, but this variable had to be placed into the experiment to ensure the overall validity of the course of the experiment. Because of this stabilizing instrumental function of the model parameters and the largely successful parallelization of the exogenous situational burden, no testable approach can be generated from this. Thus, the decisional assignment, the interdependence of partial decisions, and the environmental conditions are excluded as determinants of problem intensity in the experiment. This fact, however, is not synonymous with a lack of theoretical relevance. Experiment-conditioned peculiarities only reduce the possibilities of empirical testing.

If the consideration of the structural facts of the experiment is shifted to the problem situation as it represents itself from the narrower view of the individual decision-making units, then one gains various possibilities of operationalizing the intensity of the problem.

The economic situation of the enterprise has already been theoretically developed as an important determinant in defining the intensity of the problem. At this point it must be examined in which concrete form this variable can be quantified and thus be made available to experimental testing. A measure is required that is capable of representing the economic situation of each decision-making unit. But since this investigation is not designed to develop a reliable measure for the total assessment of business enterprises, only a much more modest concept can be taken into consideration.

Bound to the variables of the decision-making model, the individual enterprises were able to achieve several goals simultaneously. Independent from other goals, the objectives of liquidity, profit, entry of orders and sales, marketing, and product quality constituted the focal points of company policy in all decision-making units. Securing solvency and making a profit were goals that are found in the actual economic system resulting

Verification of the Theory

from the expectations of the shareholders. The three market-oriented objectives result from the competitive situation of the simulation model.

This five-element, multiple-goal conception is one of the approaches in obtaining an assessment of the situation. Since all participating decision-making units pursue principally the same strategy in their activities and since conditions are identical for the four enterprises of a testing sequence, the degree of goal attainment achieved in each case represents an objective measure of the individual situation of the enterprise in question. One could argue that this form of operationalization of problem intensity is a subjective rather than an objective assessment and thus cannot be measured objectively. It is true that the decision-making units do not have the full measure of comparative transparency that is found in the degree of goal attainment. Nevertheless, this initial lack is almost fully compensated for by the fact that there are quarterly reports on results accessible to each individual enterprise only, annual statements available to all four enterprises plus a directed demand for information. This provides a well-founded basis for comparison. Moreover, basing this on the entire duration of the test will lead to a further improvement of this operationalization of the problem intensity. The corresponding quantitative measure is determined in such a way that each enterprise is assigned a rank in each period that expresses the position the enterprise was capable of attaining within its respective testing sequence under the various economic aspects. The best position was awarded the value 1, and the last of the four positions received the rank value of 4.[2] Consequently the result of each decision-making sequence is an assessment value that, when aggregated as the sum total of five rank digits, defines the degree of economic goal attainment. This result value of a period, t, at the same time represents the situation index and thus the measure of the economic-determined problem intensity of period $t + 1$.

In addition to difficulties of the economic decision-making situation, the problem intensity is influenced by the organizational difficulties in mastering the decision tasks. Such pressures must be reckoned with, particularly under working conditions that place high qualitative and temporal demands on cooperation and communication. However, it is to be expected that during the course of repeated decisions, the internal and external working techniques of the groups will improve. A routine effect aligned with the process of problem solving reduces the problem intensity caused by organization.

It follows from these considerations that the number of repetitions of the same kind of decisions can be chosen as the direct measure for the problem intensity of the decision. Since in the experiment one experiment period corresponds to one decision-making sequence, the period itself serves as the operationalization of the technical work pressure. Accordingly, there is a higher degree of problem intensity in earlier decision-making periods than in later periods.

Testing Design: Business enterprises find themselves exposed to stronger situational pressures the more unfavorable the initial situation of the company is for decisions. This economically determined problem intensity is more noticeable the more that decisions must be made under such negative conditions. Therefore, a situational index cumulated from the total of all decisions will provide the basis for the test of theorem 1.2. With this measurement value, the problem intensity can be successfully quantified according to degree and frequency. The higher the index, the more lasting is the overall situational stress. For experimental testing, a comparison of the test results of enterprises with favorable and unfavorable initial conditions is made. In order to give due consideration to the close connection of the situational values caused by competition within a testing sequence, the values of the two best-placed decision-making units of each testing sequence are compared with the testing data of the less favorably placed enterprises. The time-pressure values from the periods with limited decision-making time are tallied into these classes of comparison as testing data.

In order to test organizationally caused problem intensity as an element for determining time pressure, periods 1–3 and periods 8–10 are compared. While little experience in the mastery of the decision tasks becomes distinct in the first interval, the routine effect caused by several repetitions becomes effective in the last interval. Testing data are the time-pressure index values of the respective periods.

The experimental test is based on the values of the staff groups of all decision-making units. Theorem 1.2 can be considered as verified if the comparison of mean values indicates a difference between the respective classes compared at a significance level of 5 percent.

Findings: First, it is to be determined whether the aggregate economic situation as reflected by the situation index can hold up as an explanation for the occurrence of time pressure. (See tables 4–3 and 4–4.)

Table 4–3
Comparison of Time-Pressure Index Values, by Problem Intensity, Periods 1–3 and 8–10

Test Values	Enterprises with Favorable Situation Index	Enterprises without Favorable Situation Index
Mean value	36.33	33.17
Standard deviation	10.92	10.39
Number (n)	36	36
Significance	$-p = 0.180$	

Note: The classifications *favorable* and *unfavorable* are based on mean situational variables of 110.67 and 139.33, respectively, which differed one level of significance of $p < 0.001$.

Table 4-4
Comparison of Time-Pressure Index Values, by Problem Intensity

Test Values	Periods with Little Decision-Making Routine	Periods with Much Decision-Making Routine
Mean value	39.22	29.53
Standard deviation	8.55	9.60
Number (n)	36	36
Significance	$p < 0.001$	

Even under distinctly different situational conditions, the statistical test reveals no significant differences in relation to the registered time pressure. Thus theorem 1.2 cannot be verified. The economically determined problem intensity does not provide an explanation for the rise of time pressure.

Without entering into an interpreting discussion of this result at this point, the effect of work-technical problem intensity is now to be investigated.

Contrary to the preceding test, the findings presented in table 4-4 support theorem 1.2 by demonstrating a highly significant difference. Problem intensity in terms of organizational stress in mastering the decision-making process clearly correlates with the respective time pressure. In the early stages of confrontation with complex decision-making tasks, temporarily high problem intensity functions as an additional condition of time pressure. Because of the low degree of process mastery, existing restrictions of decision-making time aggravate the pressure and lead to a more-intense perception of time pressure. At the same time the work technique, which becomes a routine during the course of repeated decisions, proves to be a viable explanation for the clearly discernible absorption of time pressure shown in table 4-4.

In summary, the statements made in hypothesis 1 were confirmed by the experiment. The explanatory element of decision-making time led to full verification in the testing of theorem 1.1. In the same way, problem intensity had to be secured in its work-organizational version as a condition of time pressure. The falsification of theorem 1.2 in its testing design tailored to the economic situation outlined the relevance of a dynamic approach. The proof that total situative stress remains without recognizable influence on time pressure emphasizes the necessity of an analysis that is directed to the process of problem mastery. The assumption is that varying decision-making conditions, as indicated by the situation index for the individual firms, might be compensated for by equalizing measures. Whether this interpretation can be confirmed and in which way the time and cognitive pressures are overcome must be the task of further examination.

Problem Solving under Time Pressure

The analysis of time-pressure conditions showed the importance of conducting a fundamentally dynamic investigation of decision making under time pressure. A purely comparative static approach cannot make the problem-solving process sufficiently transparent. Although time-pressure absorption already is a valuable empirical finding, the process of absorption and the individual compensatory measures cannot yet be identified. The aim of the following examination will therefore be to split the decision-making process under time pressure into its problem-solving activities. In agreement with the theoretical approach developed earlier, the achievement sectors of interaction, information, and coordination will have to be analyzed successively.

Individual Performance

First the individual mental achievement, here termed *interaction,* that the decision-making units contributed to the problem solution will be described. This encompasses both the volume of written communication and the content of the communication. For the time being, efforts to gain information from the outside are not considered. Also the direction and intensity of coordinating measures are not yet discussed.

Hypothesis 2: In complex decision-making situations, time pressure leads to the limitation of interaction within the decision-making units.

Two independently testable assertions can be derived from this theory when it is oriented simultaneously to the specific marginal conditions and results of the experiment obtained thus far:

Theorem 2.1: In experiment periods with strict limitation of the decision-making time, communication within the decision-making units is less than in periods without such restrictions.

Theorem 2.2: In experiment periods with strict limitation of the decision-making time, the degree of activity within the decision-making units is smaller than in periods free from such restrictions.

Verification of the Theory

Measurement: The documents resulting from the division of work that were exchanged between the subgroups (staff and board of directors) of the decision-making unit serve as the evidence of the contributions made to the decisions. The total mental achievement, of course, cannot be reflected in this way. By necessity all purely mental processes have to remain unconsidered. But because the exchange of documents represents the only possibility for interaction during a decision-making sequence, the material in these documents can be considered as a representative depiction of the total performance. The written exchange of information forms the common basis for determining activity, as well as for measuring communication. Different evaluation procedures permit a separate quantification of both aspects of interaction.

The analysis is based on a total of 3,253 written pieces, which allow a simple and safe identification. By this format, communication could be initially recorded as a formal process. The number of communicative acts were measured by the number of documents accrued per unit in question. A suitable measure for the volume of communication was the number of textual lines transmitted. (See the Appendix.) With this, the exchange of performance might be depicted by two variables. Because of the high correlation of $r = 0.936$, both values of measurement are equivalent to each other. Since consequently only one of the variables suffices for measurement, communication is quantified by means of the more-illustrative number of text lines.

In a second step of operationalization, activity is to be determined as the expression of the dimension of the solution to the problem. This disclosure of the concrete character of mental performance is done with the aid of document analysis.[3] In methodical agreement with Witte and by alignment with the decisional tasks of the experiment, a procedure was developed that allows recording of the activity.[4] The total decision-making achievement is differentiated by individual activities and individual objects. The technical recording was an operations matrix that contains the possible activities in the vertical position and the objects that can be combined with them in the horizontal position. For further illustration, the categories of the evaluation are presented in tables 4-5 and 4-6.

Table 4-5
Decision-Making Activities

Code	Scope	Semantic Content
11	Conveying	Active communication
12	Requesting	Passive communication
21	Determining	Positive regulation
22	Urging	Positive regulation

Table 4-5 continued

Code	Scope	Semantic Content
23	Hesitating	Negative regulation
24	Modifying	Negative regulation
31	Recommending	Positive evaluation
32	Dissuading	Negative evaluation
33	Criticizing	Negative evaluation
34	Accepting	Positive evaluation

**Table 4-6
Decision-Making Objects**

Code	Object	Equivalent
11	Comment	Report
12	Information "from outside"	Data
13	Reply	Feedback
20	Alternative	Action
31	Time period	Deadline
32	Sequence	Priority
33	Point in time	Date
34	Task	Work content
40	Goal setting	Strategy
50	Decision	Formal result
60	Actual consequence	Efficiency
70	Environment	Competition

The great combinatory variety of the possibilties of codification gained in this way guarantees a complete and valid recording of all decision-making operations.

The sum of all activities provides a reliable measure of the total activity. Depending on the testing information, either the decision-making unit and/or the decision-making period can be selected as the unit of reference. For more profound insight into the structure of activity, there are individual operations in the form of activity-object connections.

Testing Design: To test the assertion contained in theorem 2.1, communication as accumulated in the time-restricted experiment periods 1-3 and 8-10 is to be compared with the corresponding data from the unrestricted periods, 4-7. The same testing design is stipulated in theorem 2.2 with regard to the activity in these intervals of comparison. In both cases the test seeks to determine the significant differences of the respective class of values. A theorem is deemed varified if the t test discloses a difference at a maximal probability of error of 5 percent.

Verification of the Theory

Since this test is an analysis of extroverted decision-making performance and since the achievement structure in the board of directors' groups of the experiment corresponds more closely to the character of an introverted activity, the test is limited to the measurement values of the staff groups.[5]

Findings: First the reduction of communication as a result of time pressure as hypothesized in theorem 2.1 is exposed to the test. (See table 4-7.) Under the effect of time pressure, communication is essentially reduced. The statistical test indicates significant differences in the measurement values and thus confirms the restrictive statement of theorem 2.2. This result of the exchange of achievement is consistently reflected in the measurement data on the volume of achievement.[6]

The test results indicate a highly significant reduction of activity in the preparation of the decision in the periods with strict time limitation. See table 4-8. The time pressure to which the members of the staff groups are particularly exposed to a high degree leads to a reduction of problem-solving activities; the amount of achievement is reduced. That is tantamount to a renunciation of mental operations in decision finding. Theorem 2.2 could thus be verified. Hypothesis 2 is supported by the proof of the verification of both theorems. In complex decision making, time pressure leads to an essential limitation of individual performance. This result raises the questions as to the consequences of such an adaptive behavior.

Table 4-7
Comparison of Communication, by Time Limitation

Test Values	Periods without Time Limitation	Periods with Time Limitation
Mean value	53.96	36.94
Standard deviation	39.50	29.25
Number (n)	48	72
Significance	$p = 0.008$	

Table 4-8
Comparison of Decision-Making Activity, by Time Limitation

Test Values	Periods without Time Limitation	Periods with Time Limitation
Mean value	42.38	29.97
Standard deviation	9.28	10.90
Number (n)	48	72
Significance	$p < 0.001$	

The assumption of a redistribution of stress within the decision-making units can be rejected with great certainty. The partial renunciation of interaction appears to be a suitable relief measure in the problem-solving process. But because of the experiment design, which causes a virtual monopoly of information on the part of the staff, work pressure cannot be rolled over without intensification of at least the communication. The data in tables 3-9 and 3-10 attest to the plausible connection. Board of directors' groups register far less time pressure than do staff groups.

Once the roll-over thesis is rejected, the conclusion of an equality of reduction of decisions under time pressure is at hand. A limitation of achievement causes the expectation of a direct impairment of the decision results. Accordingly, there should be less economic efficiency in experiment periods with strict time limitation than in periods without time restrictions. However, the empirical finding clearly refutes this supposition.[7]

The fact that the shifting of the level of activity and of communication does not influence the economic result of the decisions made might be based on the renunciation of redundance: the existence of time pressure causes a disciplining within the framework of written argumentation. The decrease in text that was established concerns only statements that do not touch upon the quality of the documented achievement. Such an effect could be explained by the experience made in work economy. Since this experience arises from the dilemma of repeated time-pressure situations, it should be justified to expect that a limitation of redundancy can be determined particularly in later decision-making periods. Under the present conditions, the volume of communication in the last three experiment periods would have to be smaller than in the first three periods. The respective testing data lead to a clear refutation of this initially plausible assumption.[8]

These successively developing considerations are intended to afford deeper insight into the effect of the limitation of interaction. After neither a shift of the pressure nor a direct reduction of efficiency could be proved and also the redundancy thesis could not be verified, a hint of a fundamentally new orientation toward decision-making performance becomes apparent. The preceding argumentation essentially followed a quantitative concept of performance and therefore focused on the amount of performance as represented by activity and communication. An analysis under qualitative aspects of problem solving is indispensable. Therefore, an attempt should be made in a further testing step to determine thoroughly the structure of the problem-solving process in decision making under time pressure. In this way, it should be possible to obtain information about the *type* of adaptation. The interest will focus on the question as to which subactivities are limited under stress condition and which are maintained unchanged or even intensified.

Since an empirically founded norm concept of activity volume will always have to be directed to the specific problem content of the decision, first that activity is to be determined which becomes manifest in the problem-solving process in question here. The different conditions of problem intensity and decision-making time make it possible to view the average performance contributions that can be determined over all decision-making sequences as a standardized activity profile of problem solving. In order to be able to show accurately the stratification of mental performance, in the most comprehensive and illustrative manner, the various levels of activity—actions, objects, and operations—will be investigated separately. Moreover, the difference of the character of performance in both functional groups (staff and board of directors) must be proved. Therefore, the differentiation of content in the decision-making activity will be supplemented by functional differentiation. The result of this division may yield profiles of action, object, and operation that provide first indications of the explicatory bearing of the individual elements of performance. This basis is to serve the subsequent and more precise definition of the structure of performance in decision making under time pressure.

Table 4-9 comprises all elements of performance that, during the course of 120 problem-solving processes show at least 120 total entries; that is, they averaged one entry during the individual problem solution. Elements of performance that did not reach this frequency are suitable neither for the determination of activity profiles nor for the explanation of performance under time pressure.

Table 4-9
Activity Profile of Decision-Making Performance

			Decision-Making Performance			
Activity			Staff		Board of Directors	
Number	Scope	Total	Number	Percent	Number	Percent
11	Conveying	2,034	1,746	43	288	19
12	Requesting	663	105	3	558	37
21	Determining	670	381	10	289	19
22	Urging	347	205	5	142	10
31	Recommending	1,276	1,256	31	20	2
33	Criticizing	371	227	6	144	10
34	Accepting	132	81	2	51	3
Total		5,493	4,001	100	1,492	100

Note: Regulation activities 23, delaying, and 24, modifying, as well as assessment activity 32, dissuading, are not considered because of their low frequency of 7 and 0 and 89 entries.

Table 4-10
Object Profile of Decision-Making Performance

			Decision-Making Performance			
	Object		Staff		Board of Directors	
Number	Scope	Total	Number	Percent	Number	Percent
11	Comment	2,159	1,487	39	672	46
12	Information	531	421	11	110	8
13	Reply	208	52	1	156	10
20	Alternative	1,592	1,390	36	202	14
32	Sequence	142	125	3	17	1
33	Point in time	127	68	2	59	4
34	Task	279	108	3	171	11
40	Goal setting	286	201	5	85	6
Total		5,324	3,852	100	1,472	100

Note: With 17, 109, 114, and 34 from 120 possible entries, objects 31, 50, 60, and 70 do not satisfy the required frequency of occurrence and thus are not admitted as elements of the object profile.

The findings presented in tables 4-9 and 4-10 show that the activity profile and also the object profile of the staff and board of directors' groups differ from one another. Divergent performance profiles for each group result from the various functions within the work-divisional process. Both activity structure and activity volume supports this statement. There are far fewer interactive contacts in the board of directors' decision-making group with its corresponding partner than this partner has with the first group. This finding retroactively corroborates the earlier assumption, which had been made without empirical proof, that there is, respectively, an introverted and extroverted performance structure in the board of directors and staff groups of the experiment.[9] This also provides an explanation for the different degrees of time-pressure sensitivity in the two functional groups. The heavy burden of work involved in the documentation of written decision-making performances causes a higher degree of stress than those forms of problem solving that are less work intensive.

The last step of the analysis of activity is to find out first whether the profile of operations also reflects the functionally determined differences in performance. The second task of the test will be to determine to what extent the profile of operations reliably reflects the performance elements of activity and object.

Table 4-11 shows that the problem-solving activities of the two decision-making subgroups vary considerably from one another, underscoring the partially traceable heterogeneity of the functional performance struc-

Verification of the Theory

Table 4-11
Operations Profile of Decision-Making Performance

			Decision-Making Performance			
Operations			Staff		Board of Directors	
Number	Content	Total	Number	Percent	Number	Percent
11/11	Conveying/comment	1,485	1,396	39	89	10
11/12	Conveying/information	400	398	11	2	0
11/13	Conveying/reply	154	2	0	152	18
12/11	Requesting/comment	411	40	1	371	43
21/32	Determining/sequence	141	124	3	17	2
21/34	Determining/task	156	33	1	123	14
21/40	Determining/goal setting	246	171	5	75	9
31/20	Recommending/alternative	1,270	1,252	35	18	2
33/40	Criticizing/goal setting	173	161	5	12	2
Total		4,436	3,577	100	859	100

Note: Because of insufficiently frequent entries the following operations were left unconsidered in forming the profile:

Operations:	12/12	12/13	21/31	21/33	22/31	22/33	22/34	22/35
Entry:	94	27	3	92	3	19	34	0

Operations:	22/40	32/20	33/11, 12,13	33/20	33/31, 32,33	33/34
Entry	29	77	105	21	17	45

tures. Several methodic references can now be derived for the further procedure:

1. The investigation of decision-making activity or its change under time pressure must proceed separately by functional groups.
2. The profile of operations proves to be the most expressive picture of activity in the analysis of the structure of performance.
3. Total performance in decision-making activities can be reduced to a few central operations of a functional group.
4. The greatest contribution to the explanation of problem solving in decisions under time pressure can be expected from the analysis of the preparations for decision making. The members of the functional group entrusted with this task reflect a marked sensitivity to time restrictions; their mental performance receives intensive documentation. Since purely mental and only verbally articulated contributions to performance exceed the limits of the present method of investigation, the comparatively low degree of documentation of activity in the decision-making body can be valued only as a limited representation of the

specific group performance. Further analysis is therefore directed exclusively to the performance that is produced within the framework of preparation for decision making.

The expectation of a change of the content of activity due to different degrees of performance restriction remains fully within the boundaries of hypothesis 2. By contrast, the assumption of a partial activity increase would have to be viewed as a theoretical extension, for the foundation of which, however, any argumentative approach is lacking. An explicit assertion of this type therefore cannot be verified.

Directed to the theoretical tenet of hypothesis 2 and simultaneously including the experimental marginal conditions, another theorem will have to be formulated:

Theorem 2.3: The performance structure in experiment periods with strict limitation of decision-making time, as opposed to those periods devoid of restrictions, is modified.

On the basis of the profile of cooperation (table 4-11) this thesis will be tested for the activity of the staff groups. The testing measure will be the sufficiently occurring individual performance, referred to as central operations. By comparing the average number of operations in experiment periods with and without time pressure, the degree of performance under time pressure, differentiated by subperformance, can be determined.

Table 4-12 provides proof that not only the total activity is being restricted under time pressure but that this adaptive behavior can also be proved when considering the content of the structure of performance.

Table 4-12
Degree of Performance as a Function of Time Pressure

		Periods without Time Pressure		Periods with Time Pressure	
Central Operations			Degree of Performance		Degree of Performance
Number	Content	Activity	Percent	Activity	Percent
11/11	Conveying/comment	13.39	100	10.46	78
11/12	Conveying/information	4.56	100	2.49	55
21/32	Determining/sequence	1.65	100	0.65	39
21/40	Determining/goal setting	1.29	100	1.51	117
31/20	Recommending/alternative	11.85	100	9.49	80
33/40	Criticizing/goal setting	1.94	100	0.94	48

Verification of the Theory

Almost all of the individual activities reflect lesser degrees of performance under time pressure than under working conditions free from restrictions. This result unrestrictedly supports the thesis on structural performance modification expressed in theorem 2.3. The reduction of performance resulting from time pressure does not affect all problem-solving activities with the same intensity. Rather, different degrees of performance reduction can be proved.

In spite of the generally low level of activity, relatively stable elements of performance can be determined. The rendering of opinions, as well as the recommending of alternative forms of action, are the least restricted under time pressure. These largely stable operations in the experiment obviously are performances that are closely bound to the core of objective problem solving. This assumption appears to be all the more justified as at least the transmitting of opinions and proposals of action represent work-intensive forms of interaction. Goal setting under time pressure reveals an even higher degree of performance. By contrast, such operations as passing on externally obtained information, articulating goal criticism, and particularly the temporal regulation of the decision-making process must be considered as being labile contributions to performance. The questions as to how far this result of performance analysis can be founded on the conditions of information and coordination behavior must be reserved to further examination.

The theoretical statement for the explanation of problem solving under time pressure (hypothesis 2) could be ascertained by three test versions. The theorems on communication, activity, and performance structure tested in the experiment unreservedly corroborate the verification of hypothesis 2.

Demand for Information

The object of the investigation thus far has been the aspects of problem mastery classified as individual performance. The two subgroups of the decision-making units served as the points of departure for the analysis. As a consequence of the separately determined performance structure, the testing data were limited to those originating from the decision preparation by the staff. Environmental relationships, whose existence was institutionally guaranteed in the present experiment, at first intentionally remained unconsidered. They will now be included.

Each of the decision-making units could seek advisory assistance from an information center.[10] The theoretical considerations concerning information behavior under time pressure can be expressed in the following hypothesis:

Hypothesis 3: In complex decision-making situations, time pressure leads to a restriction of the demand for information on the part of the decision-making units.

In order to define this statement more precisely for the experimental test, it is necessary to split up the demand for information into measureable elements and to adjust the specific marginal conditions of the testing design. As a result, the following theorems can be derived from hypothesis 3:

Theorem 3.1: In experiment periods with strict limitation of decision-making time, a smaller amount of information is demanded than in periods free from such limitation.

Theorem 3.2: In experiment periods with strict limitation of decision-making time, less precision in the demand for information is articulated than in periods free from such limitations.

Theorem 3.3: In experiment periods with strict limitation of decision-making time, the demand for information is of a smaller scope than in periods free from such limitations.

Measurement: The delineations and measurement regulations necessary for quantification are identical with the operationalizations that Witte chooses for the experimental analysis of information behavior in decision-making processes.[11] Therefore they are to be discussed only to the extent that they appear indispensable to understand the tests that follow.

As the basis for the measurement of information, a framework of categories was developed that allowed the unequivocal identification of all questions that could occur in the context of decision-making problems. The categories correspond to the degrees of freedom of the simulation model:

business enterprise   market   period   value

Value refers to the content of the economic variable that constitutes a question. The attributes of *period, market,* and *business enterprise* characterize a question according to its temporal, spatial, and institutional distinction.

1. The core of a question is the value, which also is the unit of quantity of a piece of information. Several such units are to be counted when a specific value is to be obtained for several business enterprises. Differentiations according to different markets and periods are left unconsidered in the quantification. Consequently, the measurement of information is not based on the semantic (and therefore by necessity subjectively different) form of the question but arranges each expression of information requirement in its model-determined, syntactical elements.

2. The four elements of the information framework are more than the basis for the measurement of the amount of information. They also provide the approach for the determination of the precision of the demand for information. A question is unequivocally articulated when all characteristics necessary for a reply devoid of doubt have been explicitly named. Since full precision can be determined for each of the questions uttered, an objective norm of articulation can be set up for the respective demand for information. The degree of precision of the demand results from the relationship of the characteristics of a question with the contact characteristics of the particular information.[12]

The cognitive breadth of the demand for information is all the more marked the more different the aspects are that are made use of for the solving of the problem. Especially in complex decision-making situations, the breadth of the informatory effort represents a particular challenge. While the quantity of information is determined solely by the existence of the articulation of need as a statement of frequency, the breadth of information is directed to the recording of questions that have been uttered for the first time. The mental horizon is expanded with each problem aspect that has not yet been inquired about; here information helps to expand the perspective of the problem. This qualitative dimension of information behavior is to be measured in the following manner. Each utterance for demand is tested, independently from the recording of amount and precision, as to whether it has already been inquired about by the same decision-making unit during the course of the preceding decision-making periods. Demand for information that occurs for the first time is classified as new demand and forms the basis of the measure of information breadth.

Testing Design: Until now it had been possible to compare testing data from experiment periods with and without time limitation in order to investigate the effect of time pressure on the problem-solving behavior in decision-making processes. This procedure now faces special methodic difficulties which cannot be ignored. But they should not be viewed as insurmountable. The execution of several testing sequences not only implies a strong binding of research capacity; it also requires the securing of numerous technical research requirements. In particular, the experiment places high demands on the instrumental, personnel, and methodic stability of the testing concept. Thus, the combination of different questions within the framework of a uniform testing design becomes evident and is desirable, especially under the aspects of research economy. Here, almost no barriers of cooperation are placed on field studies and ex-post analyses. Nevertheless, because of the danger of superimposed interventions, experiments are less suitable for the investigation of several problem aspects in parallel procedures.

Despite these reservations, two conditions were varied within the framework of the testing sequences so that two different problems could be explored experimentally. Changing time allotments permitted the analysis of the decision-making process under time pressure, and alternative information conditions allowed Witte the investigation of information behavior.[13] How far the questions can be researched and depicted in isolation depends on the independence of experimental regulation. To prove this independence in the research combination treated requires the depiction of both experimental designs in the clearest form possible.

As figure 4-1 shows, there is no superimposition of interventions in the experiment. Moreover, because all inductions occur only in their impact upon the respective period of intervention, the superimposition of such effects of intervention can also be excluded.[14] This verifies the independence of the two research approaches. Methodic difficulties concerning the subquestion to be treated here consequently do not arise from factors in the experimental design but from the attempt to overcome the separation of both problem fields.

An investigation of information behavior under time pressure involving high numbers is possible only because the empirical results available thus far were able to verify the strict period delimitation of all inductions. The following testing design conceived for the testing of hypothesis 3 is based on this fact.

In the first comparison, all periods with time limitation (periods 1-3 and 8-10) are combined. The second interval of comparison encompasses the restriction-free periods 5 and 7, which had no experimental intervention and therefore represented an absolutely zero situation. This tailoring of the testing design guarantees that the stimulation of the demand for information, which is to be understood here as a potential interference, is neutralized. While direct after-effects from interventions could be negated, even uncontrolled expressions of behavior are being neutralized in this way. Since each of the period classes of comparison contains the interference error, the nature and extent of which is unknown, and since this error is thus being parallelized, there is a reliable testing design. The influence of

Project I	Information Behavior in Decision-Making Processes									
Design I	—	—	—	Appeal	—	Offer	—	—	—	—
Period	1	2	3	4	5	6	7	8	9	10
Design II	Time Limitation			—	—	—	—	Time Limitation		
Project II	Decision Making under Time Pressure									

Figure 4-1. Experimental Designs of Different Research Projects

information-stimulating inductions is eliminated; the tests exclusively ascertain the effects of time pressure.

The statistical test is done by comparison of mean values on the basis of the student t test with the significance threshold being set at a 5-percent probability of error.

Findings: As the first component of information behavior under time pressure, the limitation of the quantity of demand as hypothesized in theorem 3.1 is verified. (See table 4–13.)

Table 4–13
Comparison of Quantity of Demand for Information, by Time Limitation

Test Values	Periods without Time Limitation	Periods with Time Limitation
Mean value	12.33	9.58
Standard deviation	6.17	6.51
Number (n)	24	72
Significance	$p = 0.034$	

As the statistical test demonstrates, the differences of the quantities of information demanded are verified as significant. The validity of theorem 3.1 is supported by experimental testing: time pressure leads to a quantitative restriction of the demand for information.

A further testing step is to investigate whether this restrictive information behavior affects, in the same way, the quality of the articulation of demand, the precision of the demand for information as prognosticated by theorem 3.2.

Table 4–14
Comparison of Degree of Precision of Demand for Information, by Time Limitation

Test Values	Periods without Time Limitation	Periods with Time Limitation
Mean value	93.33	86.56
Standard deviation	8.77	17.28
Number (n)	24	72
Significance	$p = 0.185$	

As table 4–14 shows, the expectation of a lower precision in the demand as a result of time pressure must be rejected. Although an apparent difference in the values may be noticeable, this does not satisfy the requirement of significance and therefore must be regarded as coincidental. This result supports the statement that the degree of precision of demand for information follows a steady trend in the direction of an absolutely precise expression of demand.[15] Only the frequency of articulation and not stimulating or restricting measures cause a change in the precision of demand. Accordingly, the danger of a reduction of precision of demand does not exist in decisions under time pressure. The sharpness of the articulation is immune to situative pressures.

Theorem 3.3 maintains a limitation of the cognitive orientation for decisions under time pressure and, thus, a second form of quality reduction in the demand for information. The following testing step subjects this theory to the empirical test of verification.

Table 4-15 leads to a falsification of the hypothetical expectations. Because of the markedness of its values that are contrary to the hypothesis, the result of the test necessitates a rejection of the statement made in theorem 3.3. Despite time pressures, the cognitive breadth of the problem perspective remains unchanged.[16]

Table 4-15
Comparison of Breadth of Demand for Information, by Time Pressure

Test Values	Periods without Time Limitation	Periods with Time Limitation
Mean value	2.50	3.21
Standard deviation	2.57	4.03
Number (n)	24	72
Significance	$-p = 0.160$	

From the results of the tests, it can be said that hypothesis 3 was partially verified. While the assumption expressed in theorem 3.1 that the quantity of demand is reduced under time pressure could be ascertained, the attempts at verification of theorems 3.2 and 3.3 led to a rejection of the hypotheses. Obviously time pressures do lead to a reduction in the quantity of information demand in mental processes, but the qualitative elements of information behavior remain largely unaffected by the pressure. However, the proof of the constancy of the degree of precision and breadth of information does not compensate for the relevance of the first finding. By their very nature, cognitive breadth and sharpness of the articulation of need can be determined only for the demand realized and only refer to the latter.

That means that the two characteristics of information quality—precision and breadth— measured here designate distinctive features of the quantity of information that is the basis here. The combination of all three test results therefore necessitates an exacting modification of hypothesis 3: In complex decision-making situations, time pressure leads to a restriction of the quantity of information but not to a reduction of precision and cognitive breadth.

Regulation of the Decision

Decision making under time pressure places various high demands on problem solving. They require not only a mastery of the decisional content of the tasks when analyzing and assessing complex situations of action, but also coordination of the most different forms of achievement contributions.

As the results of the experimental testing clearly show, time pressure causes a restriction of the content of the decision-making performance. A corresponding assumption is made here for the coordinating efforts, founded on the considerations for the derivation of hypothesis 4, and it bases subsequent testing on the theoretical assertion formulated.

Hypothesis 4: In complex decision-making situations, time pressure leads to the limitation of coordinative activity within the decision-making units.

Despite the fact that in numerous socio-psychological investigations, there is generally a low degree of marked coordination in multipersonal achievement processes, the attempt is to be made to determine the extent of coordinative activities under alternative stress conditions.[17] To accomplish this, it is necessary to differentiate according to the objects of coordination.

If a regulative measure is directed to the course that problem solving takes—that is, if individual subactivities, temporal and spatial conditions for fulfillment, or institutional and/or personnel task assignment are definitively determined—this is called *organization*.[18] In addition to these process-directed types of regulation, a result-directed harmonization of individual performances can be subordinated under the concept of coordination. A regulation of decision by means of content specifications of the result of problem solving is called *goal setting*. It comprises all limitations of action in the form of directions of action, concrete measures, borders of discretion and selection, as well as imperatives of action that are set in order to achieve a performance result. While organization helps to arrive at a processual regulation of the decision, the coordinative instrument of goal setting affects the regulation of its content.

With this definition of the statement of hypothesis 4 and its direction to the specific marginal conditions of the experiment, two theorems can be formulated:

Theorem 4.1: In experiment periods with strict limitation of decision-making time, there is a lower degree of organization of problem solving than in periods free from such restrictions.

Theorem 4.2: In experiment periods with strict limitation of decision-making time, there is a lower degree of goal-setting articulation for problem solving than in periods free from such restrictions.

Measurement: For the operationalization of the processual and strategic coordinative measures we will revert to the empirical data of the analysis of activity done in the testing of hypothesis 2.

In principle, eight operations serve as the variables constituting organizational regulation. These operations result from the syntactical combinations of the two regulative activities of defining and urging with the four structuring objects of time period, sequence, point in time, and task. The coordinating efforts in the form of a result-oriented regulation can be recorded with the aid of two goal-setting operations. They contain determining and urging in relation to the object of goal setting.

Testing Design: In order to obtain complete insight into the regulative behavior within the experiment, a first analytical step records all regulative operations irrespective of their frequency of occurrence. Further evaluation, however, will be limited to those coordinating measures whose frequencies suggest sufficient explicative value.

The attempts at verification of theorems 4.1 and 4.2 are based on the classes of comparison of the periods with and without limitation of decision time. The corresponding testing data are computed into these two intervals and tested for essential differences by means of a comparison of the mean averages. The statistical procedure applied is a t test based on a significance requirement of a maximal 5 percent probability of error.

Findings: Once the sum of the decisional regulation determined in the experiment is demonstrated, it is possible to make empirical statements on the degree of coordinating activities by object and intensity. Only after this principle overview, which is essential for a subsequent and more profound study, may the given hypotheses be examined in a more directed manner.

Verification of the Theory

Table 4-16
Coordination of Decisions

	Operations	Decision Regulation		
Number	Content	Total	Staff	Board of Directors
21/31	Determining/time period	3	0	3
21/32	Determining/sequence	141	124	17
21/33	Determining/point in time	92	47	45
21/34	Determining/task	156	33	123
22/31	Urging/time period	3	2	1
22/32	Urging/sequence	0	0	0
22/33	Urging/point in time	19	13	6
22/34	Urging/task	34	21	13
Organizational regulation		448	240	208
21/40	Determining/goal setting	246	171	75
22/40	Urging/goal setting	29	25	4
Goal-determining regulation		275	196	79
Total		723	436	287

Several significant findings can be derived from table 4-16 that go beyond the narrow inquiry into the effect of time pressure.

As a whole the functional group of the staff entrusted with the preparation of the decision reflects a higher degree of coordinative activity than does the group that makes the final decision. This fact becomes most apparent when regulation through goals is considered. Although by definition the development of company policy in the form of goal setting is an essential task of of the company management,[19] this specific performance can be achieved only with great difficulty.[20] This assumption cannot be more closely examined: Limited access to information appears to be viewed as an unsatisfactory legitimation for goal-setting competency.

Of particular interest here is the differently oriented form of organizational regulation: The staff generally becomes aware of the need for goal regulation, obviously as a result of the generally higher temporal pressure. For the board of directors group, the task as a performance goal and object of division is prominent.[21] Although this is a result that has not yet been derived, theoretically, we want to venture, although cautiously, an assumption: A course-directed organizational policy prevails in those places that prepare decisions. Members of the final decisional agency tend to a higher degree toward a regulation by fixing competency. While the staff pays greater attention to the process of performance, the attention of the board of directors concentrates on the aspect of the responsibility for the performance.

Although the quantitative values presented in table 4-15 do not permit the determination of too low a coordination activity, they verify a distinct reservation in the regulation of the decision. The empirical fact of only a few urging regulatory operations justified this statement. The coordination ascertained in the experiment takes place with little emphasis.

Only three operations are important to coordination: The total coordination performance activated is essentially carried by the establishing of time sequences, the defining of tasks, and the setting of goals of action. These are the three core instruments of coordination.

1. The temporal regulation of the course of the decision, which is almost exclusively done by the staff, is directed most evidently to the processual aspect of problem mastery. This will be referred to as *process regulation*.
2. Coordinative measures by the board of directors concentrate on the regulation of the work content of the decision-making tasks and are mostly aimed at definite bearers of functions. This category of structuring interventions will be summarized under *function regulation*.[22]
3. The result-directed coordination of performance contributions by goal setting must also be discriminated terminologically from the organizational regulations. It is therefore labeled *goal regulation*.

Within the framework of the following testing steps, the regulative instruments are investigated separately. In this way findings on the actual use and suitability of coordinating measures with different regulative approaches are to be obtained.

Theorem 4.1 requires a comparison of the organization interventions in decision-making periods with and without time restrictions.

Table 4-17
Comparison of Activities in Organizing the Decision, by Time Limitation

Test Values	Periods without Time Limitation	Periods with Time Limitation
Process regulation (staff)		
Mean value	1.65	0.65
Standard deviation	1.30	0.97
Number (n)	48	72
Significance	$p < 0.001$	

Verification of the Theory

Table 4-17 continued

Test Values	Periods without Time Limitation	Periods with Time Limitation
Function regulation (directors)		
Mean value	1.31	0.83
Standard deviation	1.78	1.15
Number (n)	48	72
Significance	$p = 0.051$	

As table 4–17 shows, the second variable to measure for the quantification of organizational regulation barely misses the predetermined threshold of significance. An extremely strict observance of the statistical conventions, therefore, would have to exclude the verification of the validity of theorem 4.1. In view of the very minor deviation from the norm, completely rejecting this explicative tendency appears inappropriate. But even if one rejects this contribution to the support of theorem 4.1, the highly significant result on time regulation can prove its verification.

After proving a limitation of the organizational efforts as a result of time pressure in the experiment, it remains to be tested whether this expectation can also be corroborated for coordination by the predetermination of goals.

**Table 4-18
Comparison of Activities for Goal Setting, by Time Limitation**

Test Values	Periods without Time Limitation	Periods with Time Limitation
Mean value	1.29	1.51
Standard deviation	1.61	2.00
Number (n)	48	72
Significance	$-p > 0.500$	

Table 4–18 clearly shows that activities for the formulation of company policy directives are not restricted under time pressure. Because of the high probability of error and, particularly, because of the measurement values that are contrary to the hypothesis, theorem 4.2 must be rejected. On the other hand, the statistical test result does not support the antithesis of an

identifiable intensification of goal regulation. The minor differences in values are, rather, coincidental and thus unsuitable for the explanation of changes in the regulative behavior.

On the basis of the experimentally obtained results, hypothesis 4 could be partially verified. Proof of a diminishing coordination of performance under time pressure could be furnished for process regulation, which proved to be a characteristic organizational measure taken by the staff in preparing its decisions, as well as for function regulation on the part of the board of directors. The assumption of the same reduced goal regulation cannot be supported by the available data, however.

Because of the generally minor markedness of goal-regulating measures, we assume a lower degree of goal consciousness. The statement that regulation by goals is being maintained even under time pressure is suggested by the nonrefutability of the zero thesis as it results from table 4–17. Because of the coincidental nature of the test data, however, the statement appears inadequate.

The analysis of coordination behavior in problem solving under time pressure made such clear differences evident between regulation by organization and regulation by goal predetermination that the question of the efficiency of the two regulating instruments becomes central. The analysis of efficency, therefore, will pay special attention to this aspect.

Efficiency of Performance under Time Pressure

The way in which the solution to problems in decision making under time pressure takes place has been demonstrated. The performance sectors of interaction, information, and coordination, were illustrated. This provides prerequisites for an analysis of efficiency that will have to determine the degree to which factually given problem mastery is successful. In addition to the statements on the dependence of decision-making performance on temporal and situational conditions now statements regarding the effect of decision making performance on the efficiency of problem mastery are required.

For this purpose, it is necessary to discontinue the aggregate view pursued thus far and to differentiate according to decision-making units with different profiles of performance. Only after different approaches to overcoming stress-burdened decisions have been compared can empirically founded testimony on efficiency be obtained. The performance sectors of interaction, information, and coordination again serve as the points of departure.

The gradual differentiation of the decision-making units is made in accordance with their intensity of performance within these sectors of prob-

Verification of the Theory

lem solving. The assessment of performance effectiveness comprises three levels of efficiency: the personal, the temporal, and the economic efficiency of problem mastery.

Performance Satisfaction

Personal efficiency begins with the assessment of the performance of the decision-making persons. As such, it is a subjective judgment, although an overall judgment can be made for groups.

Performance satisfaction is not to be a surrogate of an objective efficiency assessment. Rather, it embodies an independent measure of personal performance success. In this sense it is to be understood as an objective measure of efficiency.

The efficiency context to be examined here corresponds to the theoretical assertion of hypothesis 5:

Hypothesis 5: In complex decisional situations under time pressure, lower personal efficiency is achieved with decreased performance than with higher performance.

When this general statement is applied to the actual experiment with simultaneous orientation to the three central sectors of performance, the following theorems can be derived:

Theorem 5.1: Decision-making units with a low degree of interaction achieve a lower degree of performance satisfaction than do decision-making units with a high degree of interaction.

Theorem 5.2: Decision-making units with little information achieve a lower degree of performance satisfaction than do units with a high demand for information.

Theorem 5.3: Decision-making units with a low degree of coordination achieve a lower degree of performance satisfaction than do decision-making units with a strong coordination.

Measurement: The empirical data on performance intensity are used to quantify the variables that are regarded as independent. Operational values for the recording of interaction, information, and coordination are the values of activity, of the quantity of demand for information, of process regulation, of function regulation, as well as of goal regulation. They are differentiated by performance units and, stratified according to little or strong markedness, form the respective comparison classes of the test. The determination of satisfaction values is based on an assessment by the decision-making persons determined by means of a questionnaire. At the end of each experiment period, the participants were asked to evaluate the success of the decision-making meeting just concluded. The exact wording and the predetermined scaling of the question was:

What is your estimate of the degree of work success of today's meeting?

```
         very                                              completely
|-----------------+-----------------+-----------------+-----------------|
         good                                              unsatisfactory
```

The graphically marked values may vary within the value limits of 10 to 60. High values represent little performance satisfaction; low values correspond to high satisfaction.[23]

The data per period were condensed to an arithmetic mean for each of the twentyfour work groups, which cooperated in pairs. In this aggregate form, the assessment values thus ascertained constitute a representative measure of performance satisfaction for each group.

Testing Design: The test of theorem 5.1 requires the determination and combination of decision-making units with a low or high degree of activity. They form the classes of comparison into which the corresponding satisfaction values are computed and tested for essential differences. Since it cannot be expected—and actually does not become manifest in the finding—that under the various aspects of performance, the same business enterprises will always occupy the class of high or low performance markedness, this procedure must be employed in an analogous way for theorems 5.2 and 5.3. The test of theorem 5.2 confronts decision-making units with a low and high quantity of demand for information. Theorem 5.3 requires the confrontation of enterprises with a high and low degree of regulative performance.

The statistical test aims at the determination of mean value differences by means of a t test. Differences in the evaluation of performance are considered as significant if they do not exceed a 5 percent probability of error. Findings that do not meet this requirement must be viewed as coincidentally caused and can make no contribution to the support of the respective expectation. The tests encompass the values of the staff groups in all experiment periods independent of the perceived intensity of time pressure.

Findings: First the satisfaction values from decision-making units with little activity must be compared with the corresponding test values of those decision-making units with an activity that was higher than average.

Table 4-19
Comparison of Satisfaction, by Degree of Activity

Test Values	Decision-Making Units with Low Activity	Decision-Making Units with High Activity
Mean value	28.98	27.81
Standard deviation	4.39	6.89
Number (n)	60	60
Significance	$p = 0.123$	

The result, shown in table 4-19, does not satisfy the required significance norm and must be regarded as coincidental. Theorem 5.1 cannot be verified by the test. Performance satisfaction as a variable of personal efficiency indicates no systematic relation to problem-solving activity.

Subsequent and further tests of hypothesis 5 are to follow immediately without attempting an interpretation of this partial result.

Table 4-20
Comparison of Satisfaction, by Quantity of Information Demand

Test Values	Decision-Making Units with Low Information Demand	Decision-Making Units with High Information Demand
Mean value	28.98	27.81
Standard deviation	4.98	6.48
Number (n)	60	60
Significance	$p = 0.123$	

Hypothesis 5 cannot be corroborated in the second verification attempt either; the empirical equivalents do not reach the required statistical significance (table 4-20). Theorem 5.2 therefore must be rejected. The intensity of the demand for information, measured by the quantity of demand, indicates no relation to personal efficiency in problem solving.

The succeeding test of performance satisfaction dependent on regulative decision-making performances is conducted separately for the three forms of coordination: process regulation, function regulation, and goal regulation.

Table 4-21
Comparison of Satisfaction, by Coordination Performance (Process, Function, and Goal Regulation)

	Process Regulation	
Test Values	Decision-Making Units with Little Process Regulation	Decision-Making Units with Much Process Regulation
Mean value	29.21	27.26
Standard deviation	5.70	5.78
Number (n)	70	50
Significance	$p = 0.036$	
	Function Regulation	
Test Values	Decision-Making Units with Little Function Regulation	Decision-Making Units with Much Function Regulation
Mean value	28.00	29.20
Standard deviation	6.13	5.01
Number (n)	80	40
Significance	$-p = 0.128$	
	Goal Regulation	
Test Values	Decision-Making Units with Little Goal Regulation	Decision-Making Units with Much Goal Regulation
Mean value	28.98	27.81
Standard deviation	4.39	6.89
Number (n)	60	60
Significance	$p = 0.123$	

The results (table 4-21) are of extraordinary significance in multiple respects.

First, they show that both the purely quantitative activity and the demand for information do not influence satisfaction in overcoming problems. Apparently these contributions to decision making are taken for granted and contribute only little to the personal evaluation of success.

Second, the fact that also the coordination of performance in the form of goal determination does not affect the performance assessment may be

Verification of the Theory

explained by the specific situation of the staff. Due to the division of competence as created in the experiment, the staff can articulate goals whose acceptance, however, remains with the board of directors, at least at the time when the assessment is made. This lack of knowledge about the taking up of goals leads to the fact that even the potential effect of regulative performance remains in doubt. Therefore, the articulation of goals by the staff appears unsuitable for the development of satisfaction.

Third, there is a significantly positive connection between the activities for process regulation and performance satisfaction. Theorem 5.3 is corroborated by this result. An intensive effort to achieve course-regulating structuring measures leads to an increase of personal efficiency. The renunciation of process-directed interventions, generally triggered by time pressure, obviously indicates the insufficient coordination of the course of the decision and is reflected in less-positive satisfaction values.

Further, attempts at coordinating performance by means of function-regulating interventions do not affect satisfaction. Neither a positive effect nor the apparent impression of a negative effect on performance satisfaction can be proved with statistical certainty.

In sum, hypothesis 5 must be regarded as falsified in its original formulation. The general assumption of a personal efficiency dependent on performance cannot be maintained. Since only the regulative performance for the organization of the problem-solving process yielded a finding that corresponds to exceptions, an explicit revision of the hypothesis is necessary:

In complex decision-making situations under time pressure, the decision-making units achieve a lower degree of personal efficiency with a low degree of process regulation than with a higher degree of process regulation. The intensity of the remaining performances, however, remains without a significant influence on the personal efficiency of the decision.

Time-Pressure Absorption

Decisions under time pressure contain two connected problem areas. In addition to the objective content of the decisional tasks, time pressures have to be overcome. Problem solving requires overcoming both cognitive and time stress. In such a pressure situation, it is virtually of existential importance to restrict performance in such a way that only a minimum loss of efficiency occurs. Therefore, empirically founded evidence is sought regarding the effectiveness of specific performances in the mastery of stress-burdened decision-making situations. They form the basis for a reliable underpinning of the practice of decision making.

First, problem-solving behavior under time pressure was investigated with respect to its effect on satisfaction. Now we will examine the temporal efficiency of the contributions to decision making. The assertion contained in hypothesis 6 serves as the theoretical basis for this examination.

Hypothesis 6: In complex decision-making situations under time pressure, a greater temporal efficiency is achieved with little performance than with high performance.

The verification test covers the three performance sectors of interaction, information, and coordination. Making this differentiation and simultaneously aligning them with the marginal conditions of the experiment allows the derivation of the following theorems for the substantiation of hypothesis 6.

Theorem 6.1: Decision-making units with a low degree of interaction achieve a higher degree of time-pressure absorption than do decision-making units with a high degree of interaction.

Theorem 6.2: Decision-making units with a low degree of information achieve a higher degree of time-pressure absorption than do decision-making units with a high demand for information.

Theorem 6.3: Decision-making units with a low degree of coordination achieve a higher degree of time-pressure absorption than do decision-making units with a high degree of coordination.

Measurement: The decision-making performances that are regarded as independent variables are operationalized by the measures of activity, of the quantity of demand for information, and of the organizational and strategic regulation already developed. They constitute the categories of comparison for the classification of the respective test data.

The qualitative measure of time-pressure absorption is the time-pressure index as determined in the last three experiment periods. The lower this measure is for a definite decision-making unit, the greater is the absorption success of the unit. Decision-making units for which comparatively high time-pressure index values can be determined despite numerous repetitions of the problem solving are, by contrast, less in a position to master the stress burden caused by the limited decision-making time; their temporal efficiency is low.[24]

Verification of the Theory

Testing Design: To test hypothesis 6, the values of decision-making units with high and low degrees of performance intensity are combined. The staffing of the classes of comparison is identical with that of the immediately preceding efficiency test of satisfaction. The verification test for theorem 6.1 requires the comparison of the time-pressure index values from periods 8 to 10 of decision-making units with high and low degrees of activity.[25] Correspondingly, theorem 6.2 requires a comparison of values for decision-making units with high and low demands for information. The test of theorem 6.3 uses the empirical data from decision-making units with high and low degrees of regulation.

The statistical testing procedure is based on a comparison of mean values with the aid of a t test. Differences in efficiency of time are regarded as proved if they do not exceed the significance value of 5 percent probability of error. Differences registered at higher error values are to be considered as coincidental and provide no contribution to the support of the assertion in question. The tests cover all experiment periods.

Finding: In the first attempt at verification, the step-by-step test of the hypothesis is directed to theorem 6.1. The significant difference in the time-pressure index values (table 4-22) confirms the relationship formulated in theorem 6.1: decision-making units that, as a result of limited decision-making time, limit their activity more strictly achieve a higher time-pressure absorption rate than do those decision-making units with a comparatively higher activity level. The adaption strategy of activity reduction can thus be verified under the aspect of temporal efficiency. Limitation of activity is an adequate instrument to overcome time pressures.

Table 4-22
Comparison of Time-Pressure Absorption (in Periods 8-10), by Degree of Activity

Test Values	Decision-Making Units with Low Activity	Decision-Making Units with High Activity
Mean value	25.83	33.22
Standard deviation	8.54	9.38
Number (n)	18	18
Significance	$p = 0.009$	

After the first verification of hypothesis 6 it must be examined how far the renunciation of information reflects the same relieving effect.

Table 4-23
Comparison of Time-Pressure Absorption (in Periods 8-10), by Demand for Information

Test Values	Decision-Making Units with Low Demand for Information	Decision-Making Units with High Demand for Information
Mean value	26.61	32.44
Standard deviation	8.58	9.80
Number (n)	18	18
Significance	$p = 0.033$	

The statistical test proves the noticeable difference in values as significant and thus supports theorem 6.2 (table 4-23). With a low demand for information, a higher temporal efficiency is achieved than with a higher quantity of demand. The limitation of the informative decision-making performance made under time pressure contributes to the reduction of time pressure. Under the absorption aspect of time-pressure mastery, the adaptive behavior of the decision-making units can thus be regarded as efficient.

The reduction of activity as well as the limitation of the demand for information proved to be instruments to reduce time pressure. We now investigate the effect of the coordinating measure on the degree of temporal pressure.

The results below (table 4-24) require a differentiated examination and interpretation of the partial findings.

Table 4-24
Comparison of Time-Pressure Absorption (in Periods 8-10), by Coordination Performance

Test Values	Process Regulation — Decision-Making Units with Little Process Regulation	Decision-Making Units with Much Process Regulation
Mean value	27.95	30.40
Standard deviation	9.89	9.52
Number (n)	21	15
Significance	$p = 0.229$	

Verification of the Theory

Table 4-24 continued

	Function Regulation	
Test Values	Decision-Making Units with Little Function Regulation	Decision-Making Units with Much Function Regulation
Mean value	29.63	29.33
Standard deviation	9.61	9.69
Number (n)	24	12
Significance	$p > 0.500$	

	Goal Regulation	
Test Values	Decision-Making Units with Little Goal Regulation	Decision-Making Units with Much Goal Regulation
Mean value	25.83	33.22
Standard deviation	8.54	9.38
Number (n)	18	18
Significance	$p = 0.009$	

Both process-oriented and function-oriented regulation are ineffective in terms of the absorption hypothesis. The minor differences in the values do not reach the required threshold of significance and must be regarded as coincidental. Process regulation and function regulation are instruments unsuitable as a means to reduce time pressure in decision making. This result is particularly significant because both regulative forms are directed to the coordination of the course of problem solving. An interpretation based solely on table 4-23 could mislead to a classification of organization as an inefficient alternative of coordination.

Course-regulating activities in themselves are work-intensive performances. This statement is supported by the information in table 4-16, which proves that organizational interventions are reduced under time pressure. The work pressure involved in organizational regulation compensates for the work relief resulting from the course regulations that were thus created. At this point it can only be presumed that certain changes in the execution of mental-performance processes take place as a result of organizational interventions in the process and function regulation. Proof is still missing.

Since the amount of organizational activity does not influence the absorption of time pressure, and the existence of time pressure generally leads to the restriction of organization performance, this behavior must be designated as inefficient. The effect of a time-pressure reduction intended with the reduction of performance is not achieved.

In contrast, goal regulation is closely connected to the absorption of time pressure. Time pressures can be reduced by renouncing rather than by intensifying goal-regulating coordination measures. The absorption hypothesis as expressed in theorem 6.3 can be verified under this partial aspect.

As can be seen from table 4-18, goal regulating measures are maintained unchanged in spite of pressures of different intensity. This result does not contradict the data in table 4-24, which reflect gradual differences in the extent of goal regulation for the individual decision-making units; however, these data do provide the basis for an assessment of regulative behavior. Because a greater absorption effect is achieved with comparatively little goal regulation, the constancy of goal regulation as determined in the comparison of periods cannot be regarded as an adequate adaptive behavior to restrictions of time. To what extent the renunciation of this adaptive behavior is justified under different considerations remains unconsidered here.

Hypothesis 6 requires explicitly differentiating modification because of the existence of two coordination performances that are completely different in their effects:

In complex decision-making situations under time pressure, a comparatively low degree of performances of interaction, information, and goal regulation brings about a higher degree of efficiency of time than do more intense performances of this kind. By contrast, the restriction of organizational regulation cannot contribute to the absorption of time pressure.

Decision Realization

The determination of efficiency criteria for the evaluation of problem solving in decision making is based on three approaches. With respect to the decision-making person, satisfaction serves as an operational measure of efficiency. Under the aspect of time pressure in the decision-making process, time-pressure absorption can be derived as a quantification of temporal efficiency. The result of decision making, that means the material consequence of problem solving, is reflected in the realization of the decision.

Particularly in the area of management decisions, the transformation of mental performance into economic success is the primary goal of all efforts. The extent to which problem-solving performance influences economic efficiency is therefore the object of the following test. For this pur-

Verification of the Theory

pose we call hypothesis 7, which formulates an assertion concerning the connection between performance under time pressure and its effects.

Hypothesis 7: In complex decisional situations under time pressure, a lower economic efficiency is achieved with little performance than with high performance.

As in the preceding testing steps, decision-making performance encompasses interaction, information, and coordination. If one specifies the statement of hypothesis 7 according to these performance sectors and transfers it to the conditions given in the experiment, the following theorems can be derived as substatements:

Theorem 7.1: Decision-making units with a low degree of interaction achieve a lower economic efficiency than do decision-making units with a high degree of interaction.

Theorem 7.2: Decision-making units with a low degree of information achieve a lower economic efficiency than do decision-making units with a high degree of information.

Theorem 7.3: Decision-making units with a low degree of coordination achieve a lower economic efficiency than do decision-making units with a high degree of coordination.

Measurement: In order to operationalize the decision-making performances we revert to the measure of activity, of the quantity of demand for information, of process regulation, of function regulation, and of goal regulation. These were already proved earlier and do not require a detailed description here.

A specific interest in the economic consequences of decision-making behavior results from the managerial character of this investigation. This fact justifies, and indeed requires, a particularly scrutinizing test even more so as the scientific results will have to satisfy the requirement of praxeologic validity. The analysis of economic efficiency of problem-solving under time pressure is therefore done on the basis of measures of effectiveness with different orientations.

The first measure of effectiveness is the overall success achieved in the course of all ten decision-making sequences. Since virtually all internal business and market-directed activities are ultimately reflected in success, particularly in the long-term, this success, gauged positively by profit and negatively by loss, guarantees a reliable measurement of the total performance realization reached.

A variable used as an operationalization aid at an earlier stage and in another form offers an alternative approach to the quantification of economic efficiency. In the framework of the analysis of the conditions of time pressure, this variable, designated as situational index, characterized the problem intensity of a period conditioned by the decision-making results of the preceding period. In the form of a nondimensional index value, this variable defines the total economic placement within the respective testing sequence. Under the criteria of liquidity, business orders received, sales, and quality of the product, each decision-making unit is ranked. The highest rank corresponds to value 1; last rank leads to an evaluative rating of 4. The five individual placements are combined to provide a reference number for overall placement. For the purpose of delineation from the situational index, the total economic result realized is called the result index. This provides a result index for the classification of economic efficiency for each decision-making unit of each decision-making period.

The total success records the economic efficiency of all individual business performances after completion of ten decision-making sequences and represents the long-term decision-making efficiency. By comparison, the result index is defined as a multivariate value, which results from the individual criteria of finance, profits, production, and acquisition of the company. The temporal unit of reference in all cases is the decision-making period. Thus, the analysis of efficiency is conducted on the basis of a long-term- and a short-term-oriented testing conception.

Testing Design: The testing data for the result index and for total success are arranged into the comparison classes of low and high performance, differentiated by activity, quantity of demand for information, and the three measures for decision-making regulation. The statistical test for mean-value differences is done with the aid of a t test. The admissible confidence measure of significance is a maximal 5 percent probability of error.

The tests are based on the measurement values from the staff groups. Within the framework of the long-term analysis of efficiency, one measuring value is included in the computation for each decision-making unit. The short-term-oriented test records the individual values from ten experiment periods. A theorem is regarded as verified if the hypothesis can be proved in one of the two testing versions.

Finding: Theorem 7.1 requires a comparison of the efficiency values at low and high degrees of activity in the decision-making units.

Verification of the Theory

Table 4-25
Comparison of Success (after Ten Experiment Periods), by Degree of Activity

Test Values	Decision-Making Units with Low Activity	Decision-Making Units with High Activity
Mean value	7.48	24.25
Standard deviation	11.27	20.00
Number (n)	6	6
Significance	$p = 0.052$	

As table 4-25 clearly shows, decision-making units with a comparatively high degree of activity realize greater total success than do those with a lower degree of activity. Although the significance value barely misses the required measure, it still appears sufficiently high, even when strict statistical test norms are applied, and it is admitted to support theorem 7.1.

But it still remains to be tested whether this result can also be verified in a differentiation by individual periods.

Table 4-26
Comparison of Result-Index Values, by Degree of Activity

Test Values	Decision-Making Units with Low Activity	Decision-Making Units with High Activity
Mean value	13.12	11.88
Standard deviation	2.45	2.18
Number (n)	60	60
Significance	$p = 0.002$	

An additional verification of theorem 7.1 can be obtained from the findings presented in table 4-26. The significant difference in efficiency for decision-making units with different degrees of activity with a high certainty proves the positive effect of decision-making activity on the economic efficiency of problem solving. At the same time, however, it becomes clear that the adaptive behavior of performance restriction occurring in stress-burdened periods must be differently appraised under two efficiency arguments. The temporal relief primarily aimed at can be achieved by a reduction of activity; the result, however, is a reduction of economic performance effectiveness.

A subsequent testing step is to determine in which way the effort in obtaining information influences the realization of the decision. The first test version confronts the result index values of decision-making units with different information behavior (table 4-27). Therefore it corresponds to a short-term-oriented analysis of efficiency.

Table 4-27
Comparison of Result-Index Values, by Demand for Information

Test Values	Decision-Making Units with Low Information Demand	Decision-Making Units with High Information Demand
Mean value	12.68	12.32
Standard deviation	2.42	2.40
Number (n)	60	60
Significance	$p = 0.207$	

In the short-term-directed testing arrangement, the efficiency hypothesis of theorem 7.2 cannot be corroborated because of insufficiently pronounced differences in values. The attempt at verification thus failed. In agreement with the stipulation made here, that hypothesis is to be recognized if it can be proved in one of the two alternative tests; this, however, does not constitute a definite failure of theorem 7.2.

The second verification will attempt to test to what extent differently pronounced information behavior reflects a relation to total success achieved over a long term. The evidently discernible difference in efficiency exceeds the fixed significance measure so barely that it still appears justified to regard theorem 7.2 as being verified. A rejection would have to be viewed as an inappropriately strict application of statistical validity norms. Moreover, verification of the efficiency hypothesis is also justified by the earlier results of empirical decision-making research. Field investigations as well as experiments proved significantly positive efficiency effects of the demand for information.[26] The examinations conducted under various testing conditions independently corroborate the economic efficiency of the demand for information.

Table 4-28
Comparison of Success (after Ten Experiment Periods), by Demand for Information

Test Values	Decision-Making Units with Low Information Demand	Decision-Making Units with High Information Demand
Mean value	7.55	24.18
Standard deviation	11.30	20.00
Number (n)	6	6
Significance	$p = 0.054$	

The data presented in table 4-28 enable a verification of theorem 7.2:

Decision-making units with a comparatively high demand for information achieve a higher degree of economic efficiency in the realization of their decisions than do decision-making units with a low demand for information.

With a view to the little willingness to demand information under time pressure, it can therefore be said that this restrictive information behavior affects economic efficiency negatively. The renunciation of informative decision-making performance leads to a relief of time pressure; time pressure, however, also corresponds to a reduction of the success of realization of the decision made. Temporal and economic efficiency again prove to be competing performance goals.

The final testing step is to determine the economic effectiveness of coordination. For a more-detailed differentiation of performance regulation, regulative measures will be split into organizational and goal-setting ones. The statistical test is done for both testing versions.

The first test will be to determine how coordination influences the total success of the decision-making units.

Table 4-29
Comparison of Success (after Ten Experiment Periods), by Coordination Performance

Test Values	Process Regulation — Decision-Making Units with Little Process Regulation	Process Regulation — Decision-Making Units with Much Process Regulation
Mean value	10.17	23.84
Standard deviation	8.81	22.47
Number (n)	7	5
Significance	$p = 0.111$	

Table 4-29 continued

	Function Regulation	
Test Values	*Decision-Making Units with Little Function Regulation*	*Decision-Making Units with Much Function Regulation*
Mean value	11.96	23.68
Standard deviation	18.29	19.09
Number (n)	8	4
Significance	$p = 0.153$	

	Goal Regulation	
Test Values	*Decision-Making Units with Little Goal Regulation*	*Decision-Making Units with Much Goal Regulation*
Mean value	7.48	24.25
Standard deviation	11.27	20.00
Number (n)	6	6
Significance	$p = 0.052$	

Table 4-29 yields different test results for the individual coordination performances. The expectation of an efficiency-promoting effect of process and function-regulating measures cannot be substantiated. On the other hand, proof of efficiency for goal-setting interventions should be regarded as confirmed. The fact that the significance threshold was missed only by the extremely small margin of $2^0/_{00}$ does not appear to justify a rejection of theorem 7.3. The value difference determined with low and high degrees of goal regulation therefore is considered still significant.

Table 4-30
Comparison of Result-Index Values, by Coordination Performance

	Process Regulation	
Test Values	*Decision-Making Units with Little Process Regulation*	*Decision-Making Units with Much Process Regulation*
Mean value	13.23	11.48
Standard deviation	2.26	2.26
Number (n)	70	50
Significance	$p < 0.001$	

Table 4-30 continued

	Function Regulation	
Test Values	Decision-Making Units with Little Function Regulation	Decision-Making Units with Much Function Regulation
Mean value	12.23	13.05
Standard deviation	2.38	2.34
Number (n)	80	40
Significance	$-p = 0.047$	

	Goal Regulation	
Test Values	Decision-Making Units with Little Goal Regulation	Decision-Making Units with Much Goal Regulation
Mean value	13.12	11.88
Standard deviation	2.45	2.18
Number (n)	60	60
Significance	$p = 0.002$	

The value differences determined in table 4-30 meet the required claim of certainty. The efficiency assumption formulated in theorem 7.3 was thus verified with regard to process regulation, as well as under the aspect of goal regulation. While economic efficiency, measured by the total success attained, could not be proved to a sufficiently reliable degree in the first testing phase, the highly significant result of the second testing version permits acceptance of the theory. The testing result on goal regulation, which was already recognized as verified, is corroborated by the statistical guarantee in table 4-29.

On the other hand, the experimental test of function regulation yields a statistically confirmed falsification of the efficiency hypothesis. The extent of function-regulating interventions with the course of decisions does not positively correlate with the economic efficiency achieved. Accordingly, hypothesis 7 cannot be verified in this testing step. The given constellation of values and their significance even justify the formulation of an antithesis:

Organizational measure in the form of function-determining regulation of the course of decision making impair the economic efficiency of the decision.

These empirical results and the results of hypothesis 6 provide a sound basis for the assessment of coordination behavior in decision making.

1. Under the aspect of economic efficiency, the fact that decision-making units do not limit their efforts for goal regulation in decision making, despite limited available time, is to be valued positively. Relinquishing goal-regulating coordination would lead to a higher time-pressure absorption rate, but would be connected with a reduction of efficiency in the realization of the decision.

2. The restriction of process regulation found in periods with strict time limitation must be valued negatively. Particularly because very high demands are placed on the execution of the performance process in bottleneck situations involving time, the renunciation of process-regulating measures constitutes an inadequate attempt at problem mastery. Insufficient time coordination is reflected in the result of the decisions realized.

3. This assessment is even more intensified by the results on personal and temporal efficiency. A low degree of organizational regulation causes a low degree of satisfaction and does not lead to the time-pressure absorption expected. Thus, the organization behavior found in the experiment, when judged by all performance criteria applied here, must be classified as inefficient. The differences in the behavior of individual decision-making units and in the corresponding efficiency values do not contradict this general conclusion.

4. A reduction of function-regulating interventions, as released by limited decision time available, cannot produce a safely provable effect of time relief; it does, however, positively affect the economic efficiency of the decision. Coordination measures, which defined the content of the tasks and/or the assignment of competency by means of function regulation, can be waived without disadvantage in a situation of temporal pressure.[27]

The limitation of function-regulating activities thus lends itself as a primary adaptation instrument for the mastery of time pressure. With one exception, the assertion contained in hypothesis 7 is supported by the testing results. Hypothesis 7 could thus be accepted as verified in principle. Because of the significance and markedness of the contradicting partial result of the test, the original formulation is explicitly modified:

In complex decisional situations under time pressure, a lower economic efficiency is achieved—when measured by means of the decision-making contributions of interaction, information, process regulation, and goal regulation—with little performance than with high performance.

Notes

1. See the discussion on the quality of the experiment, p. 75ff.
2. The determination of rank is done within each respective testing sequence in order to neutralize the small differences in the overall economic

Verification of the Theory

situation. When assigning ranking values for the goals of "orders", "sales", and "product quality", assessment followed a pure rule of maximization: the highest parameter value led to rank "1". For the bilateral variable of "success", maximum profit and minimum loss were of equal weight. Assessment under the aspect of liquidity was made in two testing steps. Business firms that were solvent received better ranking values the less they kept liquid funds open. In cases of insolvency, the extent of financial undercoverage formed the basis for the judgment.

3. For the principles of document analysis, see particularly A. Silbermann, *Inhaltsanalyse* (1967), and J. Szczepanski, *Biographische Methode* (1967).

4. See E. Witte, *Entscheidungsverläufe* (1968), p. 590ff.

5. Evidence for this statement, at this time still unproved, will be furnished in the analysis of performance structure. See p. 105ff.; M. Irle, *Macht* (1971), p. 205, arrives at a different characterization. He compares the behavior of the staff as dominantly "subject-matter oriented and less position oriented", with the behavior of the board of director groups as "derived from aspects of status and prestige".

6. Activity and communication are closely related to each other though they measure different aspects of performance. The close connection—corroborated by a correlation coefficient of $r = 0.786$—does not signify quasi-identity of the two measurement values. Rather, it expresses largely parallel development of mental performance and its conveyance to successively and supplementary acting agencies.

7. At probabilities of error of $p = 0.221$, $p = 0.123$, and $p = 0.872$ orders, sales, and success reveal no significant differences of measurement values in the two classes of comparison of periods with and without time limitation.

8. The following constellation results from the comparison of the test values for communication in the two classes of periods:

Periods	Mean Value	Standard Deviation	n
1–3	166.53	79.34	36
8–10	225.47	84.71	36

With $p = 0.003$ the statistical test indicates a significant difference, a difference that is contrary to expectations. The redundancy thesis is thus clearly rejected.

9. The statement concerning the direction of decision-making activity is not to be understood as a generalization of experimental results. It is only to offer a *plastic* designation of the experimentally designed structure of performance in the two subgroups of a decision-making unit.

10. The conditions of consultation have already been described in the information model. For this see R. Bronner, E. Witte, and P.R. Wossidlo, *Experimente* (1972), p. 169ff.

11. See E. Witte, *Informationsverhalten* (1972), p. 68ff., and Bronner, Witte, and Wossidlo, *Experimente,* p. 169ff. Under the aspect of information behavior the foregoing study represents an investigation parallel to the two works mentioned above.

12. The degree of precision can reach a maximum of 100 percent, and for borderline cases of syntactical intelligibility, a single question may sink to 25 percent. Renouncing this minimum of articulative clarity would mean that even the measurement value would remain untreated and that, thus, the question as a whole would remain unintelligible.

13. For the experimental design of the investigations by Witte, see Witte, *Informationsverhalten,* p. 77ff., and Bronner, Witte, and Wossidlo, *Experimente,* p. 166ff.

14. Time pressure as a continuing value is measured in all periods; however, it occurs to a significantly higher degree in periods with time limitation than in intervals free of pressure. The effect of measures taken to vitalize the demand for information remains limited to the period of the intervention. For this see Witte, *Informationsverhalten,* p. 79ff.

15. See ibid., p. 82ff.

16. Bronner, Witte, and Wossidlo, *Experimente,* p. 194, prove that cognitive orientation can be enlarged by a concrete supply of information. In total, it remains, however, at a lower level.

17. See particularly H.H. Kelley and J.W. Thibaut, *Problem Solving* (1954), p. 74ff.

18. See E. Witte, *Ablauforganisation* (1969), and F. Eulenburg, *Organisation* (1962).

19. See J. Bidlingmaier, *Unternehmerziele* (1964), p. 17ff.; G. Gäfgen, *Entscheidung* (1968), p. 176ff.; E. Heinen, *Zielsystem* (1966), p. 17ff.; E. Heinen, *Einführung* (1970), p. 95ff.; C. Sandig, *Betriebswirtschaftspolitik* (1966), p. 6ff.

20. W. Hamel, *Zieländerungen* (1974), arrives at the same result within the framework of a field investigation.

21. The groups of the board of directors, which register generally less stress under time pressure, reflect only a total of seventeen activities for time regulation during the course of all ten decision-making sequences. For the same time period only a total of thirty-three activities for task defining can be determined in the staff groups.

22. For a delineation of the concepts of task, work, process, function, and competence, see F. Nordsieck, *Funktion* (1969), col. 603; H. Ulrich, *Kompetenz* (1969), col. 852, and Witte, *Ablauforganisation* (1969).

23. For the content and structure of the questionnaire as well as for the placing of the question on performance assessment, see Appendix.

24. The objection could be raised against this absolute measurement of absorption ability that different initial conditions for time-pressure sensitivity were left unconsidered. It is true that the measurements of time-pressure perception in principle contain influences of sensitivity. Since, however, the statement made in hypothesis 6 can only be regarded as verified if a low degree of decision-making performance also leads to low time-pressure values—a low degree of sensitivity, however, provides no cause for limitation of activity—the testing design must be recognized as valid.

25. For the empirical obtaining of time-pressure values, see p. 74ff.

26. E. Witte, *Informationsverhalten* (1972), p. 52, succeeds in proving a connection between a high demand activity and a high degree of innovation, as well as between a low demand activity and a low degree of innovation of the decision. This finding is corroborated by Bronner, Witte, and Wossidlo, *Experimente,* p. 199ff. inasmuch as it pertains to the efficiency of the quantity of information demand.

27. In spite of its insufficiently significant markedness, the result on personal efficiency of function regulation in no way gives reason to expect negative effects on satisfaction. Quite the contrary, an increase in satisfaction would have to be assumed.

5   Consequences of the Theory of Decision Making under Time Pressure

The attempt at explanation presented here is based on a theoretical and methodological concept that finds its approach in three aspects of decision making under time pressure. The conditions for the occurrence of time pressure, behavior during problem solving under pressure, and the efficiency effect of problem-solving behavior form the parts of a system of theories. Having passed the experimental test, the now-verified hypotheses are the approach for a theory of decision making under time pressure. At the same time the question of the theoretical and praxeological consequences of these empirically substantiated statements arises.

Scientific interest was directed at two focal points of explanation: the effects of external pressures on decision-making performance and the efficiency of the decision, and the suitability of coordination measures for the regulating of decision making. The tests of the hypotheses revealed detailed relationships in these areas. Because of the isolated consideration of individual variables in certain testing intervals, it appears necessary, however, to arrive at a generalization of the statements.

The empirically ascertained fact of the existence of measures to regulate different effects makes it necessary to emphasize the performance character of the coordination instruments. Moreover, it is to be illustrated how problem intensity, which is connected generally with decision making, is reduced during the course of several repetitions of the process. A third attempt at generalization is to take up the question—independent of the specific effects of time pressure on individual performance and efficiency areas—as to whether pressures impair problem solving and whether they can be regarded as performance-stimulating elements.

The Performance Character of Decision-Making Regulation

Coordination has been differentiated analytically according to the direction of its effects. Regulative activities directed to the course of problem mastery were summarized under the concept of organization. Regulative measures determined with regard to the result of problem solving were designated as

143

goal setting. In the course of operationalization, it became necessary to differentiate by concrete structuring objects. Goal regulation, process regulation, and function regulation were considered as independent instruments of coordination. Now we will show that this differentiation is not arbitrary or made for purely terminological reasons, but that its justification results from a different aptitude. It is not a question here of the justification of conceptually or empirically determined demarcations but the instrumental way of effects, that is the different kinds of regulative quality which is in the foreground.

Goal Regulation

Compared with time restrictions, content-related determinations of the decision in the form of economic goals, criteria for evaluation, threshold values, or activity norms are extraordinarily stable. While other decision-making contributions under time pressure are restricted considerably, the efforts made in attaining result-oriented regulation remain unchanged. Obviously goal regulation is a largely problem-fixed kind of performance.

There is no recognizable relationship between goal regulation and personal efficiency. The fact of predetermined results and norms of action alone does not lead to satisfaction. This finding corroborates the assumption that goal regulation does not cause a directly discernible decision-making success. Also, the expectation that the predetermination of goals will reduce the intensity of the problem and thus facilitate the decision cannot be supported.

Time and economic efficiency are essentially determined by the extent of goal-setting coordination measures. Decision-making units with comparatively marked goal regulation generally realize more favorable values of economic result. However, they are also subject to greater time pressures than are decision-making units that regulate with less intensity. Accordingly, a coordination by predetermined decision-making goals embodies a more work-intensive type of performance, which has a positive effect on the result of problem solving.

The distinct resistance of goal-regulating coordination measures to time pressures and the clearly proved functional relationship to the economic result of decisions provide the arguments for the following characterization: goal regulation is the form of coordination that, independent of processual realities, is oriented to and affects the result of the problem solution. This statement is not intended as the formulation of the result of an empirically confirmed test. It is based on certain indications that justify such a formulation; there was, however, no explanation in the strict sense of the word, and a directed test was not undertaken. The finding determined here con-

Consequences of the Theory

cerning the performance character of goal regulation can therefore be solely understood in terms of a testable assertion, which, as a hypothesis, can be exposed to further attempts at verification.

Process Regulation

Measures emphasizing the coordination of time in the decision-making process are to a high degree unstable performances. They are essentially being restricted under time pressure and taken up again when these pressures abate. The influence of processual factors on the extent of regulation is, however, not so that requirement and fact of process regulation correspond to each other.

The requirement of course structuring is reflected in three findings:

1. In decision-making periods without pressure, there is a much stronger process coordination than in periods with strictly limited decision-making time. The necessity of time-oriented regulation is obviously recognized in situations of time distress; the regulative activity itself, however, is too exertive. With relief of time pressure, enhanced efforts to regulate the process set in. The aim is to avoid or reduce future pressures caused by time.
2. With little process regulation, there is a low degree of personal performance satisfaction. Insufficient coordination is felt to be an obstacle to performance and consequently leads to a lower degree of satisfaction.
3. However, the objective necessity of process-regulating interventions becomes visible within economic efficiency. It is higher the more measures are taken to regulate the process.

Both positive effects—an increase of satisfaction, as well as an improvement of economic efficiency—can be achieved by intensifying process-regulating measures without risking an aggravation of time pressure. In order to counter misunderstandings, the following must be emphasized: more-intensive efforts to reach a course-conscious structuring of problem-solving processes do not lead to an increase of time pressure, but neither do they lead to a decrease. Thus, process regulation is not a suitable instrument for the reduction of pressures caused by time.

Function Regulation

Structural interventions designed to determine the content of certain decision-making tasks—in the same way as process-regulating measures—are considerably reduced under time pressure. Contrary to process regulation, however, the restriction of function-regulating interventions does not have a negative effect on the economic efficiency of the decision. This means that function regulation does not contribute to efficiency. Correspondingly, a coordinating, and therefore positive, effect must be disallowed for function regulation. The fact that decision-making units with a comparatively high degree of function regulation realize less-favorable economic performance results contradicts all expectations concerning the effect of organizational efforts. There is no explanation in the sense of a deduced theory. Ex post facto attempts at explanation should therefore be undertaken with extreme caution. On the other hand, it appears inappropriate to consider such an empirical finding as purely coincidental.

On the other hand, the connection between the extent of function-regulating activities and the degree of personal performance satisfaction achieved in the individual cases can be interpreted more easily. It could even provide an approach to explaining the economic inefficiency of function regulation.

Organizational regulations aimed at the functional order of the course of decision making include instructions and norms of competency. They are to define the course of the decision under the aspect of the structural components of work content and work assignment.[1] The success of such coordinative efforts depends in two ways on the specific situational aptitude, that is, on the regulation adequacy of the structuring interventions. The expectation that instructions as formulated will be complied with, as well as their effect, will be greater when the regulation measures correspond to the regulation need, characterized primarily by the requirement for a time-adequate mastery of the decision-making tasks. It remains undisputed that this requirement may be supported by the aid of function-regulating measures; however, the necessity of process-directed coordination is more important. The more intensely the time pressures are perceived, the more pronounced the efforts are for process regulation and the less pronounced the efforts are for a function regulation.[2] If function-regulating instructions thus are given—by positions that produce less-intense pressure—these are considered to be unreasonable. They are not accepted and thus remain ignored. Moreover, the compulsion to reduce activity may prevent the compliance with function-regulating instructions.

These considerations see the explanation of economic inefficiency of function regulation in obstacles to enforcement and realization. Noncompliance with regulations is the cause of insufficient quality of performance results. By a reverse logical conclusion, however, a general efficiency of function-directed coordination measures would have to be deduced from this fact.

The Mastery of Problem Intensity

Repeated dealings with the same type of decision-making tasks lead to a reduction of problem intensity, a result of the development of an increasing decision-making routine.[3] In the course of repeated problem solving, decision makers learn to open up the cognitive fields of objective relationships and gain experience in the organizational processing of the problem-solving process.

It is not our goal here to analyze learning behavior in decision-making units systematically.[4] Moreover, the analysis of the course of individual decision-making intervals lies outside the possibilities of this experiment. Therefore, we can describe only the changes in the course of work of repeated decision-making.

The rise of problem-solving experience cannot be directly explained from modifications in the performance conditions. Nevertheless, the concrete effects of the factor of decision routine can be revealed as being a process for the reduction of problem intensity. It should be expected that a contrastive comparative analysis of the essential working conditions in the early and late periods of decision sequences provides insight into how the process of problem solving is increasingly mastered.[5]

The fact that problem intensity decreases over time is confirmed by a lower degree of time-pressure perception in the last sequences of the decision. It is again reflected in the increased interaction that occurs there. Activity, as well as the communication connected with it, reaches significantly higher values than in the first periods of decision making, which carry equal amounts of time pressure.[6]

Two central prerequisites for efficient decision finding are regarded as triggering conditions for the essential changes of the performance process: the quality of the cooperation within the decision-making units and the quality of the utilization of the information. The cognitive aspect of the exploration of the content of the problem and the organizational element of cooperation are suited to explain the mastery of the problem intensity in decision making.

Utilization of Information

The demand for information represents the basis for the mastery of the objective content of decision-making problems. We have already explained and shown the connection between the extent of the efforts to obtain information and the efficiency of decisions.[7] The quality of the utilization of the information may provide a supplementary explanation to this. It can further narrow the explicatory gap between the articulation of the need for information in decisions and the economic effect of solving the problem. References to the quality of utilization afford a deeper insight into the mastery of the cognitively caused problem intensity. Because in decision-making situations with little available time the demand for information is considerably reduced, the manner in which this quantitative reduction is connected with the qualitative level of cognitive performance is important.

The final periods of the decision-making sequences investigated here show both a small demand for information and an increasing problem mastery. Therefore the quantity of information appears to provide no explanation for the reduction of problem intensity. Rather, independent of the quantity of information available, analytical processing is improved with repeated problem solving. The lack of quantitatively insufficient cognitive orientation could then be partially compensated for by the quality of the utilization of the information.

It is difficult to measure directly the utilization of information so we will use an indirect measurement that has been employed already in the recording of time pressure. The test subjects were requested to render judgments on the assessment of information utilization at the end of each decision-making period. The objects of assessment were the receiving of necessary information—that is, the relevancy of the information received—as well as its evaluation and transmission within the decision-making unit:

The wording of the question and the scaling of possible answers are represented below:

Were you able to
(a) obtain the necessary information?

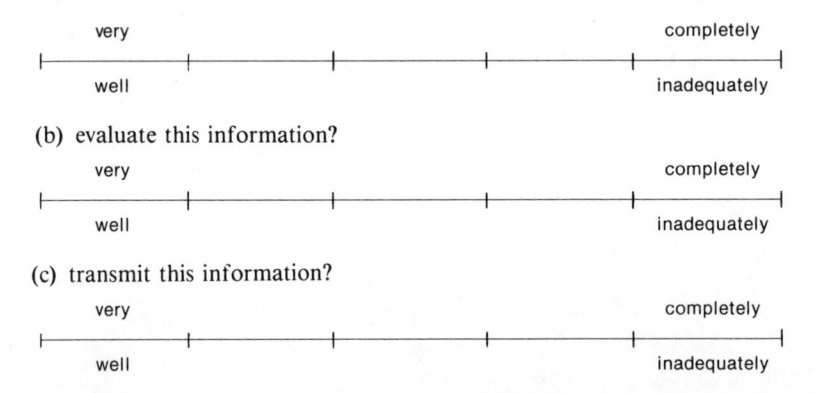

```
        very                                      completely
|-----------+-----------+-----------+-----------|
        well                                      inadequately
```

(b) evaluate this information?

```
        very                                      completely
|-----------+-----------+-----------+-----------|
        well                                      inadequately
```

(c) transmit this information?

```
        very                                      completely
|-----------+-----------+-----------+-----------|
        well                                      inadequately
```

These individual judgments by the decision makers, reduced to a group-related mean average, represented an objectivized measure of the utilization of information.

First it can be said that in the course of multiple repetitions of the deci-

Consequences of the Theory

sion-making process, the necessary information is present to an essentially greater extent than in early attempts at cognitive orientation.[8] Thus, the basis of potential mental processing is enlarged. However, this statement leaves open whether this result comes about because a greater amount of relevant information is received or because the relevancy of the information received is more clearly identified.

The quality of the evaluation of available data indicates the same positive effect. Apparently the decision makers are increasingly successful in interpreting the content of the respective information present in a more precise and more varied manner. Finally—and probably not independently from the first two effects—the transmission of the information necessary for the decision is improved.[9]

The mastery of the cognitive problem intensity of decision making exists in close connection with factors caused exclusively by the course of the decision-making situation. Processual and objective conditions influence each other mutually.

Mastery of Process

High organizational pressures that occur in initial problem solving within the framework of work-divisional decision-making processes impede the mastery of the objective tasks. Repeated dealings with performance demands of the same genre, however, lead to the mastery of the processual difficulties. The process of problem solving can be absolved easier in later repetitions than in earlier attempts. This assertion is supported by several empirical findings, which indicate unanimously that decision-making processes performed after multiple repetitions are conducted on a higher level of coordination.

Although the processes within the function groups of the decision-making units were not the focal point of interest, they gain significance in this context. The conception of the investigation therefore was intended to obtain testimony about group internal working conditions by interviewing the decision makers.

The variable is based on the judgments by the decision makers on the assessment of group internal cooperation between the team members and the cooperation between the function groups (staff and board of directors) of each decision-making unit. The test data were obtained by interviews at the end of each decision-making period. The precise text of the question including the scaling of answers is indicated below

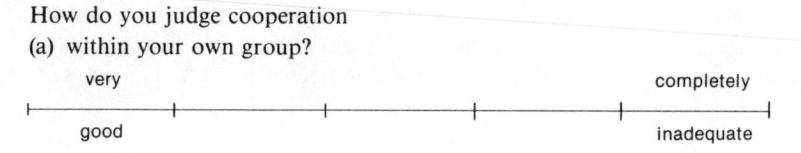

How do you judge cooperation
(a) within your own group?

very good — — — — — — completely inadequate

(b) with your staff or board of directors?

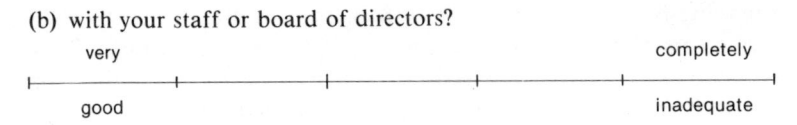

```
     very                                              completely
|-------------+-------------+-------------+-------------|
     good                                              inadequate
```

The cooperation within the work groups and the cooperation between them was greater in the last periods of the decision sequence than in the first three periods.[10] Apparently the decision makers increasingly succeed in reconciling the individual performances that, by necessity, is connected with the division of work. The same conclusion permits the clear limitation of criticism within the scope of mutual communication.[11] In sum, it is apparent that the processual component of problem intensity loses part of its pressuring effect during the course of repeated decision-making processes.

In spite of the existence of decision-regulating measures, it cannot be claimed that the reduction of the intensity of the problem, and as such the mastery of time pressure, is to be valued—alone or primarily—as the effect of empirically ascertained coordination. Such an absolute statement could hardly be proved. The partial effect of the documented goal, process, and function regulation is, however, undisputed. The reasonable assumption of undocumented, group internal coordinative efforts does not contradict this. Moreover, additional influences of intrapersonal performance regulation must be reckoned with.

There seems to be, however, a systematic connection between these three levels of problem mastery and the ordering processes that occur as a result of it. The view that "thinking and learning" is to be understood as "organizing" allows more than just analogous or conceptual considerations.[12] It emphasizes ordering as a requisite to cognitive performance.[13] Accordingly, the stronger a problem is marked by cognitive aspects, the higher the significance of ordering measures may be assessed. Ordering interventions that take place during the course of decision-making processes should thus be viewed essentially as an expression of growing problem mastery.[14]

The fact that processual organizational regulative measures are taken particularly in periods with only minor time pressure indicates the significance of intervals free from pressure. Constant time pressure implies the binding of all performance resources in the processing of the objective tasks that appear to be the most urgent. Time compulsion to achieve short-term work orientation permits only little general regulation.

Decision-making units can predetermine the course of problem solving to an increased extent only in periods devoid of pressure. In this way they create the basis for an increasing mastery of the process. The satisfaction of the decision makers and their willingness to perform are increased. The processually caused problem intensity decreases and leads to a reduction of time pressure, providing the prerequisites for a qualified solution of the problem. It becomes clear how much not only the degree of stress but also its duration determine the possibilities to master it. Constant time pressure prevents the development of effective measures of adaption.

The Effectiveness of Time Pressure

Clearly time pressure causes an essential limitation of almost all decision-making activities. Moreover, the efficiency-reducing effect of performance limitations has been verified. Accordingly, it would have to be expected that decision-making units with a high time-pressure sensitivity realize less-positive results. The empirical finding, however, clearly refutes this assumption.

**Table 5-1
Comparison of Success (after Ten Experiment Periods), by Time-Pressure Sensitivity**

Test Values	Decision-Making Units with Low Sensitivity	Decision-Making Units with High Sensivitivy
Mean value	− 0.50	27.56
Standard deviation	6.52	15.29
Number (n)	5	7
Significance	$-p < 0.001$	

The data presented in table 5-1 allow the following statement: high sensitivity to time pressure does not negatively affect the economic result of decisions. Further, decision-making units with a high degree of time-pressure sensitivity achieve a significantly greater overall success than less-sensitive decision-making units. This finding, which might seem surprising, is to be combined with the thesis of the effectiveness of time pressure. It should not be interpreted that the existence of time pressure should be viewed as desirable and virtually as a prerequisite to efficient performance results. A statement of this kind would contradict the results obtained so far. In principle, time pressure leads to a reduction in performance and causes a lower degree of efficiency in the realization of decisions made under these conditions. The effectiveness of time pressure is not confirmed in the comparison of decision-making time and decision-making efficiency but in the different forms of coping with stress.

In decision-making units that register high degrees of time limitation, the quality of problem solving is less endangered than in decision-making units that seem to ignore the existence of the same facts. The clear recognition of time pressure—the perception of a strong pressure—implies a marked awareness of the problem of time restriction and generates the ability to achieve an adequate mastery of stress. High sensitivity signifies strong time pressures; however, it also causes intensive efforts to reduce the pressure. In contrast, less sensitive decision-making units do not reach the same measure of process awareness. They develop a modest adaptive behavior by limiting performances irrespective of the effect. Process-regulating measures that have a positive influence on the course, as well as on the economic result, of the decisions are employed to a lower degree than in the more-sensitive decision-making units.[15]

Despite the different intensity of the changes in performance, the behavioral tendency of adaption for the mastery of stress remains apparent: the general limitation of the decision-making activities. It is the result of autonomous attempts at adapting to a given framework of conditions. The fact that the reduction of interventions for the purpose of process regulation cannot be valued as an adequate behavior under time pressure has already been proved in detail. Any renunciation of process-regulating coordination measures signifies a threefold inefficiency. The foremost goal of a relief from time pressure is not attained. There is a lack of instructions that could guarantee or facilitate a timely course of problem solving. The insufficient order of the course of problem solving is reflected in the personal performance judgments and endangers the willingness on the part of the decision makers to perform. Consequently, these circumstances lead to poorer economic decision-making results. It can be assumed that the difficulties created by this situation affect subsequent decision-making processes.

The existence of time pressure in otherwise freely structurable decision-making situations triggers an organizational behavior that is inimical to the situation. Mechanistic and homeostatic concepts that were useful explicative approaches in the biological, physical, and humanistic disciplines, prove to be little suited here. Decision-making processes under time pressure require directed regulation.

Notes

1. E. Witte, *Ablauforganisation* (1969), col. 24ff.
2. For this see tables 3-9 and 4-11.
3. See p. 26 and table 4-4.
4. See the comprehensive investigations by E. Kappler, *Systementwicklung* (1972), and O. Grün, *Lernverhalten* (1973).
5. V.E. Cangelosi, and W.R. Dill, *Organizational Learning* (1965-

1966), emphasize the central significance of stress as an intensifier of learning behavior.

6. With $p = 0.001$, the time-pressure index of periods 8–10 is smaller than in periods 1–3. In the same intervals the test values of activity differ significantly by $p = 0.037$. With $p = 0.003$, the communication of the late testing interval lies clearly over the communications level in the early stage of problem mastery.

7. See E. Witte, *Informationsverhalten* (1972); R. Bronner, E. Witte, and P.R. Wossidlo, *Experimente* (1972), p. 195ff.; as well as p. 134ff above.

8. With $p = 0.002$ the assessment values on the receipt of relevant information differ significantly.

9. With $p < 0.001$ the test data on the evaluation of information and with $p = 0.019$ the test data on the transmission differ significantly.

10. With $p < 0.001$ the test data on internal cooperation provide a proved, significant difference of values. The assessment values on group combining (external) cooperation differ at a significance level of $p = 0.030$.

11. The measurement values on documented criticism prove a mean value difference at $p < 0.001$.

12. K. Müller, *Denken* (1964).

13. See R. Bergius, *Produktives Denken* (1964), p. 536, and G. Kaminski, *Ordnungsstrukturen* (1964), p. 453.

14. See O. Grün, *Lernverhalten* (1973), p. 231ff.

15. Decision-making units with a high degree of time-pressure sensitivity coordinate the course of the problem-solving process at a higher level of process regulation—rated at $p = 0.012$—than do decision-making units with a low degree of time-pressure sensitivity.

Appendix

Communication Sheet

Sender   Receiver

☐ Board of Directors ☐
☐ Staff ☐

Enterprise
Game period
Number
Re: your letter
Time

☐ General ☐
☐ Plant ☐
☐ Marketing ☐
☐ Finances ☐

☐ Information Center ☐

TEXT

_____
_____
_____
_____
_____
_____
_____
_____
_____
_____
_____
_____
_____
_____
_____
_____

Cost Limit:

Operations Matrix

Operations		\multicolumn{12}{c}{Objects}
		Opinion	Information	Reply	Alternative	Period of Time	Sequence	Point in Time	Task	Goal Setting	Decision	Achieved Result	Environment
ACTIVITIES	No.	11	12	13	20	31	32	33	34	40	50	60	70
Conveying	11												
Requesting	12												
Determining	21												
Urging	22												
Delaying	23												
Modifying	24												
Recommending	31												
Dissuading	32												
Criticizing	33												
Accepting	34												

Appendix

Questionnaire

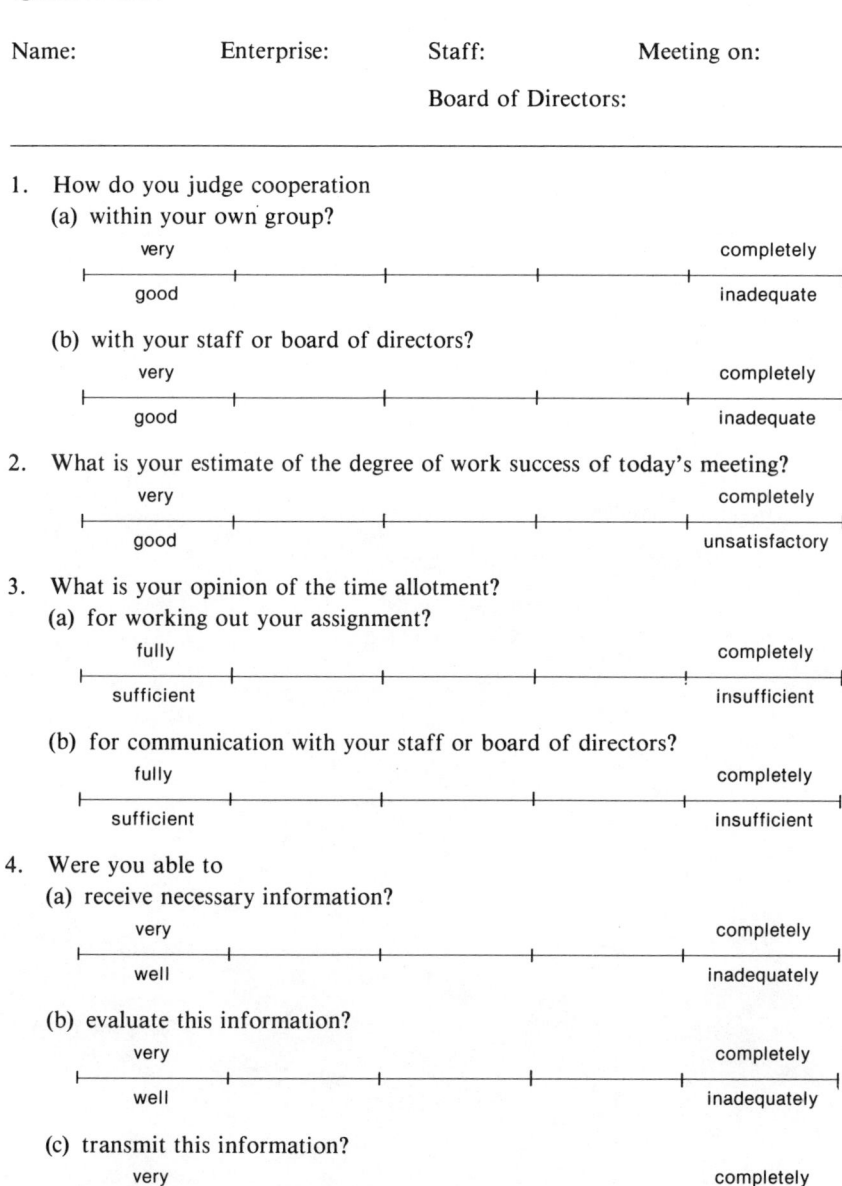

Name: Enterprise: Staff: Meeting on:

                                    Board of Directors:

---

1. How do you judge cooperation
   (a) within your own group?

   | very good | | | | completely inadequate |

   (b) with your staff or board of directors?

   | very good | | | | completely inadequate |

2. What is your estimate of the degree of work success of today's meeting?

   | very good | | | | completely unsatisfactory |

3. What is your opinion of the time allotment?
   (a) for working out your assignment?

   | fully sufficient | | | | completely insufficient |

   (b) for communication with your staff or board of directors?

   | fully sufficient | | | | completely insufficient |

4. Were you able to
   (a) receive necessary information?

   | very well | | | | completely inadequately |

   (b) evaluate this information?

   | very well | | | | completely inadequately |

   (c) transmit this information?

   | very well | | | | completely inadequately |

**Personal Data Sheet
for Participants in Business Game Topic 1**

1. Name:_____ Year of birth:_____
2. Title:_____
3. Occupation and rank:_____

4. Highest degree held:_____
5. How long have you been employed?_____

6. Employed at:_____
7. In which position/department are you currently employed?_____

8. Does this position/department have more the character of a staff or rather that of an operative department?_____

Bibliography

Abelmann, Xenia, *Beobachtung und Experiment* (1965). "Zum Verhältnis von Beobachtung and Experiment," in: *Struktur und Funktion der experimentellen Methode,* edited by Heinrich Parthey; Heinrich Vogel; Wolfgang Wächter; and Dietrich Wahl. Rostock, 1965:179-186.

Abelson, Robert P., et al. eds., *Consistency* (1968). Theories of Cognitive Consistency—A Sourcebook, edited by Robert P. Abelson; Elliot Aronson; William J. McGuire; Theodore M. Newcomb; Milton J. Rosenberg; and Percy H. Tannenbaum. Chicago, 1968.

Adam, A., *Systematische Datenverarbeitung* (1963). Systematische Datenverarbeitung bei der Auswertung von Versuchs- and Beobachtungsergebnissen. Würzburg, 1963.

Albach, Horst, *Wirtschaftlichkeitsrechnung* (1959). Wirtschaftlichkeitsrechnung bei unsicheren Erwartungen. Köln-Opladen, 1959.

——. *Entscheidungsprozess* (1961). "Entscheidungsprozess und Informationsfluss in der Unternehmensorganisation," in: *Organisation, TFB-Handbuch,* vol. 1, edited by Erich Schnaufer, and Klaus Agthe. Berlin-Baden-Baden, 1961:355-402.

Albert, Hans, *Theoriebildung* (1964). "Probleme der Theoriebildung—Entwicklung, Struktur und Anwendung sozialwissenschaftlicher Theorien," in: *Theorie und Realität,* edited by Hans Albert. Tübingen, 1964:3-70.

——. *Wissenschaftslehre* (1967). "Probleme der Wissenschaftslehre in der Sozialforschung," in: *Handbuch der Empirischen Sozialforschung,* vol. 1, edited by René König, 2d ed. Stuttgart, 1967:38-63.

——. *Traktat* (1969). Traktat über kritische Vernunft. Tübingen, 1969.

——. *Theorie* (1970). "Theorie, Verstehen und Geschichte," in: *Zeitschrift für allgemeine Wissenschaftstheorie,* vol. 1, 1970:3-23.

——. *Theorie und Prognose* (1971). "Theorie und Prognose in den Sozialwissenschaften," in: *Logik der Sozialwissenschaften,* edited by Ernst Topitsch, 7th ed. Köln-Berlin, 1971:126-143.

Alexander, F., Homöostase (1966). "Homöostase und überschüssige Energie," in: *Die Motivation menschlichen Handelns,* edited by Hans Thomae. Köln-Berlin, 1966:474-478.

Appley, Mortimer H., and Trumbull, Richard, *Stress* (1967). "On the Concept of Psychological Stress," in: *Psychological Stress—Issues in Research,* edited by Mortimer H. Appley, and Richard Trumbull. New York 1967:1-13.

Aronson, Elliot, and Carlsmith, Merrill J. *Experimentation* (1968). "Experimentation in Social Psychology," in *The Handbook of Social Psychology,* vol. 2: Research Methods, 2d ed., edited by Gardner Lindzey and Elliot Aronson. Reading, Mass.-Menlo Park, Cal.-London-Don Mills, Ont., 1968:1-79.

Aronson, Elliot, and Landy, David, *Excess Time Effect* (1967). "Further Steps Beyond Parkinson's Law: A Replication and Extension of the Excess Time Effect," in: *Journal of Experimental Social Psychology,* vol. 3, 1967:274-285.

Asch, Solomon E., *Social Pressure* (1964). "Opinions and Social Pressure," in: *Readings in Managerial Psychology,* edited by Harold J. Leavitt and Louis R. Pondy. Chicago-London, 1964:304-314.

Athos, Antony G., and Coffey, Robert E., *Behavior* (1968). Behavior in Organizations—A Multidimensional View. Englewood Cliffs, N.J., 1968.

Atteslander, Peter, *Interaktiogramm* (1963). "Das Interaktiogramm, eine Methode der Verhaltensforschung im Industriebetrieb," in: *Die Unternehmung,* 17th yr., 1963:121-130.

———. *Methoden* (1969). Methoden der empirischen Sozialforschung. Berlin, 1969.

Bales, Robert, and Borgatta, Edgar F., *Size of Group* (1962). "Size of Group as a Factor in the Interaction Profile," in: *Small Groups. Studies in Social Interaction,* edited by A. Paul Hare; Edgar F. Borgatta; and Robert F. Bales. New York, 1962:396-413.

Bartmann, Theodor, *Zeitdruck* (1963). "Der Einfluss von Zeitdruck auf die Leistung und das Denkverhalten bei Volksschülern, in: *Psychologische Forschung,* 27, 1963:1-61.

Bass, Bernard M., *Business Gaming* (1964). "Business Gaming for Organizational Research," in: *Management Science,* vol. 10, 1964:545-556.

———. *Experimental Techniques* (1964). "Production Organization Exercise: An Application of Experimental Techniques to Business Games," in: *New Perspectives in Organizational Research,* edited by W.W. Cooper; H.J. Leavitt; and M.W. Shelley II. New York-London-Sydney, 1964:97-114.

Bender, Kurt, *Führungsentscheidung* (1957). Die Führungsentscheidung im Betrieb. Stuttgart, 1957.

Bendixen, Peter, *Komplexität* (1967). "Die Komplexität von Entscheidungssituationen—Kritik am Formalismus der betriebswirtschaftlichen Entscheidungstheorie," in: *Kommunikation,* vol. 3, 1967:103-114.

Bergius, Rudolf, *Produktives Denken* (1964). "Produktives Denken—Problemlösen," in: *Handbuch der Psychologie,* vol. 2. part 2.: Lernen und Denken, edited by Rudolf Bergius, 2d. ed. Göttingen, 1964:519-563.

Bertalanffy, Ludwig v., *Theoretical Models* (1951). "Theoretical Models in Biology and Psychology," in: *Journal of Personality,* vol. 20, 1951: 24-38.

Bibliography

Bettelheim, Bruno, *Extreme Situations* (1958). "Individual and Mass Behavior in Extreme Situations," in: *Readings in Social Psychology*, edited by Eleanor E. Maccoby; Theodor M. Newcomb; and Eugene L. Hartley, 3d ed. New York, 1958:300-310.

Biasio, Silvio, *Entscheidung* (1969). Entscheidung als Prozess. Bern-Stuttgart-Wien, 1969.

Bidlingmaier, Johannes, *Unternehmerziele* (1964). Unternehmerziele und Unternehmerstrategien. Wiesbaden, 1964.

Bierfelder, Wilhelm, *Informationsverhalten* (1968). Optimales Informationsverhalten im Entscheidungsprozess der Unternehmung. Berlin, 1968.

Blalock, Hubert M., Jr., *Theory Building* (1968). "Theory Building and Causal Inferences," in: *Methodology in Social Research*, edited by Hubert M. Blalock, Jr., and Ann B. Blalock. New York-St. Louis-San Franciso-Toronto-London-Sydney, 1968:155-198.

Blau, Peter M., and Scott, W. Richard, *Organizations* (1963). Formal Organizations—A Comparative Approach. London, 1963.

Bleicher, Knut, *Simulationsmodelle* (1962). Unternehmungsspiele—Simulationsmodelle für unternehmerische Entscheidungen. Baden-Baden, 1962.

———. *Unternehmungsspiele* (1966). "Unternehmungsspiele als Erkenntnismittel für Ausbildung und Forschung," in: *Führung in der Wirtschaft*. Bad Harzburg, 1966:159-185.

Bonini, Charles P., *Simulation* (1963). Simulation of Information and Decisions Systems in the Firm. Englewood Cliffs, N.J., 1963.

———. *Simulating* (1964). "Simulating Organizational Behavior," in: *New Perspectives in Organizational Research*, edited by W.W. Cooper; H.J. Leavitt; and M.W. Shelly II. New York-London-Sydney, 1964: 276-288.

Bovard, Everett W., *Stress* (1969). "The Effects of Social Stimuli on the Response to Stress," in: *The Psychological Review*, vol. 66, 1959:267-275.

Bower, J.L., *Group Decision Making* (1965). "Group Decision Making: A Report of an Experimental Study," in: *Behavioral Science*, vol. 10, 1965:277-289.

Braybrooke, David, and Lindblom, Charles E., *Strategy* (1963). A Strategy of Decision. Policy Evaluation as a Social Process. London, 1963.

Brehm, Jack W., and Cohen, Arthur R., *Dissonance* (1962). Explorations in Cognitive Dissonance. New York-London-Sydney, 1962.

Brillouin, L., *Empirical Laws* (1962). "Empirical Laws and Physical Theories; The Respective Roles of Information and Imagination," in: *Self-Organizing Systems*, edited by Marshall C. Yovites; George T. Jacobi; and Gordon D. Goldstein. Washington, 1962:231-242.

Brim, Orville G., Jr.; Glass, David C.; Lavin, David E.; and Goodmann, Norman, *Decision Processes Studies* (1962). Personality and Decision

Processes Studies in the Social Psychology of Thinking. Stanford, Cal., 1962.
Broadbent, D.E., *Stress* (1971). Decision and Stress. London-New York, 1971.
Bronner, Rolf; Witte, Eberhard; and Wossidlo, Peter Rütger, *Experimente* (1972). "Betriebswirtschaftliche Experimente zum Informations-Verhalten in Entscheidungs-Prozessen," in: Witte, E.: *Das Informationsverhalten in Entscheidungsprozessen.* Tübingen, 1972:165-203.
Buchanan, James McGill, *Ceteris paribus* (1971). "Ceteris paribus: Einige Bemerkungen zur Methodologie," in: *Gegenstand und Methoden der Nationalökonomie,* edited by Reimut Jochimsen, and Helmut Knobel. Köln, 1971:285-296.
Buggle, Franz, *Diagnostik* (1969). "Methoden psychologischer Diagnostik," in: *Enzyklopädie der geisteswissenschaftlichen Arbeitsmethoden,* issue 7: *Methoden der Psychologie und Pädagogik.* München-Wien, 1969:72-85.
Bullis, Harry A., *Making Decisions* (1967). "Making decisions," in: *For Executives Only.* An Anthology of the Best Management Thought, edited by The Dartnell Corporation. Chicago-London, 1967:125-142.
Cangelosi, Vincent E., and Dill, William R., *Organizational Learning* (1965/66). "Organizational Learning: Observations Toward a Theory," in: *Administrative Science Quarterly,* vol. 10, 1965/66:175-203.
Carlsson, Gösta, *Funktionalismus* (1965). "Betrachtungen zum Funktionalismus," in: *Logik der Sozialwissenschaften,* edited by Ernst Topitsch, 2d ed. Köln-Berlin, 1965:236-261.
Cartwright, Dorwin, and Zander, Alvin, *Issues* (1968). "Issues and Basic Assumptions," in: *Group Dynamics—Research and Theory,* 3d ed., edited by Dorwin Cartwright and Alvin Zander. New York-Evanston-London, 1968:22-42.
Carzo, Rocco, Jr., and Yanouzas, John N., *Effects* (1969). "Effects of Flat and Tall Organization Structure," in: *Administrative Science Quarterly,* vol. 14, 1969:178-191.
Cattell, Raymond R., *Experimental Design* (1966). "The Principles of Experimental Design and Analysis in Relation to Theory Building," in: *Handbook of Multivariate Experimental Psychology,* edited by Raymond B. Cattell. Chicago, 1966:19-66.
Chapin, Stuart F., *Experiment* (1967). "Das Experiment in der soziologischen Forschung," in: *Beobachtung und Experiment in der Sozialforschung, Praktische Sozialforschung II,* 5th ed., edited by René König. Köln-Berlin, 1967:221-258.
Chapman, Robert L.; Kennedy, John L.; Newell, Allen; and Riel, William C., *Experiments* (1959). "The System Research Laboratory's Air Defense Experiments," in: *Management Science,* vol. 5, 1959:250-269.

Bibliography

Churchman, C. West, *Ungewissheit* (1970). "Ungewissheit, Wahrscheinlichkeit und Risiko," in: *Planung und Entscheidung,* edited by Walter Haseloff. Berlin, 1970:97-107.

Clausewitz, Carl v., *Vom Kriege* (1960). "Vom Kriege," in: *Die Grossen Meister der Kriegskunst,* edited by Ihno Krumpelt. Frankfurt/M., 1960:3-113.

Cohen, Arthur R., *Attitude Change* (1964). Attitude Change and Social Influence. New York-London, 1964.

Cohen, Kalman J., and Rhenman, Eric, *Management Games* (1961). "The Role of Management Games in Education and Research," in: *Management Science,* vol. 7, 1961:131-166.

Cohen, Kalman J., and Cyert, Richard M., *Simulation* (1965). "Simulation of Organizational Behavior," in: *Handbook of Organization,* edited by James G. March. Chicago, 1965:305-334.

Cohen, S.I.; Silverman, A.J.; and Shmavonian, B.M., *Human Adaptation* (1959). "The Measurement of Human Adaptation to Stressful Environments," in: *General Systems,* edited by Ludwig von Bertalanffy and Anatol Rapoport, vol. 4, 1959:231-241.

Collins, Barry E., and Guetzkow, Harold, *Group Processes* (1964). A social Psychology of Group Processes for Decision-Making. New York-London-Sydney, 1964.

Cox, D.R., *Experiments* (1958). Planning of Experiments. New York-London-Sydney, 1958.

Cranach, Mario v., *Selbstzensur* (1968). "Selbstzensur der Neugier," in: *BP-Kurier,* 20th yr, vol. 1, 1968:34-37.

Cyert, Richard M.; Simon, Herbert A.; and Trow, Donald B., *Businesss Decision* (1960). "Observation of a Business Decision," in: *Some Theories of Organization,* edited by Albert H. Rubenstein and Chadwick J. Haberstroh. Homewood, Ill., 1960:458-472.

Cyert, Richard M., and March, James G., *Behavioral Theory* (1963). A Behavioral Theory of the Firm. Englewood Cliffs, N.J., 1963.

Davis, James H., *Experimenter Presence* (1968). "Verbalization, Experimenter Presence and Problem Solving," in: *Journal of Personality and Social Psychology,* vol. 8, 1968:299-302.

Davis, R.C., *Homöostase* (1966). "Die Domäne der Homöostase," in: *Motivation menschlichen Handelns,* edited by Hans Thomae. Köln-Berlin,1966:479-487.

Dawson, Richard E., *Simulation* (1962). "Simulation in the Social Sciences," in: *Simulation in Social Science,* edited by Harold Guetzkow. Englewood Cliffs, N.J., 1962:1-15.

Dienstbach, Horst, *Anpassung* (1968). Die Anpassung der Unternehmungs-Organisation. Zur betriebswirtschaftlichen Bedeutung der Konzeption des "planned organizational change." Dissertation, München, 1968.

Dill, William R., *Decision-Making* (1962). "Administrative Decision-Making," in: *Concepts and Issues in Administrative Behavior,* edited by Sydney Mailick and Edward H. Van Ness. Englewood Cliffs, N.J., 1962:29-48.

Drabek, Thomas E., *Laboratory Simulation* (1969). Laboratory Simulation of a Police Communications System under Stress. Columbus, Ohio, 1969.

Dubin, Robert, *Stability* (1959). "Stability of Human Organizations," in: *Modern Organization Theory,* edited by Mason Haire, New York-London—Sydney, 1959:218-253.

Durkheim, Emile, *Regeln* (1965). Die Regeln der soziologischen Methode, 2d ed. Neuwied, 1965.

Eberlein, Gerald, *Experiment* (1963). "Experiment und Erfahrung in der Soziologie," in: *Experiment in Wissenschaft und Kunst,* edited by Walter Strolz. Freiburg-München, 1953:101-136.

Einstein, Albert, and Infeld, Leopold, *Physik* (1956). Die Evolution in der Physik, 1956.

Ekman, Gösta, and Lundberg, Ingvar, *Theorie und Messung* (1969). "Über Theorie und Messung in der Psychologie," in: *Enzyklopädie der geisteswissenschaftlichen Arbeitsmethoden,* edited by Manfred Thiel, issue 7: Methoden der Psychologie und Pädagogik. München-Wien, 1969:159-219.

Eulenburg, Franz, *Organisation* (1952). Das Geheimnis der Organisation, aus dem Nachlass, edited by Georg Jahn. Berlin, 1952.

Eyferth, Klaus, *Gruppenstrukturen* (1963). "Erfassung von Gruppenstrukturen, Hemmnisse experimenteller Sozialpsychologie," in: *Lehrbuch der experimentellen Psychologie,* edited by Richard Meili and Hubert Rohracher. Bern-Stuttgart, 1963:388-402.

Feger, Hubert, *Bedeutsamkeit* (1968). Untersuchungen zur Bedeutsamkeit von Entscheidungssituationen—Ein experimenteller Beitrag. Dissertation. Bonn, 1968.

Feldman, Julian, and Kanter, Herschel E., *Decision Making* (1965). "Organizational Decision Making," in: *Handbook of Organizations,* edited by James G. March. Chicago, 1965:614-649.

Festinger, Leon, *Laboratory Experiments* (1953). "Laboratory Experiments," in: *Research Methods in the Behavioral Sciences,* edited by Leon Festinger and Daniel Katz. New York-Chicago-San Francisco-Toronto-London, 1953:136-172.

———. *Comparison Processes* (1954). "A Theory of Social Comparison Processes," in: *Human Relations,* vol. 7, 1954:117-140.

———. *Dissonance* (1957). A Theory of Cognitive Dissonance. London, 1957.

———. *Social Communication* (1960). "Informal Social Communication," in: *Group Dynamics, Research and Theory,* 2d ed., edited by Dorwin Cartwright, and Alvin Xander. London, 1960:286-299.

Festinger, Leon, and Carlsmith, James M. *Kognitive Folgen* (1969). "Kognitive Folgen erzwungener Zustimmung," in: *Texte aus der experimentellen Sozialpsychologie,* edited by Martin Irle with Mario v. Granach and Hermann Vetter. Neuwied-Berlin, 1969:325-342.

Fischer, Hardi, *Forschungsmethoden* (1957). Die modernen pädagogischen und psychologischen Forschungsmethoden—Eine Einführung. Göttingen, 1957.

Flood, Merrill M. *Decision-Making Experiments* (1954). "Game-learning Theory and Some Decision-Making Experiments," in: *Decision Processes,* edited by R.M. Thrall; C.H. Coombs; and R.L. Davis. New York-London, 1954:139-158.

Francis, E.K., *Grundlagen* (1957). Wissenschaftliche Grundlagen soziologischen Denkens. München, 1957.

French, John R, *Experiments* (1953). "Experiments in Field Settings," in: *Research Methods in the Behavioral Sciences,* edited by Leon Festinger and Daniel Katz. New York-Chicago-San Francisco-Toronto-London:1953:98-135.

Freud, Sigmund, *Psychoanalyse* (1953). Abriss der Psychoanalyse. Frankfurt/M., 1953. Reprint of first edition.

———. *Psychopathologie* (1947). Zur Psychopathologie des Alltagslebens, 12th ed. London, 1947.

———. *Verdrängung* (1965). "Die Verdrängung," in: *Die Motivation menschlichen Handelns,* edited by Hans Thomae. Köln-Berlin, 1965: 311-330.

Gäfgen, Gèrard, *Entscheidung* (1968). Theorie der wirtschaftlichen Entscheidung, 2d ed. Tübingen, 1968.

Goode, William J., and Hatt, Paul K., *Methode* (1967). "Grundelemente der wissenschaftlichen Methode," in: *Beobachtung und Experiment in der Sozialforschung,* 5th ed., edited by René König. Köln-Berlin, 1967:51-75.

Goode, William J., *Rollenstress* (1967). "Eine Theorie des Rollen-Stress," in: *Moderne Amerikanische Soziologie—Neuere Beiträge zur soziologischen Theorie.* Stuttgart, 1967:269-286.

Gore, William J., *Essay on Decision-Making* (1959). "A Bibliographical Essay on Decision-Making," in: *Administrative Science Quarterly,* vol. 19, 1959:97-121.

———. *Decision-Making* (1964). Administrative Decision-Making. New York-London-Sydney, 1964.

Greenwood, Ernest, *Experiment* (1967). "Das Experiment in der Soziologie," in: *Beobachtung und Experiment in der Sozialforschung—Praktische Sozialforschung II,* 5th ed., edited by Renè König. Köln-Berlin, 1967:171-220.

Grinker, Roy R., and Spiegel, John P., *Stress* (1945). Men under Stress. Philadelphia, 1945.
Grochla, Erwin, *Modelle* (1969). "Modelle als Instrumente der Unternehmensführung," in: *Zeitschrift für betriebswirtschaftliche Forschung, N.F.,* 21st yr., 1969.
Grün, Oskar, *Lernverhalten* (1973). Das Lernverhalten in Entscheidungsprozessen der Unternehmung, Tübingen, 1973.
Grunberg, Emile, *Wirtschaftswissenschaft* (1971). "Gegenstand und externe Grenzen der Wirtschaftswissenschaft," in: *Gegenstand und Methoden der Nationalökonomie,* edited by Reimut Jochimsen and Helmut Knobel. Köln, 1971:69-87.
Guetzkow, Harold, and Simon, Herbert A., *Communication Nets* (1960). "The Impact of Certain Communication Nets upon Organization and Performance in Task-oriented Groups," in: *Some Theories of Organization,* edited by Albert H. Rubenstein and Chadwick J. Haberstroh. Homewood, Ill., 1960:259-277.
Guetzkow, Harold, and Gyr, John, *Conflict* (1964). "An Analysis of Conflict in Decision-Making Groups," in: *Human Relations,* vol. 7, 1964: 367-381.
Gzuk, Roland, *Effizienz* (1975). Messung der Effizienz von Entscheidungsprozessen. Tübingen, 1975.
Habermas, Jürgen, *Logik* (1970). Zur Logik der Sozialwissenschaften—Materialen. Frankfurt/M., 1970.
Hage, Jerald, *Organizations* (1965). "An Axiomatic Theory of Organizations," in: *Administrative Science Quarterly,* vol. 3, 1965:289-320.
Haire, Mason, *Psychology* (1964). Psychology in Management. New York-San Francisco-London-Toronto, 2d ed., 1964.
Hall, Douglas T., and Mansfield, Roger, *External Stress* (1971). "Organizational and Individual Response to External Stress," in: *Administrative Science Quarterly,* vol. 16, 1971:533-547.
Hall, Douglas, T., and Lawler, Edward E., *Job Characteristics* (1970). "Job Characteristics and Pressures and the Organizational Integration of Professionals," in: *Administrative Science Quarterly,* vol. 15, 1970: 271-281.
Hamel, Winfried, *Zieländerungen* (1974). Zieländerungen im Entscheidungsprozess. Tübingen, 1974.
Hare, Paul A., *Handbook* (1967). Handbook of Small Group Research. New York-London, 1967.
Harlow, Harry F., *Experimental Analysis* (1957). "Experimental Analysis of Behavior," in: *The American Psychologist,* vol. 12, 1957:485-490.
Hartmann, Heinz, *Sozialforschung* (1970). Empirische Sozialforschung, part 2. München, 1970.
Haseloff, Otto W., *Risiko* (1970). "Schicksalsideologie, Risiko und ratio-

Bibliography

nale Entscheidung," in: *Planung und Entscheidung,* edited by Walter Haseloff. Berlin, 1970:127-142.
Hax, Herbert, *Koordination* (1965). Die Koordination von Entscheidungen. Köln-Berlin-Bonn-München, 1965.
Hayek, F.A. *Primat* (1970). "Der Primat des Abstrakten," in: *Das neue Menschenbild,* edited by Arthur Koestler and J.R. Smythies. Wien-München-Zürich, 1970:300-313.
Heinen, Edmund, *Zielsystem* (1966). Das Zielsystem der Unternehmung. Wiesbaden, 1966.
———. *Einführung* (1970). Einführung in die Betriebswirtschaftslehre, 3d ed. Wiesbaden, 1970.
———. *Entscheidungen* (1971). Grundlagen betriebswirtschaftlicher Entscheidungen. Das Zielsystem der Unternehmung, 2d ed. Wiesbaden, 1971.
Heisenberg, Werner, *Der Teil* (1969). Der Teil und das Ganze—Gespräche im Umkreis der Atomphysik. München, 1969.
Hendrick, Clyde; Mills, Judson; and Kiesler, Charles A., *Decision Time* (1968). "Decision Time as a Function of the Number and Complexity of Equally Attractive Alternatives," in: *Journal of Personality and Social Psychology,* vol. 8, 1968:313-318.
Hermann, Charles F., *Crisis* (1963/64). "Some Consequences of Crisis Which Limit the Viability of Organizations," in: *Administrative Science Quarterly,* vol. 8, 1963/64:61-82.
Hesselbach, J., *Verhaltensforschung* (1970). "Verhaltensforschung bei unternehmerischen Entscheidungen," in: *Zeitschrift für Betriebswirtschaft,* 40th yr., 1970:647-664.
Hesseling, Pjotr, and Können, Erik, *Decision-Making Exercise* (1969). "Culture and Subculture in a Decision-Making Exercise," in: *Human Relations,* vol. 22, 1969:31-51.
Heuer, Wilhelm, *Kausalität* (1935). Vom Wesen der Kausalität—Grundfragen der Erkenntnistheorie. Heidelberg, 1935.
Heyns, Roger W., and Zander, Alvin F., *Observation* (1953). "Observation of Group Behavior," in: *Research Methods in the Behavioral Sciences,* edited by Leon Festinger, and Daniel Katz. New York-Chicago-San Francisco-Toronto-London, 1953:381-417.
Hodnett, Edward, *Problem Solving* (1955). The Art of Problem Solving. How to Improve Your Methods. New York, 1955.
Holsti, Ole R.; Loomba, Joanne K.; and North, Robert C., *Content Analysis* (1968). "Content Analysis," in: *The Handbook of Social Psychology,* vol. 2, 2d ed., edited by Gardner Lindzey, and Elliot Aronson. Reading, Mass.-Menlo Park, Cal.-London—Don Mills, Ont., 1968: 596-692.
Holzkamp, Klaus, *Theorie und Experiment* (1964). Theorie und Experi-

ment in der Psychologie—Eine grundlagen-kritische Untersuchung. Berlin, 1964.

——. *Voraussetzungen* (1970). "Wissenschaftstheoretische Voraussetzungen kritischemanzipatorischer Psychologie," in: *Zeitschrift für Sozialpsychologie,* vol. 1, 1970:5-21, 109-141.

Holzman, P.S., and Gardner, R.W., *Ausgleichen* (1966). "Ausgleichen und Verdrängen," in: *Die Motivation menschlichen Handelns,* edited by Hans Thomae. Köln-Berlin, 1966:331-338.

Homans, George C., *Gruppe* (1972). Theorie der Sozialen Gruppe, 6th ed., Opladen, 1972.

Hoppe, F., *Anspruchsniveau* (1966). "Das Anspruchsniveau," in: *Die Motivation menschlichen Handelns,* edited by Hans Thomae. Köln-Berlin, 1966:217-230.

Horvath, Fred E., *Psychological Stress* (1959). "Psychological Stress," in: *General Systems,* edited by Ludwig v. Bertalanffy, and Anatol Rapoport, vol. 4, 1959:203-230.

Irle, Martin, *Macht* (1971). Macht und Entscheidungen in Organisationen. Frankfurt/M., 1971.

Janis, Irving L., *Psychological Stress* (1958). Psychological Stress—Psychoanalytic and Behavioral Studies of Surgical Patients. New York, 1958.

Janke, Wilhelm, *Experiment* (1969). "Das Experiment in der Psychologie," in: *Enzyklopädie der geisteswissenschaftlichen Arbeitsmethoden, issue 7: Methoden der Psychologie und Pädagogik.* München-Wien, 1969:95-120.

Kahn, Robert L.; Wolfe, Donald M.; Quinn, Robert P.; Snoek, J. Diedrick; and Rosenthal, Robert A., *Organizational Stress* (1964). Organizational Stress—Studies in Role Conflict and Ambiguity. New York-London-Sydney, 1964.

Kaminski, Gerhard, *Ordnungsstrukturen* (1964). "Ordnungsstrukturen und Ordnungsprozesse," in: *Handbuch der Psychologie,* vol 1, part 2: *Lernen und Denken,* edited by Rudolf Bergius, 2d ed. Göttingen, 1964:373-492.

Kappler, Ekkehard, *Systementwicklung* (1972). Systementwicklung—Lernprozesse in betriebswirtschaftlichen Organisationen. Wiesbaden, 1972.

Karlins, Marvin, and Lamm, Helmut, *Information Search* (1967). "Information Search as a Function of Conceptual Structure in a Complex Problemsolving Task," in: *Journal of Personality and Social Psychology,* vol. 5, 1967:456-459.

Karsten, Anitra, *Motivation* (1963). "Motivation und affektives Geschehen in: *Lehrbuch der experimentellen Psychologie,* edited by Richard Meili and Hubert Rohracher. Bern-Stuttgart, 1963:264-309.

Katona, George, *Rational Behavior* (1964). "Rational Behavior and Economic Behavior," in: *The Making of Decision,* edited by William J. Gore, and J.W. Dyson. London, 1964:51-63.

Katz, Daniel, *Field Studies* (1953). "Field Studies," in: *Research Methods*

in the Behavioral Sciences, edited by Leon Festinger, and Daniel Katz. New York-Chicago-San Francisco-Toronto-London, 1953:56-97.
Katz, Daniel, and Kahn, Robert L., *Organizations* (1966). The Social Psychology of Organizations. New York-London-Sydney, 1966.
Kelley, Harold H., Thibaut, John W., *Experimental Studies* (1954). "Experimental Studies of Group Problem Solving and Process," in: *Handbook of Social Psychology,* edited by G. Lindzey, vol. 2. Cambridge, Mass., 1954:735-785.
Kelley, Harold H., and Thibaut, John W., *Problem Solving* (1969). "Group Problem Solving," in: *The Handbook of Social Psychology,* 2d ed., vol 4, edited by Gardner Lindzey, and Elliot Aronson. Reading, Mass.-Menlo Park, Cal.-London-Don Mills, Ont., 1969:1-101.
Kirsch, Werner, *Entscheidungsprozesse, I, II, III* (1970/71). Entscheidungsprozesse, vol. 1: Verhaltenswissenschaftliche Ansätze der Entscheidungstheorie, vol. 2: Informationsverarbeitungstheorie des Entscheidungsverhaltens, vol. 3: Entscheidungen in Organisationen. Wiesbaden, 1970/71.
Klaus, Georg, *Logik* (1966). Moderne Logik—Abriss der formalen Logik. Berlin, 1966.
———. *Erkenntnistheorie* (1966). Spezielle Erkenntnistheorie—Prinzipien der wissenschaftlichen Theorienbildung. Berlin, 1966.
Klausner, Samuel Z., *Stressful Situations* (1966). "Rationalism and Empiricism in Studies of Behavior in Stressful Situations," in: *Behavioral Science,* vol. 11, 1966:329-341.
Kloidt, Heinrich; Dubberke, Hans-Achim; and Göldner, Jürgen, *Entscheidungsprozess* (1959). "Zur Problematik des Entscheidungsprozesses," in: *Organisation des Entscheidungsprozesses,* edited by Erich Kosiol. Berlin, 1959:11-22.
Koelsch, F., *Arbeitsmedizin 1* (1963); *Arbeitsmedizin 2* (1966). Lehrbuch der Arbeitsmedizin. vol. 1: Allgemeine Physiologie—Pathologie—Fürsorge. Stuttgart, 1963; vol. 2: Berufsgefährdungen und Schutzmassnahmen. Stuttgart, 1966.
König, René, *Interview* (1957). Das Interview. Formen, Technik, Auswertung. Praktische Sozialforschung, vol. 1, 2d ed. Köln, 1957.
———. *Beobachtung und Experiment* (1967). "Beobachtung und Experiment in der Sozialforschung," in: *Beobachtung und Experiment,* 5th ed., edited by René König. Köln-Berlin, 1967:17-47.
———. *Beobachtung* (1967). "Die Beobachtung," in: *Handbuch der Empirischen Sozialforschung,* vol. 1, 2d ed., edited by René König. Stuttgart, 1967:107-135, Appendix:697-706.
Kolb, Josef, *Erfahrung im Experiment* (1963). "Erfahrung im Experiment und in der Theorie der Physik," in: *Experiment und Erfahrung in Wissenschaft und Kunst,* edited by Walter Strolz. Freiburg-München,1963:9-39.
Koller, Horst, *Simulation* (1969). Simulation und Planspieltechnik—

Berechnungsexperimente in der Betriebswirtschaft. Wiesbaden, 1969.
Korch, H., *Hypothese* (1972). Die wissenschaftliche Hypothese. Berlin, 1972.
Kosiol, Erich, *Organisation* (1962). Organisation der Unternehmung. Wiesbaden, 1962.
Kotarbinski, Tadeusz, *Praxiology* (1965). Praxiology. An Introduction to the Sciences of Efficient Action. Oxford, 1965.
Kraft, Victor, *Erkenntnislehre* (1960). Erkenntnislehre. Wien, 1960.
Kreikebaum, Hartmut, *Geltungsdauer* (1971). "Überlegungen zur Geltungsdauer organisatorischer Regelungen," in: *Zeitschrift für Organisation*, 40th yr., 1971:14–18.
Kreutz, Henrik, *Sozialforschung* (1972). Soziologie der empirischen Sozialforschung—Theoretische Analyse von Befragungstechniken und Ansätze zur Entwicklung neuer Verfahren. Stuttgart, 1972.
Kuehn, A.A., *Realism* (1962). "Realism in Business Games," in: *Proceedings of the Conference on Business Games in Teaching Devices,* edited by Jackson S. Dill. Sweeney, 1962:56–60.
Langer, Thomas S., and Michael, Stanley T., *Life Stress* (1963). Life Stress and Mental Health. London, 1963.
Lanzetta, John T., *Stress* (1955). "Group Behavior under Stress," in: *Human Relations,* vol. 8, 1955:29–52.
Lazarsfeld, Paul F., *Methodische Probleme* (1967). "Methodische Probleme der empirischen Sozialforschung," in: *Moderne Amerikanische Soziologie—Neuere Beiträge zur soziologischen Theorie,* edited by Heinz Hartmann. Stuttgart, 1967:95–117.
———. *Wissenschaftslogik* (1971). "Wissenschaftslogik und empirische Sozialforschung," in: *Logik der Sozialwissenschaften,* edited by Ernst Topitsch, 7th ed. Köln-Berlin, 1971:37–49.
Lazarus, Richard S., *Psychological Stress* (1963/64). "A Laboratory Approach to the Dynamics of Psychological Stress," in: *Administrative Science Quarterly,* vol. 8, 1963/64:192–213.
———. *Stress* (1966). Psychological Stress and the Coping Process. New York-St. Louis-San Francisco-Toronto-London-Sydney, 1966.
Leinfellner, Werner, *Wissenschaftstheorie* (1967). Einführung in die Erkenntnis- und Wissenschaftstheorie, 2d ed. Mannheim, 1967.
Levi, Lennart, *Stress* (1964). Stress. Körper, Seele und Krankheit-Eine Einführung in die psychosomatische Medizin. Göttingen-Berlin-Frankfurt/M.-Zürich, 1964.
Levitt, Eugene E., *Angst* (1971). Die Psychologie der Angst. Stuttgart-Berlin-Köln-Mainz, 1971.
Lewin, Arie Y., and Weber, Wesley L., *Risk Taking* (1969). "Management Game Teams in Education and Organization Research: An

Experiment on Risk Taking," in: *Academy of Mangement Journal,* vol. 12, 1969:49-58.

Liebermann, Bernhard, *Experimental Studies* (1962). "Experimental Studies of Conflict in Some Two-Person and Three-Person Games," in: *Mathematical Methods in Small Group Processes,* edited by Joan H. Criswell, Herbert Solomon, Patrick Suppes. Stanford, Cal., 1962: 203-220.

Lienert, Gustav A., *Belastung* (1964). Belastung und Regression. Versuch einer Theorie der systematischen Beeinträchtigung der intellektuellen Leistungsfähigkeit. Meisenheim am Glan, 1964.

———. *Testaufbau* (1969). Testaufbau und Testanalyse, 3d ed. Weinheim-Berlin-Basel, 1969.

Lindemann, Peter, and Koller, Horst, et al., (Unternehmungsspiel, 1969). IBM Unternehmungsspiel TOPIC 1, 1969.

Löther, R., *Vergleich* (1969). "Vergleich, Klassifikation und Analogie," in: *Wege des Erkennens—Philosophische Beiträge zur Methodologie der naturwissenschaftlichen Erkenntnis,* edited by H. Laitko, and R. Bellman. Berlin, 1969:91-106.

Machlup, Fritz, *Marginalanalyse* (1971). "Marginalanalyse und empirische Forschung," in: Gegenstand und Methoden der Nationalökonomie, edited by Reimut Jochimsen, and Helmut Knobel. Köln, 1971:297-320.

Malewski, Andrzej, *Reduktion* (1965). "Zur Problematik der Reduktion— Stufen der Allgemeinheit in Theorien über menschliches Verhalten," in: *Logik der Sozialwissenschaften,* edited by Ernst Topitsch, 2d ed. Köln-Berlin, 1965:367-383.

March, James G., and Simon, Herbert A., *Organizations* (1958). Organizations. New York-London, 1958.

Marschak, Jacob, and Radner, Roy, *Teams* (1972). Economic Theory of Teams. New Haven-London, 1972.

Marx, Melvin H., *Theory Construction* (1963). "The General Nature of Theory Construction,": *Theories in Contemporary Psychology,* edited by Melvin H. Marx. London, 1963:4-43.

Mayntz, Renate, *Soziale Organisation* (1958). Die soziale Organisation des Industriebetriebes. Stuttgart, 1958.

———. *Soziologie* (1963). Soziologie der Organisation. Reinbek bei Hamburg, 1963.

Mayntz, Renate; Holm, Kurt; and Hübner, Peter, *Methoden* (1969). Einführung in die Methoden der empirischen Soziologie. Köln-Opladen, 1969.

McGrath, Josef E., *Theory of Method* (1964). "Toward a Theory of Method for Research on Organisations," in: *New Perspectives in Organization Research,* edited by W.W. Cooper; Harold J. Leavitt; and M.W. Shelly II. New York-London-Sydney, 1964:533-556.

McGrath, Josef E., and Altman, Irvin, *Small Group Research*. (1966). Small Group Research. A Synthesis and Critique of the Field. New York-Chicago-San Francisco-Toronto-London, 1966.
McGuire, Josef W., *Theories* (1964). Theories of Business Behavior. Englewood Cliffs, N.J., 1964.
Mechanic, David, *Methodology* (1962). "Some Considerations in the Methodology of Organizational Studies," in: *The Social Science of Organizations,* edited by Harold J. Leavitt. Englewood Cliffs, N.J., 1962:137-182.
———. *Stress* (1962). Students under Stress—A Study in the Social Psychology of Adaptation. New York, 1962.
Meier, Albert, *Koordination* (1969). "Koordination," in: *Handwörterbuch der Organisation,* edited by Erwin Grochla. Stuttgart, 1969:893-899.
Meier, Robert C.; Newell, William T.; and Pazer, Harold L., *Simulation* (1969). Simulation in Business and Economics. Englewood Cliffs, N.J., 1969.
Meili, Richard, *Experiment* (1963). "Das Psychologische Experiment," in: *Lehrbuch der experimentellen Psychologie,* edited by Richard Meili, and Hubert Rohracher. Bern-Stuttgart, 1963:1-18.
Meimberg, Rudolf, *Willkür* (1964). "Über das Element der Willkür in sozialökonomischen Werturteilen," in: *Jahrbuch für Sozialwissenschaft,* vol. 15, 1964:312-336.
Meltzer, Morton F., *Information Center* (1967). The Information Center. Management's Hidden Assex, 1967.
Mertens, Peter, *Simulation* (1969). Simulation. Stuttgart, 1969.
Mesarović, Mihajlo D., *Systems* (1962). "On Self Organizational Systems." in: *Self-Organizing Systems,* edited by Marshall C. Yovits; George T. Jacobi; and Gordon D. Goldstein. Washington, 1962:9-48.
Miller, James G., *Living Systems* (1965). "Living Systems: Basis Concepts, Structure and Process. Cross-Level Hypotheses," in: *Behavioral Science,* vol. 10, 1965:193-237; 337-379; 380-411.
Miller, Norman, *Time* (1968). "As Time Goes By," in: *Theories of Cognitive Consistency. A Sourcebook,* edited by Robert P. Abelson et al. Chicago, 1968:589-598.
Miottke, Peter, *Marktmodell* (1967). Das Marktmodell des Unternehmungsspieles TOPIC 1, 1967.
Mittenecker, Erich, *Auswertung* (1970). Planung und statistische Auswertung von Experimenten, 8td ed. Wien, 1970.
Mize, Joe H., and Cox, J. Grady, *Simulation* (1968). Essentials of Simulation. Englewood Cliffs, N.J., 1968.
Moltke, Helmuth v., *Militärische Werke* (1960). "Aus Moltkes Militärischen Werken," in: *Die Grossen Meister der Kriegskunst,* edited by Ihno Krumpelt, Frankfurt/M., 1960:117-206.

Morgenstern, Oskar, *Wirtschaftsprognose* (1928). Wirtschaftsprognose—Eine Untersuchung ihrer Voraussetzungen und Möglichkeiten. Wien, 1928.
———. *Strategie* (1962). Strategie—heute. Frankfurt/M., 1962.
———. *Vollkommene Voraussicht* (1964). "Vollkommene Voraussicht und wirtschaftliches Gleichgewicht," in: *Theorie und Realität,* edited by Hans Albert. Tübingen, 1964:251-271.
Morris, William T., *Management Decision* (1964). The Analysis of Management Decision, revised edition. Homewood, Ill., 1964.
———. *Management Science* (1968). Management Science. A Bayesian Introduction. Englewood Cliffs, N.J., 1968.
———. *Management Decisions* (1969). "Management Decisions, Art or Science," in: *Management Decision-Making,* edited by Gordon A. Yewdall. London, 1969:1-36.
Mott, Paul E., *Effective Organizations* (1972). The Characteristics of Effective Organizations. New York-Evanston-San Francisco-London, 1972.
Müller, Johannes, *Isolation* (1965). "Zum Problem der Isolation beim Experimentieren und zur Stellung des Experiments in den technischen Wissenschaften," in: *Struktur und Funktion der experimentellen Methode,* edited by Heinrich Parthey; Heinrich Vogel; Wolfgang Wächter; and Dietrich Wahl. Rostock, 1965:171-205.
Müller, Kurt, *Denken* (1964). "Denken und Lernen als Organisieren," in: *Handbuch der Psychologie,* vol. 1, part 2: *Lernen und Denken,* edited by Rudolf Bergius, 2d ed. Göttingen, 1964:118-143.
Münch, Richard, *Mentales System* (1972). Mentales System und Verhalten—Grundlagen einer allgemeinen Verhaltenstheorie. Tübingen, 1972.
Münch, Richard, and Schmid, Michael, *Konventionalismus* (1970). "Konventionalismus und empirische Forschungspraxis," in: *Zeitschrift für Sozialpsychologie,* 1st yr., 1970:299-310.
Myrdal, Gunnar, *Objektivität* (1971). Objektivität in der Sozialforschung. Frankfurt/M., 1971.
Naschold, Frieder, *Organisation* (1969). Organisation und Demokratie. Stuttgart-Berlin-Köln-Mainz, 1969.
———. *Systemsteuerung* (1969). Systemsteuerung. Stuttgart-Berlin-Koln-Mainz, 1969.
Nordsieck, Fritz, *Funktion* (1969). "Funktion," in: *Handwörterbuch der Organisation,* edited by Erwin Grochla. Stuttgart, 1969:602-616.
Norris, Eleanor L., *Stress* (1968). "Verbal Indices of Psychological Stress," in: *Theories of Cognitive Consistency—A Sourcebook,* edited by Robert P. Abelson et al. Chicago, 1968:417-424.
Oaklander, Harold, and Fleishman, Edwin A., *Organizational Stress*

(1963/64). "Patterns of Leadership Related to Organizational Stress in Hospital Settings," in: *Administrative Science Quarterly,* vol. 8, 1963/64:520-532.
Opp, Karl-Dieter, *Anwendung* (1967). "Zur Anwendung sozialwissenschaftlicher Theorien für praktisches Handeln, in: *Zeitschrift für die gesamte Staatswissenschaft,* vol. 123, 1967:393-418.
———. *Methodologie* (1970). Methodologie der Sozialwissenschaften—Einführung in Probleme ihrer Theorienbildung. Reinbek bei Hamburg, 1970.
Pagés, Robert, *Experiment* (1967). "Das Experiment in der Soziologie," in: *Handbuch der Empirischen Sozialforschung,* vol. 1, edited by René König, 2d ed. Stuttgart, 1967:415-450, Appendix:740-752.
Pareto, Vilfredo, *Gesellschaft* (1971). "Gesellschaft als empirisches Sozialsystem," in: *Soziale Systeme—Materialien zur Dokumentation und Kritik soziologischer Ideologie,* edited by K.H. Tjaden. Neuwied-Berlin, 1971:70-79.
Parthey, Heinrich, *Empirische Basis* (1969). "Die empirische Bases naturwissenschaftlicher Erkenntnis," in: *Wege des Erkennens,—Philosophische Beiträge zur Methodologie der naturwissenschaftlichen Erkenntnis,* edited by H. Laitko and R. Bellman. Berlin, 1969:74-90.
Parthey, Heinrich, and Wächter, Wolfgang., *Theorie* (1965). "Bemerkungen zur Theorie der experimentellen Methode," in: *Struktur und Funktion der experimentellen Methode,* edited by Heinrich Parthey; Heinrich Vogel; Wolfgang Wächter; and Dietrich Wahl. Rostock, 1965:23-46.
Peak, Helen, *Objective Observation* (1953). "Problems of Objective Observation," in: *Research Methods in the Behavioral Sciences,* edited by Leon Festinger and Daniel Katz. New York-Chicago-San Francisco-Toronto-London, 1953:243-299.
Pepinsky, Pauline N.; Pepinsky, Harold B.; and Pavlik, William B., *Time Pressure* (1960). "The Effects of Task Complexity and Time Pressure upon Team Productivity," in: *Journal of Applied Psychology,* vol. 44, 1960:34-38.
Pepinsky, Harold B., and Pepinsky, Pauline N., *Productivity* (1961). "Organization, Management Strategy, and Team Productivity," in: *Leadership and Interpersonal Behavior,* edited by Luigi Petrullo and Bernard Bass. New York, 1961:216-237.
Pfiffner, John N., and Sherwood, Frank P., *Organization* (1960). Administrative Organization. Englewood Cliffs, N.J., 1960.
Philipp, Fritz, *Risiko* (1967). Risiko und Risikopolitik. Stuttgart, 1967.
Picot, Arnold, *Organisationsforschung* (1972). Grundfragen experimenteller Organisationsforschung—Ein wissenschafts- und methodentheoretischer Beitrag zur empirischen Betriebswirtschaftslehre. Dissertation. München, 1972.

Pollay, Richard W., *Decision Times* (1970). "The Structure of Executive Decisions and Decision Times," in: *Administrative Science Quarterly,* vol. 15, 1970:459-471.

Popper, Karl R., *Naturgesetze* (1964). "Naturgesetze und theoretische Systeme," in: *Theorie und Realität—Ausgewählte Aufsätze zur Wissenschaftslehre der Sozialwissenschaften,* edited by Hans Albert. Tübingen, 1964:87-102.

———. *Erfahrungswissenschaft* (1964). "Die Zielsetzung der Erfahrungswissenschaft," in: *Theorie und Realität—Ausgewählte Aufsätze zur Wissenschaftslehre der Sozialwissenschaften,* edited by Hans Albert. Tübingen, 1964:73-86.

———. *Theories* (1968). "Theories, Experience and Probabilistic Intuitions," in: *The Problem of Inductive Logic,* edited by Imre Lakatos. Amsterdam, 1968:285-303.

———. *Logik* (1969). Logik der Forschung, 3d ed. Tübingen, 1969.

———. *Historizismus* (1969). Das Elend des Historizismus, 2d ed. Tübingen, 1969.

Radloff, Roland, and Helmreich, Robert, *Stress* (1968). Groups under Stress: Psychological Research in Sealab II. New York, 1968.

Rapoport, Anatol, *Self Organization* (1960). "Some Self-Organization Parameters in Three-Person-Groups," in: *General Systems,* edited by Anatol Rapoport and Ludwig von Bertalanffy, vol. 5, 1960:129–143.

Rapoport, Anatol, and Orwant, C., *Experimental Games* (1962). "Experimental Games—A Review," in *Behavioral Science,* vol. 7, 1962: 1-37.

Reinermann, Heinrich, *Systeme* (1970). "Betriebliche und Biologische Systeme—Ein Beitrag zur interdisziplinären Systemanalyse und zur Organisationsforschung," in: *Kommunikation,* vol. 6, 1970:72-91.

Richter, F., *Vereinfachung* (1969). "Vereinfachung und Idealisierung," in: *Wege des Erkennens,—Philosophische Beiträge zur Methodologie der naturwissenschaftlichen Erkenntnis,* edited by H. Laitko and R. Bellman. Berlin, 1969:107-118.

Richter, Rudolf, *Methodologie* (1971). "Methodologie aus der Sicht des Wirtschaftstheoretikers," in: *Gegenstand und Methoden der Nationalökonomie,* edited by Reimut Jochimsen and Helmut Knobel. Köln, 1971:188-203.

Riecken, Henry W. *Experiments* (1962). "A Program for Research on Experiments in Social Psychology," in: *Decisions, Values and Groups,* vol. 2, Proceedings of a Conference held at the University of New Mexico, edited by Norman F. Washburne. New York-Oxford-London-Paris, 1962:25-41.

Rohn, Walter E. *Unternehmensplanspiel* (1964). Führungsentscheidungen im Unternehmensplanspiel. Essen, 1964.

Rokeach, Milton, *Mind* (1960). The Open and Closed Mind—Investigations into the Nature of Belief Systems and Personality Systems. New York, 1960.

Rosenthal, Robert, *Experimenter's Hypothesis* (1968). "The Experimenter's Hypothesis as unintended Determinant of Experimental Results," in: *Organizational Experiments: Laboratory and Field Research*, edited by William M. Evan. New York-Evanston-London, 1968:25-32.

Rubenstein, Albert H., and Haberstroh, Chadwick, J., *Communication* (1966). "Communication," in: *Some Theories of Organization*, edited by Albert H. Rubenstein, and Chadwick J. Haberstroh. Homewood, Ill., 1966:367-382.

Rubinstein, S.L., *Denken* (1968). Das Denken und die Wege seiner Erforschung. Berlin, 1968.

Rudner, Richard S., *Philosophy* (1966). Philosophy of Social Science. Englewood Cliffs, N.J., 1966.

Ruff, George E., and Korchin, Sheldon J., *Stress Behavior* (1967). "Adaptive Stress Behavior," in: *Psychological Stress—Issues in Research*, edited by Mortimer H. Appley and Richard Trumbull. New York, 1967:297-323.

Runzheimer, Bodo, *Experiment* (1966). Das Experiment in der betriebswirtschaftlichen Forschung. Dissertation. Karlsruhe, 1966.

———. *Situationskontrolle* (1968). "Die Situationskontrolle im Experiment," in: *Zeitschrift für Betriebswirtschaft*, 38th yr., 1968:58-74.

Sachs, Lothar, *Auswertungsmethoden* (1968). Statistische Auswertungsmethoden. Berlin-Heidelberg-New York, 1968.

Sandig, Curt, *Betriebswirtschaftspolitik* (1966). Betriebswirtschaftspolitik, 2d ed. Stuttgart, 1966.

Sarnoff, Irving, and Zimbardo, Philipp G., *Angst* (1969). "Angst, Furcht, und soziale Gesellung," in: *Texte aus der experimentellen Sozialpsychologie*, edited by Martin Irle with Mario v. Cranach and Hermann Vetter. Neuwied-Berlin, 1969:133-153.

Sauermann, Heinz, and Selten, Reinhard, *Experimentelle Wirtschaftsforschung* (1967). "Zur Entwicklung der experimentellen Wirtschaftsforschung," in: *Beiträge zur experimentellen Wirtschaftsforschung*, edited by Heinz Sauermann. Tübingen, 1967:1-8.

Sauermann, Heinz, ed., *Wirtschaftsforschung* (1967, 1970). Beiträge zur experimentellen Wirtschaftsforschung, vols. 1 and 2. Tübingen, 1967 and 1970.

Scherhorn, Gerhard, *Information* (1964). Information und Kauf, Empirische Analyse der "Markttransparenz." Köln-Opladen, 1964.

Scheuch, Erwin K., *Interview* (1967). "Das Interview in der Sozialforschung," in: *Handbuch der Empirischen Sozialforschung*, vol. 1, 2d ed., edited by René König. Stuttgart, 1967:136-196, Appendix:707-715.

Schneeweiss, Hans, *Entscheidungskriterien* (1967). Entscheidungskriterien bei Risiko. Berlin-Heidelberg-New York, 1967.
Schneider, Dieter, *Investition* (1970). Investition und Finanzierung. Köln-Opladen, 1970.
Schutz, William C., *Groups* (1955). "What Makes Groups Productive?" in: *Human Relations,* vol. 8, 1955:429-465.
Schwartzbaum, Allan, and Gruenfeld, Leopold, *Subject-Observer Interaction* (1969). "Factors Influencing Subject-Observer Interaction in an Organizational Study," in: *Administrative Science Quarterly,* vol. 14, 1969:443-450.
Scott, Richard W., *Field Methods* (1965). "Field Methods in the Study of Organizations," in: *Handbook of Organizations,* edited by James G. March. Chicago, 1965:261-304.
Segeth, Wolfgang, *Logik* (1971). Elementare Logik, 6th ed. Berlin, 1971.
Selltiz, Claire; Jahoda, Marie; Deutsch, Morton; and Cook, Stuart W., *Untersuchungsmethoden* (1972). Untersuchungsmethoden der Sozialforschung, part 1. Neuwied-Darmstadt, 1972.
Selye, Hans, *Stress* (1957). Stress beherrscht unser Leben. Düsseldorf, 1957.
Shubik, Martin, *Decision-Making* (1964). "Approaches to the Study of Decision-Making Relevant to the Firm," in: *The Making of Decisions,* edited by William J. Gore and J.W. Dyson. London, 1964: 31-50.
———. *Experimental Gaming* (1964). "Experimental Gaming and Some Aspects of Competitive Behavior," in: *New Perspectives in Organization Research,* edited by W.W. Cooper; Harold J. Leavitt; and M.W. Shelly II. New York-London-Sydney, 1964:449-463.
———. *Gaming* (1972). "On the Scope of Gaming," in: *Management Science,* vol. 18, 1972:20-36.
Siebel, Wigand, *Logik des Experiments* (1965). Die Logik des Experiments in den Sozialwissenschaften. Berlin, 1965.
Sieber, Eugen H., *Planspiel* (1963). "Das Planspiel unternehmerischer Entscheidungen," in: *Betriebsführung und Operations Research,* edited by Adolf Angermann. Frankfurt/M., 1963:80-123.
Sieber, Joan D., and Lanzetta, John T., *Individual Differences* (1966). "Some Determinants of Individual Differences in Predecision Information-processing Behavior," in: *Journal of Personality and Social Psychology,* vol. 4, 1966:561-571.
Siegel, Sidney, *Level of Aspiration* (1964). "Level of Aspiration and Decision Making," in: *Contributions of Sidney Siegel,* edited by Samuel Messick and Arthur H. Brayfield. New York-San Francisco-London-Toronto, 1964:113-126.
Siegel, Sidney, and Harnett, D.L., *Bargaining Behavior* (1964). "Bargain-

ing Behavior. A Comparison between Mature Industrial Personnel and College Students, in: *Operations Research,* vol. 12, 1964:334-343.

Silbermann, Alphons, *Inhaltsanalyse* (1967). "Systematische Inhaltsanalyse" in: *Handbuch der empirischen Sozialforschung,* vol. 1, 2d ed., edited by René König. Stuttgart, 1967:570-600.

Simon, Herbert A., *Behavior* (1957). Administrative Behavior, 2d ed. New York, 1957.

———. *Models* (1957). Models of Man—Social and Rational. New York-London-Sydney, 1957.

———. *Management Decision* (1960). The New Science of Management Decison. New York-Evanston, 1960.

———. *Rational Choice* (1964). "A Behavioral Model of Rational Choice," in: *The Making of Decisions,* edited by William J. Gore and J.W. Dyson. London, 1964:111-127.

Sixtl, Friedrich, *Messmethoden* (1967). Messmethoden der Psychologie—Theoretische Grundlagen und Probleme. Weinheim, 1967.

Skinner, B.F., *Laboratory* (1963). "The Flight from the Laboratory," in: *Theories in Contemporary Psychology,* edited by Melvin H. Marx. London, 1963:323-338.

Spinner, Helmut F., *Modelle und Experimente* (1969). "Modelle und Experimente," in: *Handwörterbuch der Organisation,* edited by Erwin Grochla. Stuttgart, 1959:col. 1000-1010.

Spreen, Otfried, *Stress* (1964). "Die Stellung von vier motorischen Variablen in einer Faktorenanalyse und ihre Beziehungen zu Angst und Stress," in: *Psychologische Forschung* 27, 1964:403-418.

Stahlknecht, Peter, *Operations Research* (1970). Operations Research, 2d ed. Braunschweig, 1970.

Stegmüller, Wolfgang, *Gegenwartsphilosophie* (1960). Hauptströmungen der Gegenwartsphilosophie, 2d ed. Stuttgart, 1960.

———. *Kausalität* (1960). "Das Problem der Kausalität," in: *Probleme der Wissenschaftstheorie, Festschrift für Victor Kraft,* edited by Ernst Topitsch. Wien, 1960:171-190.

———. *Wissenschaftliche Erklärung* (1969). Wissenschaftliche Erklärung und Begründung. Probleme und Resultate der Wissenschaftstheorie und Analytischen Philosophie, vol. 1. Berlin-Heidelberg-New York, 1969.

———. *Theorie und Erfahrung* (1970). "Theorie und Erfahrung. Probleme und Resultate der Wissenschaftstheorie und Analytischen Philosophie," vol. 2. Berlin-Heidelberg-New York, 1970.

Stogdill, Ralph M., *Group Achievement* (1959). Individual Behavior and Group Achievement—A Theory. New York, 1959.

Szczepanski, Jan, *Biographische Methode* (1967). "Die Biographische Methode," in: *Handbuch der Empirischen Sozialforschung,* vol. 1, 2d ed., edited by René König. Stuttgart, 1967:551-569.

Tannenbaum, Percy H., *Stress* (1968). "Comment: Models of the Role of Stress," in: *Theories of Cognitive Consistency—A Sourcebook,* edited by Robert P. Abelson et al. Chicago, 1968:432-435.
Taylor, Donald W., and Faust, William L., *Efficiency* (1962). "Twenty Questions: Efficiency in Problem Solving as a Function of Size of Group," in: *Small Groups. Studies in Social Interaction,* edited by A. Paul Hare; Edgar F. Borgatta; and Robert F. Bales. New York, 1962:208-220.
Taylor, Donald W., *Decision Making* (1965). "Decision Making and Problem Solving," in: *Handbook of Organizations,* edited by James G. Marsh. Chicago, 1965:48-86.
Thomae, Hans, *Entscheidung* (1960). Der Mensch in der Entscheidung. München, 1960.
Tjaden, K.H., *Sozialsystem* (1971). "Die Entwicklung des Begriffs des Sozialsystems als Entfaltung soziologischer Ideologie, Einleitung" in: *Soziale Systeme—Materialien zur Dokumentation und Kritik soziologischer Ideologie,* edited by K.H. Tjaden. Neuwied-Berlin, 1971: 11-52.
Torrance, E. Paul, *Behavior Under Stress* (1961). "A Theory of Leadership and Interpersonal Behavior under Stress," in: *Leadership and Interpersonal Behavior,* edited by Luigi Petrullo, and Bernhard Bass. New York, 1961:100-117.
Trull, Samuel G., *Decision Success* (1966). "Some Factors Involved in Determining Total Decision Success," in: *Management Science,* vol. 12, 1966:B270-B280.
Ulrich, Hans, *Unternehmung* (1968). Die Unternehmung als produktives soziales System. Bern, 1968.
———. *Kompetenz* (1969). "Kompetenz," in: *Handwörterbuch der Organisation,* edited by Erwin Grochla. Stuttgart, 1969:col. 852-856.
Vickers, Sir Geoffrey, *Stress* (1959). "The Concept of Stress in Relation to the Disorganization of Human Behavior," in: *General Systems,* edited by Ludwig v. Bertalanffy, and Anatol Rapoport, vol. 4, 1959: 243-247.
Vogel, Heinrich, *Experimente und Theorie* (1965). "Zum Verhältnis von Experiment und Theorie (unter besonderer Berücksichtigung der Ansichten Max Borns)," in: *Struktur und Funktion der experimentellen Methode,* edited by Heinrich Parthey; Heinrich Vogel; Wolfgang Wächter; and Dietrich Wahl. Rostock, 1965:47-75.
Vroom, Victor H., *Organizational Control* (1964). "Some Psychological Aspects of Organizational Control," in: *New Perspectives in Organizational Research,* edited by W.W. Cooper; Harold J. Leavitt; and M. W. Shelly II. New York-London-Sydney, 1964:72-86.
Wahl, Dietrich, *Anwendung* (1965). "Probleme der Anwendung der experimentellen Methode in den Gesellschaftswissenschaften," in: *Struktur*

und Funktion der experimentellen Methode, edited by Heinrich Parthey; Heinrich Vogel; Wolfgang Wächter; and Dietrich Wahl. Rostock, 1965:103-149.

Walster, Elaine, and Berscheid, Ellen, *Time* (1968). "The Effects of Time," in: *Cognitive Consistency—A Sourcebook,* edited by Robert P. Abelson et al. Chicago, 1968:599-608.

Weick, Karl E., *Laboratory Experimentation* (1965). "Laboratory Experimentation with Organizations," in: *Handbook of Organizations,* edited by James G. March. Chicago, 1965:194-260.

———. Observational Methods (1968). "Systematic Observational Methods," in: *The Handbook of Social Psychology,* vol. 2, 2d ed., edited by Garner Lindzey and Elliot Aronson. Reading, Mass.-Menlo Park, Cal.-London-Don Mills, Ont., 1968:357-451.

Wherry, Robert J., Jr., and Curran, Patrick M., *Psychological Stress* (1966). "A Model for the Study of Some Determiners of Psychological Stress: Initial Experimental Research," in: *Organizational Behavior and Human Performance,* vol. 1, 1966:226-251.

White, Ralph K., and Lippitt, Ronald, *Autocracy and Democracy* (1960). Autocracy and Democracy. An Experimental Inquiry. New York, 1960.

Wiggins, James A., *Laboratory Methods* (1968). "Hypothesis Validity and Experimental Laboratory Methods," in: *Methodology in Social Research,* edited by Hubert M. Blalock, Jr., and Ann B. Blalock. New York-St. Louis-San Francisco-Toronto-London-Sydney, 1968:390-427.

Wild, Jürgen, *Grundlagen und Probleme* (1966). Grundlagen und Probleme der betriebswirtschaftlichen Organisationslehre. Berlin, 1966.

Winer, B.J., *Statistical Principles* (1970). Statistical Principles in Experimental Design. London-New York-Sydney-Toronto-Düsseldorf-Mexico-Johannesburg-Panama-Singapore-Ljubljana, 1970.

Witte, Eberhard, *Entscheidung* (1964). "Analyse der Entscheidung. Organisatorische Probleme eines geistigen Prozesses," in: *Organisation und Rechnungswesen—Festschrift für Erich Kosiol,* edited by Erwin Grochla. Berlin, 1964:101-124.

———. *Lehre und Spiel* (1965). "Lehre und Spiel," in: *IBM-Nachrichten,* 15th yr., 1965, vol. 175:2848-2851.

———. *Phasentheorem* (1968). "Phasen-Theorem und Organisation komplexer Entscheidungsverläufe," in: *Zeitschrift für betriebswirtschaftliche Forschung,* 20th yr., 1968:625-647.

———. *Entscheidungen* (1968). "Organisierbare Entscheidungen," in: UNIVAC. Die Lochkarte, 32nd yr. 1968:3-6.

———. *Entscheidungsverläufe* (1968). Die Organisation komplexer Entscheidungsverläufe—ein Forschungsbericht. Mannheim, 1968.

———. *Ablauforganisation* (1969). "Ablauforganisation," in: *Hand-*

wörterbuch der Organisation, edited by Erwin Grochla. Stuttgart, 1969:col.20–30.

———. *Entscheidungsprozesse* (1969). "Entscheidungsprozesse," in: *Handwörterbuch der Organisation,* edited by Erwin Grochla. Stuttgart, 1969:col. 497–596.

———. *Informationsverhalten* (1972). Das Informationsverhalten in Entscheidungsprozessen. Tübingen, 1972.

———. *Innovationsentscheidungen* (1972). Organisation für Innovationsentscheidungen—Das Promotorenmodell. Göttingen, 1972.

Wittman, Waldemar, *Information* (1959). Unternehmung und unvollkommene Information—Unternehmerische Voraussicht—Ungewissheit und Planung. Köln-Opladen, 1959.

Wossidlo, Peter Rütger, *Reservierung* (1970). Unternehmenswirtschaftliche Reservierung—Eine realtheoretische und praxeologische Untersuchung. Berlin, 1970.

———. *Reihenfolgen* (1976). Die Gestaltung von Reihenfolgen in geistigen Arbeitsprozessen. Habilitationsschrift. München, 1976.

Zelditch, Morris, Jr., and Hopkins, Terence K., *Experiments* (1971). "Laboratory Experiments with Organizations," in: *Organizational Experiments: Laboratory and Field Research,* edited by William M. Evan. New York-Evanston-London., 1971:39–45.

Zepf, Günter, *Führungsstil* (1972). Kooperativer Führungsstil und Organisation—Zur Leistungsfahigkeit und organisatorischen Verwirklichung einer kooperativen Führung in Unternehmungen. Wiesbaden, 1972.

Zetterberg, Hans L., *Theorie* (1962). "Theorie, Forschung und Praxis in der Soziologie," in: *Handbuch der Empirischen Sozialforschung,* vol. 1, edited by René König. Stuttgart, 1962:64–104.

Zieleniewski, Jan, *Organisation* (1966). "Die Begriffe Organisation und Handlung im Zusammenhang mit einigen anderen allgemeinen Begriffen," in: *Praxeologie,* edited by Kurd Alsleben, and Wolfgang Wehrstedt. Quickborn, 1966:35–70.

———. *Leistungsfähigkeit* (1966). "Die Leistungsfähigkeit des Handelns," in: *Praxeologie,* edited by Kurd Alsleben, and Wolfgang Wehrstedt. Quickborn, 1966:71–86.

Index

Index

Accuracy, material/formal, 56
Acute analysis, 51–52
Albert, H., 50

Behavior of groups, 6–7
Biological-physical stress, 2–3
Bounded rationality, concept of, 10
Broadbent, D.E., 8
Business games, 59; design of economic framework, 68–70

Cangelosi, V.E., and Dill, W.R., 13
Communication time pressure, 71
Coordinative activity, 32–33
Critical experiment, 53
"Critical transparence," 58

Davis, R.C., 7
Decision, internal/external weight of, 26
Decision complexity, 25
Decision experiment, 53
Decision-making model, 59–61
Decision-making regulation, 115–120; performance character of, 143–146
Decision-making time, 24, 94–95
Decision realization, 130–138
Definiteness, degree of, 49
Dissonance theory (Festinger), 4–5
Document analysis, 52

Economic efficiency, 38–40
Elementary stress, 11
Experiment: characteristics, 52–58; design, 58–75; as method of research, 50–52; quality of, 75–84
Experiment directors, 63–64; neutrality of, 57
Experiment groups, 64–66
Experimental tasks: total duration and periodization, 67–68

Feger, H., 58
Festinger, L., 4–5
Findings: decision-making time, 94–95; decision realization, 132–138; demand for information, 113–115; functional validity, 83–84; individual performance, 103–109; performance satisfaction, 122–125; personal validity, 77–81; problem intensity, 98–99; regulation of decision, 116–120; situative validity, 84–85; time-pressure absorption, 127–130
"Formal accuracy" (reliability), 56
Freud, S., 3
Function regulation, 118, 145–146
Functional validity, 81–83

General adaptations syndrome, 2–3
Generality, degree of, 49
Goal regulation, 118, 144–145
Goal setting, 115
Gzuk, R., 34

Hall, D.T., and Lawler, E.E., 12–13
Hall, D.T., and Mansfield, R., 6
Hamel, W., 34
Hare, P.A., 33
Historical analysis, 51, 52
Homeostasis, principle of, 3

Immunity (personal neutrality), 57, 63–64
Individual performance, 100
Information, demand for, 109–115; limitation of, 30–31
Information, utilization of, 147–149
Informational model, 61–63
Interaction, 28–29, 100
Interference experiment, 53

Lienert, G.A., 53

March, J.G., and Simon, H., 7, 12
"Material accuracy" (validity), 56
Mayntz, R., 7
Measurement, 55-58; decision-making time, 94; decision realization, 131-132; demand for information, 110-111; functional validity, 82; individual performance, 101-102; performance satisfaction, 121-122; personal validity, 77; problem intensity, 96-97; regulation of decision, 116; situative validity, 84; time pressure, 74-75; time-pressure absorption, 126
Miller, J.G., 33
Morgenstern, O., 22
Morris, W.T., 12

Neutrality of research methods, 55-58

Organization, 115

Pareto, V., 7
Performance efficiency, 34-40, 120-138
Performance satisfaction, 121-125
Performance time pressure, 71
Permanent testability, scientific theory of, 54
Personal disposition, 8-9
Personal efficiency, 36-37
Personal validity, 76-81
Personnel requirements, 57, 63-64
Popper, K.R., 49-50
"Principle of arbitrariness," 53
Problem intensity, 25-26, 95-99, 147-151
Problem solving under time pressure, 27-33, 100-120, 149-151
Psychic-cognitive stress, 3-5

Reliability of measurement procedure, 56-57
Representativeness, 54-55
Rubenstein, A.H., and Haberstroh, C.J., 12

Sauermann, H., and Selten, R., 64

Scherhorn, E.K., 9
Scheuch, E.K., 56
Selye, H., 2-3, 33
Sensitivity (to time pressure), 24-25
Sensitivity analysis, 76-81
Simon, H.A., 10
Simulation model, 58-63
Situative complexity, 9-11
Situative validity, 83-85
Social-interactive stress (social pressure), 5-8
Social systems, behavior of, 6-8
Spinner, H.F., 51
Stress, elements of, 8-14
Stress, sensitivity to, 76-81

Testing design: decision-making time, 94; decision realization, 132; demand for information, 111-113; functional validity, 82; individual performance, 102-103; performance satisfaction, 122; personal validity, 77; problem intensity, 98; regulation of decision, 116; situative validity, 84; time-pressure absorption, 127
Thomae, H., 8-9
Time efficiency, 37-38
Time pressure, conditions of, 23-26, 93-99
Time pressure, effectiveness of, 151-152
Time pressure, forms of, 71-72
Time pressure, induction of, 70-75
Time pressure, measurement of, 74-75
Time-pressure absorption, 125-130
Time-pressure index, 75. See also Time pressure, measurement of
Time-pressure sensitivity, 76-81
Time-pressure variation, 72-74
Time restrictions, 11-14

Validity, 56; functional, 81-83; personal, 76-81; situative, 83-85
Verification, 50, 93-138

Witte, E., 9, 22, 101, 110, 112
Wossidlo, P.R., 37

About the Author

Rolf Bronner has worked in both public administration and private industry. After graduating from the University of Mannheim, he became the assistant of Eberhard Witte at the Institute for Empirical Decision Research. Currently he is professor of economics and business administration at the University of Paderborn. His area of research and teaching is human problem solving, especially information behavior, decision making, coping with stress, conflict and complexity, learning behavior, and management performance.